UNIVERSIT...
WOLVER...

...us Lib...

Postmodernity and its Discontents

Postmodernity and its Discontents

ZYGMUNT BAUMAN

Polity Press

The right of Zygmunt Bauman to be identified as author of this work
has been asserted in accordance with the Copyright, Designs and Patents Act 1988.

First published in 1997 by Polity Press
in association with Blackwell Publishers Ltd.

Editorial office:
Polity Press
65 Bridge Street
Cambridge CB2 1UR, UK

Marketing and production:
Blackwell Publishers Ltd
108 Cowley Road
Oxford OX4 1JF, UK

ISBN 0-7456-1790-5
ISBN 0-7456-1791-3 (pbk)

A CIP catalogue record for this book is available from the British Library.

Typeset in 10 on 12 pt Garamond
by Best-set Typesetter Ltd., Hong Kong
Printed in Great Britain by TJ Press Ltd, Padstow, Cornwall

This book is printed on acid-free paper.

Contents

Introduction: Discontents – Modern and Postmodern   1

1   The Dream of Purity   5
2   The Making and Unmaking of Strangers   17
3   The Strangers of the Consumer Era: from the Welfare State to Prison   35
4   Morality Begins at Home: or the Rocky Road to Justice   46
5   Parvenu and Pariah: the Heroes and Victims of Modernity   71
6   Tourists and Vagabonds: the Heroes and Victims of Postmodernity   83
7   Postmodern Art, or the Impossibility of the Avant-garde   95
8   The Meaning of Art and the Art of Meaning   103
9   On Truth, Fiction and Uncertainty   112
10   Culture as Consumer Co-operative   127
11   On the Postmodern Redeployment of Sex: Foucault's *History of Sexuality* Revisited   141
12   Immortality, Postmodern Version   152
13   Postmodern Religion?   165
14   On Communitarianism and Human Freedom, or How to Square the Circle   186

Afterword: The Last Word – and it Belongs to Freedom   199

Notes   209

Index   218

Introduction:
Discontents – Modern and
Postmodern

In 1930 a book called first *Das Unglück in der Kultur*, and later renamed *Das Unbehagen in der Kultur*, appeared in Vienna. Its author was Sigmund Freud. Almost simultaneously, the English translation appeared – for which Freud suggested a title *Man's Discomfort in Civilization*. As Freud's English editor James Strachey informs us, Joan Riviere, the book's English translator, played instead for a time with the concept of *malaise*, but chose finally the title *Civilization and its Discontents*. It is under this title that Freud's provocative challenge to the folklore of modernity entered our collective consciousness and in the end framed our thinking about the consequences – both intended and unintended – of the modern adventure. (We know now that it was the story of *modernity* which the book told, even if its author preferred to speak of *Kultur* or civilization; only modern society thought of itself as of an activity of 'culture' or 'civilization', and acted on such self-knowledge, with the results Freud set out to explore; the phrase 'modern civilization' is, for this reason, a pleonasm.)

You gain something, but usually you lose something in exchange: so went Freud's message. As 'culture' or 'civilization', modernity is about beauty ('this useless thing which we expect civilization to value'), cleanliness ('dirtiness of any kind seems to us incompatible with civilization') and order ('Order is a kind of compulsion to repeat which, when a regulation has been laid down once and for all, decides when, where and how a thing shall be done, so that in every similar circumstance one is spared hesitation and indecision'). Beauty (that is, whatever gives the sublime pleasure of harmony and perfection of form), purity and order are gains not to be played down and certainly not likely to be given up without an outcry, breast-beating and remorse. But neither are they to be had without paying a heavy price. Nothing predisposes humans 'naturally' to seek or preserve beauty, to keep clean and to observe the routine called order. (If they seem here and there to display such an 'instinct', it must be a contrived and acquired, *trained* inclination, the surest sign of a civilization at work.) Humans need be forced to respect and appreciate harmony, cleanliness and order. Their freedom to act on their own impulses must be trimmed. Constraint is painful: defence against suffering generates sufferings of its own.

'Civilization is built upon a renunciation of instinct.' In particular – so Freud tells us – civilization (read: modernity) 'imposes great sacrifices' on man's sexuality and aggressivity. 'The urge for freedom, therefore, is directed against particular forms and demands of civilization or against civilization altogether.' And it cannot be otherwise. The pleasures of civilized life come in a package deal, so Freud insists, with sufferings, satisfaction with discontents, submission with rebellion. Civilization – the order imposed upon naturally disorderly humanity – is a compromise, a trade-off, continually challenged and forever nudged to be renegotiated. The pleasure principle is here cut down to the measure of the reality principle and the rules spell out that reality which is the measure of the realistic. 'Civilized man has exchanged a portion of his possibilities of happiness for a portion of security.' However well justified and realistic may be our attempts to improve on specific flaws of the present-day solutions, 'perhaps we may also familiarize ourselves with the idea that there are difficulties attaching to the nature of civilization which will not yield to any attempt at reform'.

Of that order which was the pride of modernity and the cornerstone of all its other accomplishments (whether appearing under the same rubric of order or hiding under the code-names of beauty and cleanliness), Freud spoke in terms of 'compulsion', 'regulation', 'suppression' or 'forced renunciation'. Those discontents which were the trade-mark of modernity arose from the 'excess of order' and its inseparable companion – the dearth of freedom. Security from the triple threat hidden in the frail body, the untamed world and the aggressive neighbours called for the sacrifice of freedom; first and foremost, the individual's freedom to seek pleasure. Within the framework of a civilization bent on security, more freedom meant less discontent. Within the framework of a civilization that chose to limit freedom in the name of security, more order meant more discontent.

Ours, however, is the time of deregulation. The reality principle has today to defend itself in the court of justice in which the pleasure principle is the presiding judge. 'The idea that there are difficulties attaching to the nature of civilization which will not yield to any attempt at reform' seems to have lost its pristine obviousness. Compulsion and forced renunciation has turned from an irritating necessity into an unwarranted assault launched against individual freedom.

Sixty-five years after *Civilization and its Discontents* was written and published, individual freedom rules supreme; it is the value by which all other values came to be evaluated, and the benchmark against which the wisdom of all supra-individual rules and resolutions are to be measured. This does not mean, though, that the ideals of beauty, purity and order which sent men and women on their modern voyage of discovery have been forsaken, or lost any of their original lustre. Now, however, they are to be pursued – and fulfilled – through individual spontaneity, will and effort. In its present, postmodern version, modernity seems to have found the philosophers' stone which Freud dismissed as a naive and harmful fantasy: it set out to smelt the precious metals of clean order and orderly cleanliness straight from the ore of the human, all-too-human bid for pleasure, ever more pleasure and ever more pleasurable pleasure – a bid once decried as base and condemned as self-destructive. As if unscathed, perhaps even strengthened, by two centuries of concentrated efforts to keep it in the iron glove of reason-dictated rules and regulations, the 'invisible hand' regained trust and is once more in favour. Individual freedom, once a liability and a problem (perhaps *the* problem) for all order-builders, became the major asset and resource in the perpetual self-creation of the human universe.

You gain something, you lose something else in exchange: the old rule holds as true today as it was true then. Only the gains and the losses have changed places: *postmodern men and women exchanged a portion of their possibilities of security for a portion of happiness.* The discontents of modernity arose from a kind of security which tolerated too little freedom in the pursuit of individual happiness. The discontents of postmodernity arise from a kind of freedom of pleasure-seeking which tolerates too little individual security.

Any value is a value (as Georg Simmel long ago observed) only thanks to the loss of other values one must suffer in order to obtain it. But you need most what you lack most. The splendours of freedom are at their brightest when freedom is sacrificed at the altar of security. When it is the turn of security to be sacrificed in the temple of individual freedom, it steals much of the shine of its former victim. If dull and humdrum days haunted the seekers of security, sleepless nights are the curse of the free. In both cases, happiness goes by the board. Listen to Freud again: 'We are so made that we can derive intense enjoyment only from a contrast and very little from a state of things.' Why? Because 'what we call happiness . . . comes from the (preferably sudden) satisfaction of needs which have been dammed up to a high degree, and it is from its nature only possible as an episodic phenomenon'. And so: freedom without security assures no more steady a supply of happiness than security without freedom. A different arrangement of human affairs is not necessarily a step forward on the road to greater happiness – it only seems to be such at the moment it is being made. Re-evaluation of all values is a happy, exhilarating *moment*, but the re-evaluated values do not necessarily guarantee a *state* of bliss.

There are no gains without losses, and the hope of a wondrous purification of gains from losses is as futile as the proverbial dream of a free lunch – but the gains and losses specific to any arrangement of human cohabitation need to be carefully counted, so that the optimal balance between the two can be sought even if (or rather because) the hard-won sobriety and wisdom prevents us, postmodern men and women, from indulging in a daydream about a balance sheet that has only a credit side.

This book is intended as a collection of small, and partial, contributions to this task.

This book has a special significance for me, since for the first time in the last quarter of a century some of its chapters were originally written in Polish, my native language, and presented to, as well as discussed with, Polish academics and students. My links with my Alma Mater, the University of Warsaw, have been restored. And so too has been the enlightening and stimulating exchange with my friends and colleagues, Polish sociologists and philosophers, all insightful and perceptive, sharp and challenging, too numerous to be mentioned by name, to whom I am in debt for clarifying and polishing many of the ideas this book contains.

My special thanks go to Anthony Giddens: without his continuous interest in my work, his gentle yet relentless, friendly yet determined pressure, this book would never have been put together.

And, as with each successive work of mine for ten years now, I wish to thank my editor, David Roberts. I guess no author could wish for a better understanding with his editor; we both struggle for the same purpose – which, as Roberts himself put it, is to produce a text 'demanding that the reader should look at things s/he would rather leave unexamined', the role of the editor being 'to remove unnecessary impediments to the reader's understanding without depriving the author of his individual voice'. And no one I know makes these words into flesh more capably than David Roberts.

1

The Dream of Purity

Great crimes often start from great ideas. Few great ideas prove completely innocent when their inspired followers try to make the word flesh – but some can hardly ever be embraced without the teeth being bared and daggers sharpened. Among this class of ideas, pride of place belongs to the vision of purity.

'The German Final Solution', observed the American writer Cynthia Ozick, 'was an aesthetic solution; it was a job of editing, it was the artist's finger removing a smudge; it simply annihilated what was considered not harmonious.'[1] The German psychologist Klaus Dörner calls his readers 'die Nazis auch als Bürger zu sehen, die genauso wie die Bürger vor und nach, ihre Antwort auf die Soziale Frage gesucht haben'[2] – the 'social question' to which they sought the answer being the question of 'pollution', of the stubborn presence of people who 'did not fit', who were 'out of place', who 'spoiled the picture' – and otherwise offended the aesthetically gratifying and morally reassuring sense of harmony. In the early years of the modern era, as Michel Foucault reminded us, madmen were rounded up by the city authorities, loaded into *Narrenschiffen* and sent to sea; madmen stood for 'a dark disorder, a moving chaos . . . which opposes the mind's luminous and adult stability'; and the sea stood for water, which 'carries off, but does more: it purifies'.[3]

Purity is an ideal; a vision of the condition which needs yet to be created, or such as needs to be diligently protected against the genuine or imagined odds. Without such a vision, neither the concept of purity makes sense, nor the distinction between purity and impurity can be sensibly drawn. A forest, a mountain range, a meadow, an ocean ('nature' in general, as distinguished from culture, the human product) is neither pure nor impure – that is, until it is spattered with the leftovers of a Sunday picnic or infused with the waste of chemical factories. Human intervention does not just soil nature and make it filthy; it introduces into nature the very distinction between purity and filth, it creates the very possibility of a given part of the natural world being 'clean' or 'dirty'.

Purity is a vision of things put in places *different* from those they would occupy if not prompted to move elsewhere, pushed, pulled or goaded; and it is a vision of *order* – that is, of a situation in which each thing is in its rightful place and nowhere else. There is no way of thinking about purity without having an image of 'order', without assigning to things their 'rightful', 'proper' places – which happen to be such places as they would not fill 'naturally', of their own accord. The opposite of 'purity' – the dirt, the filth, 'polluting agents' – are things 'out of place'. It is not the intrinsic quality of things which makes them into 'dirt', but solely their location; more precisely, their location in the order of things envisaged by the purity-seekers. Things which are 'dirt' in one context may become pure just by being put in another place – and vice versa. Beautifully polished, shining shoes become dirt when put on the dining table; returned to the shoe-stack, they recover their pristine purity. An omelette, a mouth-watering work of culinary art when on the dinner plate, becomes a nasty stain when dropped on the pillow.

There are, however, things for which the 'right place' has not been reserved in any fragment of man-made order. They are 'out of place' everywhere; that is, in all places for which the model of purity has been designed. The world of the purity-seekers is simply too small to accommodate them. It won't be enough to move them to another place; one needs to get rid of them once and for all – to burn them out, poison them, shatter them in pieces, put them to the sword. More often than not these are mobile things, things that will not stick to their assigned place, that change places of their own accord. The trouble with such things is that they will cross boundaries whether invited to or not. They control their own location, and thus deride the purity-seekers' efforts to 'put things in their place', and in the end lay bare the incurable fragility and shakiness of all placements. Cockroaches, flies, spiders or mice, which at any time may decide to share a home with its legal (human) residents without asking the owners' permission, are for that reason always, potentially, uninvited guests, and so cannot be incorporated into any imaginable scheme of purity.

The situation becomes yet more threatening and calls for yet more vigilance in the case of things which do not just move of their own accord, but do it moreover without drawing attention to themselves; they defy not just the model of purity, but the very effort of its protection, since without being aware of the invasion one does not know that the time of action has arrived, and one can be easily lulled into the illusion of security. Carpet mites, bacteria and viruses belong to that category of things from which nothing is safe, including the pursuit of safety itself. The writers of advertising copy for washing powders and detergent products sense the difference very well – promising future customers that they will be able to smother and destroy 'the dirt you see and the germs you don't'.

We may gather from what has been said thus far that the interest in purity, and the associated interest in 'hygiene' (that is, keeping the dirt away) has more than an accidental relation to the fragility of order; to a situation in which we feel that we cannot rely on order taking care of itself, that we cannot expect order to survive our laxity, our doing nothing about it, by its own momentum. 'Order' means a regular, stable environment for our action; a world in which the probabilities of events are not distributed at random, but arranged in a strict hierarchy – so that certain events are highly likely to occur, others are less probable, some others virtually impossible. Only such an environment do we understand. Only in such surroundings (according to Wittgenstein's definition of understanding) do we 'know how to go on'. Only here can we select our actions properly – that is, with a reasonable hope that the results we have in mind will indeed be achieved. Only here can we rely on the habits and expectations we have acquired in the course of our being-in-the-world. We humans are endowed with memory and a capacity for learning, and for this reason we have vested interests in an 'orderliness' of the world. Learned abilities to act are powerful assets in a stable and predictable world; they would become downright suicidal, though, if the events were suddenly to break out of the causal sequences and thus defy all prediction and take us by surprise.

No one perhaps explained better what all this fuss about purity and fighting dirt is about than the great British anthropologist Mary Douglas, in her eye-opening book *Purity and Danger* (first published in 1966). Dirt, Douglas suggested,

> is essentially disorder. There is no such thing as absolute dirt; it exists in the eye of the beholder . . . Dirt offends against order. Eliminating it is not a negative movement, but a positive effort to organize the environment . . .
>
> In chasing dirt, in papering, decorating, tidying, we are not governed by anxiety to escape disease, but are positively re-ordering our environment, making it conform to an idea. There is nothing fearful or unreasoning in our dirt-avoidance: it is a creative movement, an attempt to relate form to function, to make unity of experience . . .
>
> To conclude, if uncleanliness is matter out of place, we must approach it through order. Uncleanliness or dirt is that which must not be included if a pattern is to be maintained.[4]

From Mary Douglas's analysis, the interest in purity and the obsession with the struggle against dirt emerge as universal characteristics of human beings: the models of purity, the patterns to be preserved change

from one time to another, from one culture to another – but each time
and each culture has a certain model of purity and a certain ideal pattern
to be kept intact and unscathed against the odds. Also, all concerns with
purity and cleaning emerge from that analysis as essentially alike. Sweeping the floor and stigmatizing traitors or banishing strangers appear to
stem from the same motive of the preservation of order, of making or
keeping the environment understandable and hospitable to sensible
action. This may well be so; but the explanation in such universal,
extratemporal and species-wide terms does not go far towards evaluating
various forms of purity-pursuits from the point of view of their social and
political significance and the gravity of their consequences for human
cohabitation.

    If we focus our attention on the latter, we will immediately note that
among the numerous incarnations of the pattern-sapping 'dirt' one case,
sociologically speaking, is of a very special, indeed unique, importance:
namely, the case of when it is *other human beings* who are conceived of
as an obstacle to the proper 'organization of environment' – when, in
other words, it is other people, or more specifically a certain category of
other people, who become 'dirt' and are treated as such.

    The founder of phenomenological sociology, Alfred Schütz,[5] made us
aware of the characteristics of human life which seem obvious the
moment they are pointed out: that if we humans may 'find our bearings
within our natural and socio-cultural environment and to come to terms
with it', it is thanks to the fact that this environment has been 'preselected
and preinterpreted . . . by a series of common-sense constructs of the
reality of daily life'. Each of us, in our daily activities, and without much
thinking about it, uses a tremendous number of products of that
preselection and preinterpretation, which combine into what Schütz calls
the 'stock of knowledge at hand'. Without such knowledge, living in the
world would be inconceivable. None of us is able to build the world of
significations and meanings from scratch; each of us enters a 'prefabri-
cated' world, in which certain things are important and others are not; in
which the established relevances bring certain things into focus and
leave others in the shadow. Above all, we enter a world in which an
awful lot of aspects are obvious to the point of not being consciously
noticed any more and in need of no active effort, not even spelling them
out, to be invisibly, yet tangibly present in everything we do – and
thereby endowing our actions, and the things we act upon, with the
solidity of 'reality'.

    Among the tacit, yet indispensable ingredients of the 'stock of knowl-
edge at hand', that commonsensical wisdom which all of us receive, to
use Schützian terms, as a gift from the 'intersubjective world of culture',

from that 'treasure house of ready-made pre-constituted types' – pride of place belongs to the assumption of 'reciprocal perspectives'. What we believe without thinking (and, above all, as long as we do not think about it) is that our experiences are *typical* – that is, that whoever looks at the object 'out there' sees 'the same' as we do, and that whoever acts, follows 'the same' motives which we know from introspection. We also believe in the 'interchangeability of standpoints'; to whit, if we put ourselves in another person's place, we will see and feel exactly 'the same' as he or she sees and feels in his or her present position – and that this feat of empathy may be reciprocated.

This assumption seems pretty straightforward and innocuous; perhaps even deeply moral in its consequences, since it postulates the essential similarity of human beings and assigns to the others the qualities of subjects just like our own subjectivity. And yet, to hold fast, this assumption of 'reciprocal perspectives' must rest on a still deeper presupposition: that it is not just me who assumes reciprocity of perspective and behaves accordingly – but that this assumption of reciprocity is itself reciprocated. If a suspicion arises that the latter is not the case then the rock-solid construction of daily security falls to pieces. 'I am able to understand other people's acts', says Schütz, 'only if I can imagine that I myself would perform analogous acts if I were in the same situation, directed by the same because motives, or oriented by the same in-order-to motives – all these terms understood in the same restricted sense of the "typical" analogy, the "typical" sameness . . .'[6] The undetachable corollary of this ability to imagine myself in the situation of the other is, of course, the ability to imagine the other in my own position: the expectation that, if cast in my situation, the other would think and behave just as I do . . . In other words, the idea of the essential unity between me and the other, which the assumption of the reciprocity of standpoints ostensibly promotes, precedes rather than follows this assumption. I must first be able to accept unproblematically our mutual similarity, the readiness of the other to think and behave along lines identical with my own, for the assumption of our reciprocity of standpoints to hold.

The recipes attached to routine situations I am likely to encounter in the course of daily life combine in what Max Scheler called the *relativ-natürliche Weltanschauung*. Armed with these recipes, I feel secure. For most things I do, and all things I do routinely, they offer a reliable and sufficient guidance. They have all 'the appearance of a *sufficient* coherence, clarity, and consistency to give anybody a reasonable chance of understanding and of being understood'. But they boast this salutary and wondrous quality only because they are 'evident', accepted matter of factly, without much reflection – and this happy-go-lucky situation may exist only as long as no one around begins to question them, ask about their grounds and reasons, points out the discrepancies, lays bare their arbitrariness. This is why the arrival of a Stranger has the impact of an earthquake . . . The Stranger shatters the rock on which the security of daily life rests. He comes from afar; he does not share the local assumptions – and so 'becomes essentially the man who has to place in question nearly everything that seems to be unquestionable to the members of the approached group'.[7] He 'has to' commit this damaging and deplorable act because he has no status within the approached group which would make the pattern of that group look 'natural' to him, and because even if he tried his best, and successfully, to behave outwardly in the fashion that pattern requires, he would not be accorded by the group the credit of reciprocating the group's standpoint.

If 'dirt' is an element which defies the purpose of the ordering efforts, and the self-acting, self-moving and self-directing dirt is an element which defies the very possibility of effective efforts, then the Stranger is the very epitome of the latter. No wonder the locals of all times and places, in their frenzied efforts to separate, confine, exile or destroy the strangers compared the objects of their exertions to vermin and bacteria. No wonder either, that they compared the meaning of their own action to hygienic routines; they fought the 'strangers', convinced that they defended health against the carriers of disease.

This is what 'the locals' (who, to be sure, could think of themselves as 'locals' and constitute themselves into 'locals' only in as far as they opposed themselves to the 'strangers' – that is, to some other people who were not 'locals') did, let me repeat, at all times and places. But in certain situations the preoccupation with Strangers assumed a particularly important role among many activities involved in the daily care of purity, the daily reproduction of an inhabitable, orderly world. This happened once the work of purifying, or 'order-making', had become a conscious/purposeful activity, when it had been conceived as a *task*; when the objective of cleaning, instead of keeping intact the way in which things were, became *changing the way* in which things used to exist yesterday, *creating* a new order that challenged the present one; when, in other words, the care of order meant the introduction of a new and, by the same token, *artificial* order – making, so to speak, a *new beginning*. This momentous change in the status of order coincided with the advent of the *modern era*. Indeed, we can define modernity as the time, or the way of life, in which order-making consists of the dismantling of the 'traditional', inherited and received, order; in which 'being' means a perpetual new beginning.

Each order has its own disorders; each model of purity has its own dirt that needs to be swept away. But in a durable, lasting order which pre-empts the future and also involves, among other prerequisites, the prohibition of change, even the cleaning and sweeping pursuits are parts of order. They belong to the daily routine, and like everything routine they tend to be repeated monotonously, in a thoroughly habitualized fashion that renders reflection redundant. It is not so much the dirt-eliminating routine, as the prevention of an occasional, unusual *interruption* of the routine, that reaches the level of consciousness and arouses attention. The care for purity focuses not so much on fighting the 'primary dirt', as on the fight against the 'meta-dirt' – against slackening, or altogether neglecting, the effort to keep things as they are . . . The situation changes drastically, though, when ordering means the dismant-ling of the extant order and replacing it with a new model of purity. Now, keeping purity cannot be reduced to the maintenance of daily routine; worse still, the routine itself has the awesome tendency to turn into 'dirt' which needs to be stamped out in the name of the new purity. All in all, the state of 'perpetual beginning' generates ever new, 'improved' targets of purity, and with each new target cuts out new categories of 'dirt' – an unheard-of dirt and an unprecedented dirt. A new condition appears, in which even ordinary, boringly familiar things may turn into dirt at short notice or without notice. With models of purity changing too fast for the purifying skills to catch on, nothing seems secure any more; uncertainty and suspicion rule the day.

We may go a step further and say that the 'order-making' now becomes indistinguishable from announcing ever new 'abnormalities', drawing ever new dividing lines, identifying and setting apart ever new 'strangers'. Thoroughly familiar and unproblematic 'neighbours next door' may turn overnight into terrifying strangers once a new order is envisaged; a new game is devised which the neighbours-of-yesterday are unlikely to play placidly for the simple reason that the new order is about making them into strangers and the new game is about eliminating them – 'cleansing the site'. Doing something about the strangers moves into the very centre of ordering concerns. Strangers are no longer routine, and thus the routine ways of keeping things pure do not suffice. In a world constantly on the move the anxiety which condensed into the fear of strangers saturates the totality of daily life – fills every nook and cranny of the human condition.

In the modern world, notoriously unstable and constant solely in its hostility to everything constant, the temptation to arrest the movement, to bring the perpetual change to a halt, to install an order secure against all further challenges, becomes overwhelming and very difficult to resist.

Almost all modern fantasies of a 'good world' were deep down anti-modern, in that they visualized the end of history understood as a process of change. Walter Benjamin said of modernity that it was born under the sign of suicide; Sigmund Freud suggested that it was driven by Thanatos – the instinct of death. Modern utopias differed in many of their detailed prescriptions, but they all agreed that the 'perfect world' would be one remaining forever identical with itself, a world in which the wisdom learnt today will remain wise tomorrow and the day after tomorrow, and in which the life skills acquired will retain their usefulness forever. The world depicted in the utopias was also, expectedly, a transparent world – one in which nothing dark or impenetrable stood in the way of the eye; a world with nothing spoiling the harmony; nothing 'out of place'; a world without 'dirt'; a world without strangers.

No wonder that throughout the modern era there was a strict correlation between the scale and radicality of the 'new and final order' imagined, dreamt of and tried in practice, and the passion with which the 'problem of strangers' was approached, as well as the severity of treatment reserved for the strangers. What was 'totalitarian' about totalitarian political programmes, themselves thoroughly modern phenomena, was more than anything else the comprehensiveness of the order they promised, the determination to leave nothing to chance, the simplicity of the cleaning prescriptions, and the thoroughness with which they approached the task of removing anything that collided with the postulate of purity. Totalitarian ideologies were remarkable for their proclivity to condense the diffuse, pinpoint the elusive, make the uncontrollable into a target within reach and, so to speak, within bullet-range; the dispersed and ubiquitous anxiety exhaled by equally dispersed and ubiquitous threats to comprehension and to the sense of order were thereby squeezed and compressed so that they could be 'handled', and dealt with wholesale in a single, straightforward procedure. Nazism and communism excelled in pushing the totalitarian tendency to its radical extreme – the first by condensing the complexity of the 'purity' problem in its modern form into that of the purity of race, the second into that of the purity of class. Yet totalitarian cravings and leanings made their presence visible, albeit in a slightly less radical form, also in the tendency of the modern nation-state as such to underpin and reinforce the uniformity of state citizenship with the universality and comprehensivess of national membership.

For reasons which I have analysed elsewhere[8] and which are too complex and numerous to be spelled out here, the tendency to collectivize and centralize the 'cleansing' activities aimed at the preservation of purity, while by no means extinct or exhausted, tends in our time to be ever more often replaced with the strategies of deregulation and privatization. On the one hand, we note in many places a growing indifference of the state to its past task of promoting a singular as well as a comprehensive model of order, and the unprecedented equanimity with which the co-presence of a variety of such models is contemplated by the powers that be. On the other hand, one can discern the waning of the 'forward push' so crucial to the modern spirit, the relaxation of the modern war of attrition waged against received tradition, the lack of enthusiasm for (even resentment of) all-embracing schemes of decreed order that promise to put and fix everything in its place – and, indeed, the appearance of *sui generis* vested interest in the continuing diversification, under-determination, 'messiness' of the world. An ever growing number of postmodern men and women, while by no means immune to the fear of being lost and ever so often carried away by the recurring waves of 'homesickness', find the open-endedness of their situation attractive enough to outweigh the anguish of uncertainty. They revel in the pursuit of new and untested experience, are willingly seduced by offers of adventure, and on the whole prefer keeping options open to all fixity of commitment. In this change of mood they are aided and abetted by a market organized entirely around consumer demand and vitally interested in keeping that demand permanently unsatisfied and thus preventing the ossification of any acquired habits and whipping up the consumers' appetite for ever more intense sensations and ever new experience.

The consequence of that sea-change, most relevant to our topic, has been well captured by Georges Balandier: 'Aujourd'hui, tout se brouille, les frontières se déplacent, les catégories deviennent confuses. Les différences perdent leur encadrement; elles se démultiplient, elles se trouvent presque à l'état libre, disponibles pour la composition de nouvelles configurations, mouvantes, combinables et manipulables.'[9]

Differences pile up one upon the other, distinctions previously not considered relevant to the overall scheme of things and therefore invisible now force themselves upon the canvas of the *Lebenswelt*. Differences once accepted as non-negotiable are thrown unexpectedly into the melting pot or become objects of contention. Competitive charts overlap or clash, barring all chance of an 'official' and universally binding Ordnance Survey map. Yet since each scheme of purity generates its own dirt and each order generates its own strangers, making up the stranger in its own likeness and measure – the stranger is now as resistant to fixation as the social space itself: 'L'Autre se révèle *multiple*, localisable partout, changeant selon les circonstances.'

Does this augur the end of the Stranger's victimization and martyrdom in the service of purity? Not necessarily, contrary to many enthusiastic eulogies of the new postmodern tolerance, or even its assumed love of difference. In the postmodern world of freely competing styles and life patterns there is still one stern test of purity which whoever applies for admission is required to pass: one needs to be capable of being seduced by the infinite possibility and constant renewal promoted by the consumer market, of rejoicing in the chance of putting on and taking off identities, of spending one's life in the never ending chase after ever more intense sensations and even more exhilarating experience. Not everybody can pass that test. Those who do not are the 'dirt' of postmodern purity.

Since the criterion of purity is the ability to partake in the consumerist game, those left outside as a 'problem', as the 'dirt' which needs to be 'disposed of', are *flawed consumers* – people unable to respond to the enticements of the consumer market because they lack the required resources, people unable to be 'free individuals' according to the sense of 'freedom' as defined in terms of consumer choice. They are the new 'impure', who do not fit into the new scheme of purity. Looked at from the now dominant perspective of the consumer market, they are redundant – truly 'objects out of place'.

The job of separating and eliminating that waste of consumerism is, like everything else in the postmodern world, deregulated and privatized. The shopping malls and supermarkets, the temples of the new consumerist creed and the stadiums where the game of consumerism is played, bar entry to the flawed consumers at their own expense, surrounding themselves with surveillance cameras, electronic alarms and heavily armed guards; so do the neighbourhoods where lucky and happy consumers live and enjoy their new freedoms; so do the individual consumers, viewing their homes and their cars as ramparts of permanently besieged fortresses.

These deregulated, privatized, diffuse concerns with guarding the purity of consumerist life also come together in two contradictory, yet mutually reinforcing political demands directed towards the state. One is the demand to further enhance consumer freedoms of free consumers: to privatize the use of resources by 'rolling back' all collective intervention in private affairs, dismantling politically imposed constraints, cutting taxes and public expenditure. Another demand is to deal more energetically with the consequences of the first demand: surfacing in the public discourse under the name of 'law and order', this second demand is about the prevention of the equally deregulated and privatized protest of the victims of deregulation and privatization. Those whom the expansion of consumer freedom deprived of consumer skills and powers need to be checked and kept at bay; being a drain on public funds, and therefore indirectly on 'taxpayers' money' and the freedom of free consumers, they need to be checked and kept at bay at the least possible cost. If waste-disposal proves to be less costly than waste-recycling, it should be given priority; if it is cheaper to exclude and incarcerate the flawed consumers to keep them from mischief, this is preferable to the restoration of their consumer status through thoughtful employment policy coupled with ramified welfare provisions. And even the ways of exclusion and incarceration need to be 'rationalized', preferably subjected to the severe discipline of market competition: let the cheapest offer win . . .

In his eye-opening study of the ways in which the 'defence of law and order' is today carried on in the affluent countries, Nils Christie draws the following nightmarish picture of where the present tendency, if unchecked, is likely to lead:

> There are no natural limits. The industry is there. The capacity is there. Two thirds of the population will have a standard of living vastly above any found – for so large a proportion of a nation – anywhere else in the world. Mass media flourish on reports on the dangers of the crimes committed by the remaining one third of the population. Rulers are elected on promises to keep the dangerous third behind bars. Why should this come to stop? There are no natural limits for rational minds . . .
>
> The worst nightmare will never materialize. The dangerous population will not be exterminated, except for those killed by capital punishment. But the risks are great that those seen as core members of the dangerous population may be confined, warehoused, stored away, and forced to live their most active years as consumers of control. It can be done democratically, and under the strict control of the legal institutions.

'And the theoreticians in criminology and law', Christie observes gloomily, 'are there with a helping hand. Nobody believes in treatment any more, but incapacitation has been a favourite . . .'[10] The present-day concern with the purity of postmodern enjoyment expresses itself in the ever more pronounced tendency to criminalize its socially produced problems.

That every order tends to criminalize resistance to itself and outlaw its assumed or genuine enemies is evident to the point of triviality. What is less obvious, yet seems to emerge from our brief survey of the forms which the pursuit of purity has taken in modern and postmodern times, is that the object of particularly zealous and intense outlawing flurry are the radical consequences of the order's own constitutive principles. Modernity lived in a state of permanent war against tradition, legitimized by the urge to collectivize human destiny on a new and higher level, to substitute a new, better order for the old, jaded and outlived. It had therefore to purify itself of those who threatened to turn its inherent irreverence against its own principles. One of the most vexing 'impurities' in the modern version of purity was the *revolutionaries*, which the modern spirit could not but generate: revolutionaries were, after all, nothing but zealots of modernity, the most faithful among the believers in modern revelation, eager to draw the most radical lessons from the message, and push the order-making effort beyond the boundary of what the order-making mechanism was able to sustain. Postmodernity, on the other hand, lives in a state of permanent pressure towards dismantling of all collective interference into individual fate, towards deregulation and privatization. It tends to fortify itself therefore against those who – following its inherent tendency to disengagement, indifference and free-for-all – threaten to expose the suicidal potential of the strategy by pushing its implementation to the logical extreme. The most obnoxious 'impurity' of the postmodern version of purity is not revolutionaries, but those who either disregard the law or take the law into their own hands – muggers, robbers, car-thieves and shoplifters, as well as their *alter egos* – the vigilantes and the terrorists. Again, they are but the zealots of postmodernity, avid learners and pious believers in the postmodern revelation, keen to bring the life-recipes which the lesson suggests to their radical conclusion.

The pursuit of modern purity expressed itself daily in punitive action against dangerous classes; the pursuit of postmodern purity expresses itself daily in punitive action against the residents of mean streets and no-go urban areas, vagabonds and layabouts. In both cases, the 'impurity' at the focus of the punitive action is the extremity of the form promoted as pure; the stretching to the limits of what should have been, but could not be, kept in bounds; the waste-product that is but a disqualified mutation of the product passed as meeting the standards.

2

The Making and Unmaking of Strangers

All societies produce strangers; but each kind of society produces its own kind of strangers, and produces them in its own inimitable way. If the strangers are the people who do not fit the cognitive, moral, or aesthetic map of the world – one of these maps, two or all three; if they, therefore, by their sheer presence, make obscure what ought to be transparent, confuse what ought to be a straightforward recipe for action, and/or prevent the satisfaction from being fully satisfying; if they pollute the joy with anxiety while making the forbidden fruit alluring; if, in other words, they befog and eclipse the boundary lines which ought to be clearly seen; if, having done all this, they gestate uncertainty, which in its turn breeds the discomfort of feeling lost – then each society produces such strangers. While drawing its borders and charting its cognitive, aesthetic and moral maps, it cannot but gestate people who conceal borderlines deemed crucial to its orderly and/or meaningful life and so are accused of causing the discomfort experience as the most painful and the least bearable.

The most oppressive of nightmares that has haunted our century, notorious for its horrors and terrors, gory deeds and dreary premonitions, was best captured in George Orwell's memorable image of the jackboot trampling a human face. No face was secure – as everyone was prone to be charged with the crime of trespassing or transgressing. And since humanity bears ill all confinement while the humans who transgress the boundaries turn into strangers – everyone had reasons to fear the jackboot made to trample the strange face in the dust, squeeze the strange out of the human and keep those not-yet-trampled-but-about-to-be-trampled away from the mischief of illegal frontier-crossing.

Jackboots are parts of uniforms. Elias Cannetti wrote of 'murderous uniforms'. At some point of our century it became common knowledge that men in uniforms are to be feared most. Uniforms were the insignia of the servants of the State, that source of all power, and above all the coercive power aided and abetted by the absolving-from-inhumanity power; wearing uniforms, men become that power in action; wearing jackboots, they trample, and trample on behest and in the name of the State. The State which dressed men in uniforms so that they might be allowed and instructed to trample and absolved in advance from the guilt of trampling, was the State which saw itself as the fount, the guardian and the sole guarantee of orderly life: the dam protecting order from chaos. It was the State that knew what the order should look like, and which had enough strength and arrogance not only to proclaim all other states of affairs to be disorder and chaos, but also force them to live down to such a condition. This was, in other words, the modern state – one which legislated order into existence and defined order as the clarity of binding divisions, classifications, allocations and boundaries.

The typical *modern* strangers were the waste of the State's ordering zeal. What the modern strangers did not fit was the vision of order. When you draw dividing lines and set apart the so divided, everything that blurs the lines and spans the divisions undermines your work and mangles its products. The semantic under- and/or over-determination of the strangers corrupted neat divisions and marred the signposts. Merely by being around they interfered with the work which the State swore to accomplish, and undid its efforts to accomplish it. The strangers exhaled uncertainty where certainty and clarity should have ruled. In the harmonious, rational order about to be built there was no room – there could be no room – for 'neither–nors', for the sitting astride, for the cognitively ambivalent. Order-building was a war of attrition waged against the strangers and the strange.

In this war (to borrow Lévi-Strauss's concepts) two alternative, but also complementary strategies were intermittently deployed. One was *anthropophagic*: annihilating the strangers by *devouring* them and then metabolically transforming into a tissue indistinguishable from one's own. This was the strategy of *assimilation*: making the different similar; smothering of cultural or linguistic distinctions; forbidding all traditions and loyalties except those meant to feed the conformity to the new and all-embracing order; promoting and enforcing one and only one measure of conformity. The other strategy was *anthropoemic*: *vomiting* the strangers, banishing them from the limits of the orderly world and barring them from all communication with those inside. This was the strategy of *exclusion* – confining the strangers within the visible walls of the ghettos or behind the invisible, yet no less tangible, prohibitions of *commensality*, *connubium* and *commercium*; 'cleansing' – expelling the strangers beyond the frontiers of the managed and manageable territory; or, when neither of the two measures was feasible – destroying the strangers physically.

The most common expression of the two strategies was the notorious clash between the liberal and the nationalist/racist versions of the modern project. People are different, implied the liberal project, but they are different because of the diversity of local, particularistic traditions in which they grew and matured. They are products of education, creatures of culture, and hence pliable and amenable to reshaping. With the progressive universalization of the human condition, which means nothing else but the uprooting of all parochiality together with the powers bent on preserving it, and consequently setting human development free from the stultifying impact of the accident of birth – that predetermined, stronger-than-human-choice diversity will fade away. Not so – objected the nationalist/racist mind. Cultural remaking has limits which no human effort could transcend. Certain people will never be converted into something else than they are. They are, so to speak, beyond repair. One cannot rid *them* of their faults; one can only get rid *of them* themselves, complete with their inborn and eternal oddities and evils.

In the modern society and under the aegis of the modern state, cultural and/or physical annihilation of strangers and of the strange was a *creative destruction*; demolishing, but building at the same time; mutilating, but also straightening up . . . It was part and parcel of the ongoing order-building, nation-building, state-building effort, its necessary condition and accompaniment. And, obversely, whenever building-order-by-design is on the agenda, certain inhabitants of the territory to be made orderly in the new way turn into strangers that need to be eliminated.

Under the pressure of the modern order-building urge, the strangers lived, so to speak, in a state of suspended extinction. The strangers were, by definition, an anomaly to be rectified. Their presence was defined *a priori* as temporary, much as the current/fleeting stage in the prehistory of the order yet to come. A permanent coexistence with the stranger and the strange, and the pragmatics of living with strangers, did not need to be faced point-blank as a serious prospect. And it would not need, as long as modern life remained a life-towards-a-project, as long as that project remained collectivized into a vision of a new and comprehensive order, and as long as the construction of such an order remained in the hands of a State ambitious and resourceful enough to pursue the task. Not everywhere do these conditions seem to be holding today, however: at a time which Anthony Giddens calls 'late modernity', Ulrich Beck 'reflexive modernity', George Balandier 'surmodernity', and I have (together with many others) chosen to call 'postmodern': the time we live now, in our part of the world (or, rather – living in such a time defines what we see as 'our part of the world' . . .).

From disembedding to setting afloat

In its order-building pursuits, the modern State set about discrediting, disavowing and uprooting *les pouvoirs intermédiaires* of communities and traditions. If accomplished, the task would 'disembed' (Giddens) or 'disencumber' (MacIntyre) the individuals, give them the benefit of an absolute beginning, set them free to choose the kind of life they wish to live and to monitor and manage its living in the framework of legal rules spelled out by the sole legitimate legislating powers – those of the State. The modern project promised to free the individual from inherited identity. Yet it did not take a stand against identity as such, against having *an* identity, even a solid, resilient and immutable identity. It only transformed the identity from the matter of *ascription* into the *achievement* – thus making it an individual task and the individual's responsibility.

Much like that global order which collectively underwrote individual life-efforts, the orderly (comprehensive, cohesive, consistent and continuous) identity of the individual was cast as a *project*, the *life project* (as Jean-Paul Sartre, with wisdom fast becoming retrospective, articulated it). Identity was to be erected systematically, level by level and brick by brick, following a blueprint completed before the work started. The construction called for a clear vision of the final shape, careful calculation of the steps leading towards it, long-term planning and seeing through the consequences of every move. And so there was a tight and irrevocable bond between social order as a project and the individual life as a project; the latter was unthinkable without the former. Were it not for the collective efforts to secure a reliable, lasting, stable, predictable setting for individual actions and choices – constructing a clear and lasting identity and living one's life towards such an identity would be all but impossible.

Settings appear reliable (1) if their calculated life-expectancy is more or less commensurate with the duration of the individual identity-building process; and (2) if their shape is seen as immune to the vagaries of fads and foibles promoted singly or severally (in sociological jargon – if the 'macro-level' is relatively independent of what goes on at the 'micro-level'), so that individual projects can be sensibly inscribed in a tough, trustworthy, unyielding external frame. This was the case, by and large, through most of modern history, the notorious modern acceleration of change notwithstanding. 'Structures' (from physical neighbourhoods to currencies) appeared to be endowed with enough resilience and solidity to withstand all inroads of individual endeavours and survive all individual choice, so that the individual could measure himself against the rock-hard and finite set of opportunities (that is, convinced that his choices can be, in principle, *rationally* calculated and *objectively* evaluated). When compared to the biologically limited span of individual life, the institutions embodying collective life and the powers guaranteeing their authority appeared truly immortal. Professions, occupations and related skills did not age quicker than their carriers. Neither did the principles of success: delaying gratifications paid off in the long run, and the savings book epitomized the prudence and wisdom of long-term planning. In the modern society which engaged its members primarily in the role of producers/soldiers,[1] adjustment and adaptation pointed one way only: it was the fickle individual choice which needed to take stock as well as notice of the 'functional prerequisites' of the whole – which in more than one sense it had to perceive, to use Durkheim's apt phrase, as 'greater than itself'.

If these are indeed the conditions of the reliability of settings, or of the appearance of the settings as reliable – the context of postmodern life does not pass the test. The individual life-projects find no stable ground in which to lodge an anchor, and individual identity-building efforts cannot rectify the consequences of 'disembedding' and arrest the floating and drifting self. Some authors (notably Giddens) point to the widely fashionable efforts of 're-embedding'; being, however, postulated, rather than pre-given, and sustained solely by the notoriously erratic supplies of emotional energy, the sites of the sought 're-embedment' are plagued with the same unsteadiness and eccentricity which prompts the disembedded selves to seek them in the first place. The image of the world daily generated by present-day life concerns is devoid of genuine or assumed solidity and continuity which used to be the trade-mark of modern 'structures'. The dominant sentiment is now the feeling of a new type of uncertainty – not limited to one's own luck and talents, but concerning as well the future shape of the world, the right way of living in it, and the criteria by which to judge the rights and wrongs of the way of living. What is also new about the postmodern rendition of uncertainty (by itself not exactly a newcomer in a world with the modern past) is that it is no longer seen as a mere temporary nuisance, which with due effort may be either mollified or altogether overcome. The postmodern world is bracing itself for life under a condition of uncertainty which is permanent and irreducible.

Dimensions of the present uncertainty

Many a feature of contemporary living contributes to the overwhelming feeling of uncertainty: to the view of the future of the 'world as such' *and* the 'world within reach' as essentially undecidable, uncontrollable and hence frightening, and of the gnawing doubt whether the present contextual constants of action will remain constant long enough to enable reasonable calculation of its effects . . . We live today, to borrow the felicitous expression coined by Marcus Doel and David Clarke,[2] in the atmosphere of *ambient fear*. Let us name just a few of the factors responsible.

1 The new world disorder. After half a century of clear-cut divisions, obvious stakes and indubitable political purposes and strategies came the world devoid of visible structure and any – however sinister – logic. Power-bloc politics, which not so long ago dominated the world, frightened by the awesomeness of its possibilities; whatever came to replace it frightens however by its lack of consistency and direction – and so by the boundlessness of possibilities it forebodes. Hans Magnus Erzensberger of Germany fears the impending era of the civil war (he has counted about forty such wars being waged today from Bosnia through Afghanistan to Bougainville). In France, Alain Minc writes of the coming of New Dark Ages. In Britain, Norman Stone asks whether we are not back in the medieval world of beggars, plagues, conflagrations and superstitions. Whether this is or is not the tendency of our time remains, of course, an open question, which only the future will answer – but what truly matters now is that auguries like these can be publicly made from the most prestigious sites of contemporary intellectual life, listened to, pondered and debated.

The 'Second World' is no more; its former member countries woke up, to use Claus Offe's felicitous phrase, to the 'tunnel at the end of the light'. But with the demise of the Second World, the 'Third World' too, once in the Bandung era constituting itself as the third force, a force in opposition to both power blocs and to the very principle of power-bloc politics (and proving to be such a force through playing up the fears and inanities of the two power-greedy world empires), quit the world political stage. Today twenty or so wealthy, but worried and unself-assured, countries confront the rest of the world which is no longer inclined to look up to their definitions of progress and happiness, yet grows by the day ever more dependent on them for preserving whatever happiness or merely survival it can scrape together by its own means. Perhaps the concept of the 'secondary barbarization' best sums up the overall impact of the present-day metropoly on the world periphery.

2 The universal deregulation – the unquestionable and unqualified priority awarded to the irrationality and moral blindness of market competition, the unbound freedom granted to capital and finance at the expense of all other freedoms, the tearing up of the socially woven and

societally maintained safety nets, and the disavowal of all but economic reasons, gave a new push to the relentless process of polarization, once halted (only temporarily, as it now transpires) by the legal frameworks of the welfare state, trade union bargaining rights, labour legislation, and – on a global scale (though in this case much less convincingly) – by the initial effects of world agencies charged with the redistribution of capital. Inequality – inter-continental, inter-state, and most seminally the inner-societal (regardless of the level of the GNP boasted or bewailed by the country) reaches once more proportions which the yesteryear world confident of its ability to self-regulate and self-correct seemed to have left behind once for all. By cautious and, if anything, conservative calculations, rich Europe counts among its citizens about three million homeless, twenty million evicted from the labour market, thirty million living below the poverty line. The switch from the project of community as the guardian of the universal right to decent and dignified life, to the promotion of the market as the sufficient guarantee of the universal chance of self-enrichment, deepens further the suffering of the new poor – adding insult to their injury, glossing poverty with humiliation and with denial of consumer freedom, now identified with humanity.

The psychological effects, though, reach far beyond the swelling ranks of the dispossessed and the redundant. Only the few powerful enough to blackmail the other powerfuls into the obligation of a golden handshake can be sure that their home, however prosperous and imposing it may seem today, is not haunted by the spectre of tomorrow's downfall. No jobs are guaranteed, no positions are foolproof, no skills are of lasting utility, experience and know-how turn into liability as soon as they become assets, seductive careers all too often prove to be suicide tracks. In their present rendering, human rights do not entail the acquisition of the right to a job, however well performed, or – more generally – the right to care and consideration for the sake of past merits. Livelihood, social position, acknowledgment of usefulness and the entitlement to self-dignity may all vanish together, overnight and without notice.

3 The other safety nets, self-woven and self-maintained, these second lines of trenches once offered by the neighbourhood or the family, where one could withdraw to heal the bruises left by the marketplace skirmishes – if they have not fallen apart, then they have at least been considerably weakened. The changing pragmatics of interpersonal relations (the new style of 'life politics', as described with great conviction by Anthony Giddens), now permeated by the ruling spirit of consumerism and thus casting the other as the potential source of pleasurable experience, is partly to blame: whatever else the new pragmatics is good at, it cannot generate lasting bonds, and most certainly not the bonds which

are *presumed* as lasting and *treated* as such. The bonds which it does generate in profusion have in-built until-further-notice and unilateral-withdrawal-at-will clauses and promise neither the granting nor the acquisition of rights and obligations.

The slow yet relentless dissipation and induced forgetting of social skills bears another part of the blame. What used to be put together and kept together by individual skills and with the use of indigenous resources tends to be mediated now by technologically produced tools purchasable in the market. In the absence of such tools partnerships and groups disintegrate (if they had the chance to emerge in the first place). Not just the satisfaction of individual needs, but the presence and resilience of teams and collectivities become to an ever greater extent market-dependent, and so duly reflect the capriciousness and erraticism of the marketplace.

4 As David Bennett recently observed,[3] 'radical uncertainty about the material and social worlds we inhabit and our modes of political agency within them . . . is what the image-industry offers us . . .'. Indeed, the message conveyed today with great power of persuasion by the most ubiquitously effective cultural media (and, let us add, easily read out by the recipients against the background of their own experience, aided and abetted by the logic of consumer freedom) is a message of the essential indeterminacy and softness of the world: in this world, everything may happen and everything can be done, but nothing can be done once for all – and whatever happens comes unannounced and goes away without notice. In this world, bonds are dissembled into successive encounters, identities into successively worn masks, life-history into a series of episodes whose sole lasting importance is their equally ephemeral memory. Nothing can be known for sure, and anything which is known can be known in a different way – one way of knowing is as good, or as bad (and certainly as volatile and precarious) as any other. Betting is now the rule where certainty was once sought, while taking risks replaces the stubborn pursuit of goals. And thus there is little in the world which one could consider solid and reliable, nothing reminiscent of a tough canvas in which one could weave one's own life itinerary.

Like everything else, the self-image splits into a collection of snapshots, each having to conjure up, carry and express its own meaning, more often than not without reference to other snapshots. Instead of constructing one's identity, gradually and patiently, as one builds a house – through the slow accretion of ceilings, floors, rooms, connecting passages – a series of 'new beginnings', experimenting with instantly assembled yet easily dismantled shapes, painted one over the other; a *palimpsest identity*. This is the kind of identity which fits the world in which the art of forgetting is an asset no less, if no more, important than the art of memorizing, in which forgetting rather than learning is the condition of continuous fitness, in which ever new things and people enter and exit without much rhyme or reason the field of vision of the stationary camera of attention, and where the memory itself is like video-tape, always ready to be wiped clean in order to admit new images, and boasting a life-long guarantee only thanks to that wondrous ability of endless self-effacing.

These are some, certainly not all, of the dimensions of postmodern uncertainty. Living under conditions of overwhelming and self-perpetuating uncertainty is an experience altogether different from a life subordinated to the task of identity-building and lived in a world bent on the building of order. The oppositions which in that other experience underlay and endorsed the meaning of the world, and of life lived in it, lose in the new experience much of their meaning and most of their heuristic and pragmatic potency. Baudrillard has written profusely about this implosion of the sense-giving oppositions.

Yet alongside the collapse of the opposition between reality and its simulation, truth and its representation – comes the blurring and the watering down of the difference between the normal and the abnormal, the expectable and the unexpected, the ordinary and the bizarre, domes-ticated and wild – the familiar and the strange, 'us' and the strangers. The strangers are no longer authoritatively preselected, defined and set apart, as they used to be in times of the state-managed, consistent and durable programmes of order-building. They are now as unsteady and protean as one's own identity; as poorly founded, as erratic and volatile. *L'ipséité*, that difference which sets the self apart from the non-self, and 'us' apart from 'them', is no longer given by the pre-ordained shape of the world, nor by command from on high. It needs to be constructed, and recon-structed, and constructed once more, and reconstructed again, on both sides at the same time, neither of the sides boasting more durability, or just 'givenness', than the other. Today's strangers are by-products, but also the means of production, in the incessant, because never conclusive, process of identity building.

Freedom, uncertainty, and freedom from uncertainty

What makes certain people 'strangers' and therefore vexing, unnerving, off-putting and otherwise a 'problem', is – let us repeat – their tendency to befog and eclipse boundary lines which ought to be clearly seen. At different times and in different social situations, different boundaries ought to be seen more clearly than others. In our postmodern times, for reasons spelled out above, the boundaries which tend to be simultaneously most strongly desired and most acutely missed are those of *a rightful and secure position in society*, of a space unquestionably one's own, where one can plan one's life with the minimum of interference, play one's role in a game in which the rules do not change overnight and without notice, act reasonably and hope for the better. As we have seen, it is the widespread characteristic of contemporary men and women in our type of society that they live perpetually with the 'identity problem' unsolved. They suffer, one might say, from a chronic absence of resources with which they could build a truly solid and lasting identity, anchor it and stop it from drifting.

Or one can go yet further and point out a more incapacitating feature of their life situation, a genuine double-bind, which defies the most ardent efforts to make identity clear-cut and reliable. While *making* oneself an identity is a strongly felt need and an activity eloquently encouraged by all authoritative cultural media – *having* an identity solidly founded and resistant to cross-waves, having it 'for life', proves a handicap rather than an asset for such people as do not sufficiently control the circumstances of their life itinerary; a burden that constrains the movement, a ballast which they must throw out in order to stay afloat. This, we can say, is a universal feature of our times – and hence the anxiety related to the problems of identity and the disposition to be concerned with everything 'strange', on which anxiety may be focused and by being focused made sense of, is potentially universal. But the specific gravity of that feature is not the same for everybody; the feature affects different people to a different degree and brings consequences with varying importance for their life-pursuits.

In her eye-opening study of *Purity and Danger*,[4] Mary Douglas taught us that what we perceive as uncleanness or dirt and busy ourselves scrubbing and wiping out is that anomaly or ambiguity 'which must not be included if the pattern is to be maintained'. She added a sociological perspective to Jean-Paul Sartre's brilliant and memorable analysis of *le visqueux*, 'the slimy'.[5] The slimy, says Sartre, is docile – or so it seems to be.

Only at the very moment when I believe that I possess it, behold by a curious reversal, it possesses me . . . If an object which I hold in my hands is solid, I can let go when I please; its inertia symbolizes for me my total power . . . Yet here is the slimy reversing the terms; [my self] is suddenly *compromised*, I open my hands, I want to let go of the slimy and it sticks to me, it draws me, it sucks at me . . . I am no longer the master . . . The slime is like a liquid seen in a nightmare, where all its properties are animated by a sort of life and turn back against me . . .

If I dive into the water, if I plunge into it, if I let myself sink in it, I experience no discomfort, for I do not have any fear whatsoever that I may dissolve in it; I remain a solid in its liquidity. If I sink in the slimy, I feel that I am going to be lost in it . . . To touch the slimy is to risk being dissolved in sliminess.

Feeling the alterity of the water in which I swim (if I know how to swim, that is, and if the waves are not too strong for my skills and muscles) is not only freedom from fear; it is positively pleasurable. The joy obtained from an uncommon or rare sensual experience is unclouded by the apprehension that something important to me and more lasting than the pleasure may be given up as a result. If anything, immersing myself in the lake or the sea reasserts my power to keep my shape intact, my control over my body, my freedom and mastery: at any time I may come back if I wish, dry myself, not for a moment dreading the compromise, the discreditation of my being myself, being what I think/want myself to be. But imagine taking a bath in a barrelful of resin, tar, honey or treacle . . . Unlike water, the substance will stick, cling to my skin, would not let go. Rather than exuberantly invading a foreign, novel element – I feel invaded and conquered by an element from which there is no escape. I am no longer in control, no longer a master of myself. I have lost my freedom.

Thus the sliminess stands for the loss of freedom, or for the fear that freedom is under threat and may be lost. But, let us note, freedom is a *relation* – a power relation. I am free if and only if I can act according to my will and reach the results I intend to reach; this means, though, that some other people will be inevitably restricted in their choices by the actions I have taken, and that they will fail to reach the results *they* wished. In fact, I cannot measure my own freedom in absolute terms – I can measure it only *relatively*, comparing it with other people's ability to get it their way. Thus, ultimately, freedom depends on who is stronger – on the distribution of the skills and material resources which the effective action requires. What follows is that the 'sliminess' (stickiness, stubbornness, resilience, potency of compromising, of transforming possession into being possessed, mastery into dependency) of another substance (and this includes, more than anything else, other *people*) is *a function of my own skills and resources*. What seems slimy resin to some, may be fresh, pleasant, exhilarating sea-water to some others. And the purest of waters may act the 'slimy style' against a person ignorant of the art of swimming, but also a person too weak to defy the powerful element, to withstand the torrent, to steer safely through the rapids, to stay on course among the eddies and tidal waves. One is tempted to say that, much as beauty is in the eye of beholder, the sliminess of the slimy is in the muscles (or in the wallet?) of the actor.

The stranger is hateful and feared the way the slimy is, and for the same reasons (not everywhere, to be sure, and not at all times; as Max Frisch caustically observed in his essay 'Foreignization 1', musing on our feelings about foreigners coming to stay in our cities, 'there are just too many of them – not at the construction sites and not in the factories and not in the stable and not in the kitchen, but during after-hours. Especially on Sunday there are suddenly too many of them'). If this is so, then the same relativity principle which rules the constitution of 'sliminess' regulates the constitution of resented strangers, strangers as people to be resented: the acuity of strangehood, and the intensity of its resentment, grow up with the relative powerlessness and diminish with the growth of relative freedom. One can expect that the less people control and can control their lives and their life-founding identities, the more they will perceive others as slimy, and the more frantically they will try to disentangle, detach themselves from the strangers they experience as an enveloping, suffocating, sucking-in, formless substance. In the post-modern city, the strangers mean one thing to those for whom 'no-go area' (the 'mean streets', the 'rough districts') means 'I won't go in', and those to whom 'no go' means 'I can't go out'.

For some residents of the modern city, secure in their burglar-proof homes in leafy suburbs, fortified offices in the heavily policed business centres, and cars bespattered with security gadgets to take them from homes to offices and back, the 'stranger' is as pleasurable as the surfing beach, and not at all slimy. The strangers run restaurants promising unusual, exciting experiences to the taste-buds, sell curious-looking, mysterious objects suitable as talking points at the next party, offer services other people would not stoop or deign to offer, dangle morsels of wisdom refreshingly different from the routine and boring. The strangers are people whom you pay for the services they render and for the right to terminate their services once they no longer bring pleasure. At no point do the strangers compromise the freedom of the consumer of their services. As the tourist, the patron, the client, the consumer of services is always in charge: s/he demands, sets the rules, and above all decides when the encounter starts and when it ends. Unambiguously, the strangers are purveyors of pleasures. Their presence is a break in the tedium. One should thank God that they are here. So what is all that uproar and outcry for?

The uproar and the outcry comes, let there be no mistake, from other areas of the city, which the pleasure-seeking consumers never visit, let alone live in. Those areas are populated by people unable to choose whom they meet and for how long, or to pay for having their choices respected; powerless people, experiencing the world as a trap, not as an adventure park; incarcerated in a territory from which there is no exit for them, but which others may enter or leave at will. Since the only tokens for securing the freedom of choice which is a legal tender in the consumer society are in short supply or are denied them altogether, they need to resort to the only resources they possess in quantities large enough to impress; they defend the territory under siege through (to use Dick Hebdidge's pithy description) 'rituals, dressing strangely, striking bizarre attitudes, breaking rules, breaking bottles, windows, heads, issuing rhetorical challenges to the law'. They react in a wild, rabid, distraught and flustered fashion, as one reacts to the incapacitating pulling/dissolving power of the slimy. The sliminess of strangers, let us repeat, is the reflection of their own powerlessness. It is their own lack of power that crystallizes in their eyes as the awesome might of the strangers. The weak meet and confront the weak; but both feel like Davids fighting Goliaths. Each is 'slimy' to the other; but each fights the sliminess of the other in the name of the purity of its own.

Ideas, and the words which convey them, change their meaning the further they travel – and travelling between the homes of the satisfied consumers and the dwellings of the powerless is a long-distance voyage. If the contented and the secure wax lyrical about the beauty of nationhood, the New Jerusalem, the glory of heritage and the dignity of tradition – the insecure and hounded bewail the defilement and humiliation of the race. If the first rejoice in the variety of guests and pride themselves on their open minds and open doors, the second gnash their teeth at the thought of lost purity. The benign patriotism of the first rebounds as the racism of the second.

Nothing spurs into action as frenzied, licentious and disorderly as the fear of the dissembly of order, embodied in the figure of the slimy. But there is a lot of energy boiling in this chaos; with a degree of skill and cunning it can be gathered and redeployed to give the unruliness a direction. The fear of the slimy, precipitated by powerlessness, is always a tempting weapon to be added to the armoury of the power-greedy. Some of the latter come from the ranks of the frightened. They may try to use the heaps of accumulated fear and anger to climb out of the besieged ghetto, or, as Ervin Goffman wittily suggested, to make the crutch into a golf club. The diffuse resentment of the weak they may try to condense into an assault against equally weak strangers, thus kneading the fear and anger into the foundation of their own power, as tyrannical and intolerant as power can be, while all the time claiming to defend the weak against their oppressors. But other power-seekers are also attracted. One needs, after all, only to drive a few miles to refill the empty tank of nationalism with racist fuel. Not much navigating skill is needed to make the nationalist sails gather the wind blowing from racist hatred; to enlist, by the same token, the powerless in the service of the power-greedy. What one needs is but to remind them of the sliminess of strangers . . .

Theorizing the difference, or the twisted road to shared humanity

The essential difference between the socially produced modality of modern and postmodern strangers, for reasons listed before, is that, while modern strangers were earmarked for annihilation, and served as bordermarks for the advancing boundary of the order-under-construction, the postmodern ones are, joyfully or grudgingly, but by common consent or resignation, here to stay. To paraphrase Voltaire's comment on God – if they did not exist, they would have to be invented . . . And they are, indeed, invented, zealously and with gusto – patched together from protruding and salient or minute and inobtrusive distinction marks. They are useful precisely in their capacity as strangers; their strangehood is to be protected and caringly preserved. They are indispensable sign-posts on the itinerary with no plan or direction – they must be as many and as protean as the successive and parallel incarnations of identity in the never ending search for itself.

In an important respect, and for important reasons, ours is a *heterophilic* age. For the sensation-gatherers or experience-collectors as at least the better-off among us are, concerned (or, more exactly, forced to be concerned) with flexibility and openness, rather than with fixity and self-closure, difference comes at a premium. There is a resonance and a harmony between the way we go about our identity problems and plurality and differentiation of the world in which the identity problems are dealt with, or which we conjure up in the process of that dealing. It is not just that we need the strangers around, because, due to the way we are culturally shaped, we would miss precious life-enhancing values in a uniform, monotonous and homogeneous world; more than that – such a world without difference could not, by any stretch of the imagination, evolve out of the way in which our lives are shaped and carried on. The question is no longer how to get rid of the strangers and the strange once and for all, or declare human variety but a momentary inconvenience, but how to live with alterity – daily and permanently. Whatever realistic strategy of coping with the unknown, the uncertain and the confusing can be thought of – it needs to start from recognizing this fact.

And, indeed, all intellectually conceived strategies still in competition today seem to accept this. One may say: a new theoretical/ideological consensus is emerging, to replace another one, more than a century old. If the left and right, the progressivists and the reactionary of the modern period agreed that strangehood is abnormal and regrettable, and that the superior (because homogenous) order of the future would have no room for the strangers, postmodern times are marked by an almost universal agreement that difference is not merely unavoidable, but good, precious and in need of protection and cultivation. In the words of that towering figure of the postmodern intellectual right, Alain de Benoist:[6] 'We see reasons for hope only in the affirmation of collective singularities, the spiritual reappropriation of heritages, the clear awareness of roots and specific cultures.' The spiritual guide of the Italian neo-fascist movement, Julius Evola, is yet more blunt:[7] 'The racists recognize difference and want difference.' Pierre-André Taguieff sums up the process of the postmodern rearticulation of the racist discourse, coining the term 'differentialist racism'.

Note that these self-admittedly right-wing, even fascist, professions of faith, unlike their precursors, no longer propose that differences between people are immune to cultural interference and that it is beyond human power to make someone into someone else. Yes, they say, differences – our differences as much as the differences of the others – are all human products, culturally produced. But, they say, different cultures make their members in different shapes and colours – and *this is good*. Thou shalt not tie together what cultures, in their wisdom, have set apart. Let us, rather, help cultures – any culture – to go their own separate and, better still, inimitable ways. The world will be so much richer then . . .

The striking thing, of course, is that a reader unaware that the author of the first quotation was Benoist could be forgiven for mistaking it for a left programmatic statement; and that Evola's sentence would lose none of its conviction if the word 'racist' were replaced by 'progressive', 'liberal', or – for that matter – 'socialist' . . . Are we not all *bona fide* 'differentialists' today? Multiculturalists? Pluralists?

And so it happens that both right and left agree today that the preferable mode of living with strangers is to keep apart . . . Though perhaps for different reasons, both resent and publicly denigrate the universalist/imperialist/assimilationist ambitions of the modern state, now debunked as innately proto-totalitarian. Disenchanted or repelled by the idea of legislated uniformity, the left, which – being left – cannot live without hope, turns its eyes towards 'community', hailed and eulogized as the long-lost, now rediscovered, true home of humanity. To be a born-again communitarian is widely considered today as the sign of a critical standpoint, leftism and progress. Come back community, from the exile to which the modern state confined you; all is forgiven and forgotten – the oppressiveness of parochiality, the genocidal propensity of collective narcissism, the tyranny of communal pressures and the pugnacity and despotism of communal discipline. It is, of course, a nuisance that one finds in this bed some unwelcome and thoroughly repulsive fellows . . . How to keep the bed to oneself, how to prove that the unwelcome fellows have no right to be in it? This seems to be the question . . .

I propose that the racist bedfellows in the bed of communitarianism are perhaps a nuisance for its new occupants, but not at all a surprise. They were there first, and it is their birthright to be there. Both sets of occupants, the old ones and the new, have been lured into that bed by the same promise and the same desire – of 're-embedding' of what has been 'disembedded', of the release from the formidable task of individual self-construction, and from even more awesome and burdensome individual responsibility for its results.

The old racism turned its back on the emancipatory chance entailed in the modern project. I propose that, true to its nature, it turns its back now on the emancipatory chance which the changed, postmodern context of life holds. Only now, for the reason of curious amnesia or myopia, it is not alone in doing so. It sings in chorus with the lyrical voices of a growing number of social scientists and moral philosophers, who extol the warmth of the communal home and bewail the trials and tribulations of the unencumbered, homeless self.

This is a type of critique of the emancipatory failure of modernity which itself does not hold hope for emancipation: this is a misdirected, and – I would say – retrograde critique of the modern project, as it only proposes the shifting of the site of disablement and subordination from the universalist state to the particularist tribe. It only replaces one 'essentialism', already discredited, by another, not yet fully unmasked in all its disempowering potential. True, communal self-determination may assist the initial stages of the long process of re-empowerment of human subjects – their resolve to resist the disciplinary pressures currently experienced as the most obnoxious and overwhelming. But there is a dangerous, and easily overlooked point, where re-empowerment turns into a new disempowerment, and emancipation into a new oppression. Once on this road, it is difficult to sense where to stop, and as a rule it is too late to stop once the point has been recognized after the fact. We would all be well advised to heed the recent reminder of Richard Stevers:[8]

Martin Luther King Jr. understood perfectly well that racial and ethnic relations would deteriorate markedly if the cultural value of integration declined. Indeed, this is precisely what has happened in the United States. The various gender, racial and ethnic groups have almost come to occupy mutually exclusive social spaces . . . [T]he struggle for equality becomes a struggle for power – but power left to itself does not recognize equality.

But there is a genuine emancipatory chance in postmodernity, the chance of laying down arms, suspending border skirmishes waged to keep the stranger away, taking apart the daily erected mini-Berlin Walls meant to maintain distance and to separate. This chance does not lie in the celebration of born-again ethnicity and in genuine or invented tribal tradition – but in bringing to its conclusion the 'disembedding' work of modernity, through focusing on the right to choose one's identity as the sole universality of the citizen/human, on the ultimate, inalienable individual responsibility for the choice – and through laying bare the complex state- or tribe-managed mechanisms aimed at depriving the individual of that freedom of choice and that responsibility. The chance of human togetherness depends on the rights of the stranger, not on the question who – the state or the tribe – is entitled to decide who the strangers are.

Interviewed by Robert Maggiori for *Liberation* on 24 November 1994, Jacques Derrida appealed for rethinking rather than abandoning the modern idea of humanism. The 'human right', as we begin to see it today, but above all as we may and ought to see it, is not the product of legislation, but precisely the opposite: it is what sets the limit 'to force, declared laws, political discourses' and 'founded' rights (regardless of who has, or demands, or usurps the prerogative to 'found' them authoritatively). 'The human' of the traditional humanist philosophy, including the Kantian subject, is – so suggests Derrida – 'still too "fraternal", subliminally virile, familial, ethnic, national etc.' What – as I suggest – follows from here, is that the modern theorizing of human essence and human rights erred on the side of leaving too much, rather than too little, of the 'encumbered' or 'embedded' element in its idea of the human – and it is for this fault, rather than for siding too uncritically with the homogenizing ambitions of the modern state and hence placing the 'encumbering' or 'embedding' authority on the wrong site, that it ought to be subjected to critical scrutiny and reassessment.

That reassessment is a philosophical task. But saving the possibility of emancipation from being stillborn sets, besides the philosophical, also a political task. We have noted that the odious 'sliminess' of the stranger progresses as the freedom of the individuals faced with the duty of self-assertion declines. We have also noted that the postmodern setting does not so much increase the total volume of individual freedom, as redistribute it in an increasingly polarized fashion: intensifies it among the joyfully and willingly seduced, while tapering it almost beyond existence among the deprived and panoptically regulated. With this polarization uncurbed, one can expect the present duality of the socially produced status of strangers to continue unabated. At one pole, strangehood (and difference in general) will go on being constructed as the source of pleasurable experience and aesthetic satisfaction; at the other, as the terrifying incarnation of the unstoppably rising sliminess of the human condition – as the effigy for all future ritual burning of its horrors. And power politics will offer its usual share of opportunities for short-circuiting the poles: to protect their own emancipation-through-seduc-tion, those close to the first pole would seek domination-though-fear over those to the second pole, and so would aid and abet their cottage industry of horrors.

The sliminess of strangers and the politics of exclusion stem from the logic of polarization – from the increasingly 'two nations, mark two' condition;[9] and this is the case because the polarization arrests the process of individualization, of genuine and radical 'disembedding' for the 'other nation' – for the oppressed who have been denied the resources for identity-building and so (for all practical intents and purposes) also the tools of citizenship. It is not merely income and wealth, life expectation and life conditions, but also – and perhaps most seminally – the right to individuality, that is being increasingly polarized. And as long as it stays this way, there is little chance for the desliming of the strangers.

3

The Strangers of the Consumer Era: from the Welfare State to Prison

In 1981, 2.9 million criminal offences were recorded in England and Wales. In 1993, 5.5 million. In the last three years, the prison population has risen from 40,606 to 51,243. Between 1971 and 1993, public expenditure on the police rose from £2.8 billion to £7.7 billion. From 1984 to 1994, the number of practising solicitors went up from 44,837 to 63,628, and of practising barristers from 5,203 to 8,093.

In 1994, 5.6 million people in Britain claimed income support. 2,700,000 drew unemployment benefit; but by other accounts, than official governmental ones, the numbers of those who needed employment but had been barred by legal rules from claiming unemployment benefit (and thus from the official statistics of the unemployed) were twice as many.

For the last quarter of a century the population of prison inmates and all those who derive their livelihood from the prison industry – the police, the lawyers, the suppliers of prison equipment – has grown steadily. So has the population of the indolent – deprived, left behind, cast outside economic and social life. And so, expectedly, grew the popular feeling of insecurity; 85 per cent of the population of Britain today think that it was safe to walk the streets at night thirty years ago, but 95 per cent think that it is not safe now.

Those last thirty years or so were indeed fateful and seminal years in the history of the way in which the 'Western' – industrial, capitalist, democractic, modern – society was shaped and maintained. It is that way which determines the names people tend to give to their fears and anxieties, and to the spots where they suspect the threat to their security to lie. And that way – let me repeat – underwent a most profound change.

The very term 'unemployed' by which those unable to make their living used to be (and still are – though now misleadingly) described, made them into the proverbial exception that confirms the rule – obliquely reasserting the principle that 'being employed' is the norm which the state of 'being out of work' violates. The 'unemployed' were the 'reserve army of labour'. Temporarily out of job for reason of health, infirmity or current economic trouble, they were to be groomed to resume employment when fit – and grooming them was, by and large, the recognized task and the explicit or tacit undertaking of political powers.

This is no longer the case. Except in the nostalgic and increasingly demagogic copies of electoral commercials, those out of work have ceased being a 'reserve army of labour'. Economic upturns no longer signal the end to unemployment. 'Rationalizing' now means *cutting* not creating jobs, and technological and managerial progress is measured by 'slimming down' the work force, *closing down* branches and staff *reductions.* Updating the fashion in which business is run consists in making work 'flexible' – shedding labour and abandoning production lines and production sites at a moment's notice, whenever greener grass is sighted elsewhere: whenever more profitable commercial possibilities, or more docile and less costly labour, beckon from afar. Once tied down to steel and concrete, to heavy factory buildings and unwieldy machinery, capital has itself already become the embodiment of flexibility; it has mastered the tricks of pulling itself, like a rabbit, out of the hat or vanishing without a trace – with the information super-highway playing the role of the magic wand. Yet some people's meat being some other people's poison, changes which mean rationalization and flexibility for capital rebound at the receiving end as catastrophes – as inexplicable, as beyond human power; and as the stiffening of opportunities into the solid wall of fate. Jobs *for life* are no more. As a matter of fact jobs *as such*, as we once understood them, are no more. Without them, there is little room for life-lived-as-a-project, for long-term planning and far-reaching hopes. Be grateful for the bread you eat today and do not think too far ahead . . . The symbol of wisdom is no longer the savings book; it is now, at least for those able to afford being wise, the credit cards, and a walletful of them.

Few of us remember now that the Welfare State was originally conceived as a state-wielded tool to groom back the *temporarily* unfit into fitness and to encourage those who were fit to try harder, by saving them from fear of losing their fitness in the process . . . Welfare provisions were seen then as a safety net, drawn by the community as a whole, under every one of its members – giving everyone the courage to face the challenge of life; so that fewer and fewer members would ever need to use it, and those who did would use it less and less often. The community took it upon itself to make sure that the unemployed would have enough health and skills to become employed again, and to insure them against the temporary hiccups and vagaries of the ups and downs of fortune. The Welfare State was conceived not as *charity*, but a citizen's *right*, and not as the provision of individual handouts, but a form of *collective insurance*. (Who considers the payment from a life- or property-insurance company as charity or a handout?!) As I said, few of us remember this now . . .

This was the case – this *could* be the case – in those times when *industry* provided work, living and the insurance, for the majority of the population. The Welfare State had to reach where industry did not; it had to bear the marginal costs of capital's race for profit, to make the left-behind labour employable again – an effort which capital itself would not or could not undertake. Today, with a growing sector of the population never likely to enter production again, and thus being of no present or prospective interest to those who run the economy, the 'margin' is no longer marginal, and the collapse of capital's interest makes it seem yet less marginal – bigger and more awkward and cumbersome – than it is. This new perspective is expressed in the fashionable phrase: 'Welfare State? We can no longer afford it' . . .

As a result, welfare provisions have been transformed from the exercise of citizens' rights into the stigma of the impotent and the improvident. 'Focused on those who need it', subject to ever stricter and ever more humiliating means tests, vilified for being a drain on 'taxpayers' money', associated in the public mind with sponging, reprehensible negligence, sexual laxity or drug abuse – they turn ever more into the contemporary version of the wages of sin; and wages of sin which we not only 'cannot afford', but for which there is no moral reason why we should try to do so. The sins for which the original Welfare State was meant to pay were the sins of the capitalist economy and market competition, of capital which could not stay solvent without enormous social costs in shattered existences and broken lives – the costs which it refused, however, to pay, or could not pay under the threat of insolvency. It was that damage for which the Welfare State promised to idemnify the present victims and to insure the prospective ones. If we hear now that we, the 'taxpayers', 'cannot afford this any more', it only means that the state, the community, does not see it fit or desirable any more to countersign the social, human costs of economic solvency (which under market conditions is equivalent to profitability). Instead, it shifts the payment to the victims themselves, present and future. It refuses the responsibility for their ill fate – just as it has abandoned the old task of the 'recommodification' of labour. No more collective insurance against the risks; the task of coping with the collectively produced risks has been *privatized*.

Every type of social order produces some visions of the dangers which threaten its identity. But each society spawns visions made to *its own measure* – to the measure of the kind of social order it struggles to be. On the whole, these visions tend to be mirror images of the society which spawns them, while the image of the threat tends to be a self-portrait of the society with a minus sign. Or, to put this in psychoanalytical terms, the threat is a projection of the inner *ambivalence* of the society about its own ways and means; about the fashion in which it lives and perpetuates its living. The society unsure of the survival of its order develops the mentality of a besieged fortress; but the enemies who had laid siege to its walls are its own, its very own 'inner demons' – the suppressed, ambient fears which permeate its daily life, its 'normality', yet which, in order to make daily reality endurable, must be squashed and squeezed out of the lived-through quotidianity and moulded into an alien body: into a tangible enemy whom one can fight, and fight again, and even hope to conquer.

In line with this rule, the danger which haunted the classic modern state was that of the *revolution*. The enemies were the revolutionaries or all-too-radical reformists, the subversive forces trying to replace the extant state-managed order with another state-managed order, with a counter-order reversing upside down each and any principle by which the current order lived or aimed to live. As Michel Foucault has shown, the classic modern state, firmly in charge of the daily order-making efforts, collectivized and 'demographized' its tasks; the order-making was, above all, the job of generalizing, classifying, defining and setting apart categories. From that perspective, the counter-order could appear only as another, opposing classification and a reversal of categorial hierarchy. Those bent on doing the reversal could be seen only as aspiring alternative classifiers and legislators of categories. The 'inner demon', thus exorcized and reincarnated in the body of the revolutionary conspiracy, was the self-destructive tendency of the state's own legislating effort: the discontent, dissent and heresy which that effort could not but spawn in an ever growing volume among those cast at the receiving end of the present-day classifications.

If the state no longer presides over the reproduction of systemic order, having now left the task to the deregulated, and thus no longer politically accountable, market forces, the point of gravity in the process of order-making has shifted away from the legislating/generalizing/classifying/categorizing activities. Gradually yet steadily, fears related to the precariousness of order cease to be state-centred. Political power, the question of who rules the state and who makes the laws of the land, ceases to be the main bone of contention. The enemy is no longer the revolutionary conspiracy of the would-be state administrators. Since no tangible, well-defined agency seems to be in charge of the *present* order, it is difficult, nay impossible, to imagine any not-yet-existing power which would cure the ills of the current order in the *future* by replacing it with another order – placing it under, so to speak, 'new management'. When the American politologist Peter Drucker declared 'no more salvation by society', this was a programmatic, ideological statement; but it was also, even if not self-consciously, a product of stock-taking, an assertion of new realism. 'No more salvation by society' means that there are no visible collective, joint agencies in charge of the global societal order. The care for the human plight has been privatized, and the tools and practices of care deregulated. One comprehensive and universal categorial grid has fallen apart. Self-aggrandizement is replacing socially sponsored improvement, and self-assertion takes the place of the collective cure for class deprivation. It is now individual wit and muscle that must be stretched in the daily struggle for survival and improvement.

When it managed the disciplined conduct of its members through their *productive roles*, society prompted joining forces and the search for advancement through collective efforts. The society which obtains order-stabilizing behavioural patterns from its members who have been evicted or are about to be evicted from their statuses as *producers* and defined instead as, first and foremost, *consumers*, discourages the anchoring of hope in *collective* actions. Thoughts emerging within the cognitive horizon framed by the daily practices of the consumers invariably enhance the acute interest in the consumer market and extend its seductive powers. Unlike production, consumption is a thoroughly *individual* activity: it also sets individuals at cross purposes, often at each other's throats.

The 'inner demons' of this type of society are born out of the seductive powers of the consumer market. The society of consumers can no more do without that *seduction* than the society of producers could do without thanks to the enforcement of *normative regulation*. For this very reason it cannot afford to declare a war, even less to wage a war, against the market tendency to beef up consumer dreams and desires to a state of frenzy and to raise them sky-high – however detrimental such a tendency may prove to the form of order in which it is rooted.

And detrimental to order it is – as much as it is indispensable to it; there is no novelty in this paradox – as, since the moment when order turned into a task to be performed, any strategy of order-making proved to be charged with the same incurable ambivalence. What is, however, novel is the *type* of order and the *method* it needs for its own smooth functioning and perpetuation. The method is new, and so are the *discontents* it breeds and the *risks* it incubates. As the feasibility of a socially initiated redistribution of consumer desirables is fading, even those who cannot partake of the consumer feast, and thus are not properly regulated by the powers of market seduction, have only one course of action left to take in order to attain the standards the consumer society promotes: to reach for the ends directly, without first deploying the means. After all, one cannot deploy what one does not possess . . .

Whatever has been registered in recent years as *rising criminality* (a process, let us note, parallel to the falling of the membership of the communist or other radical parties of 'alternative order') is not a product of malfunctioning or neglect – let alone of factors external to society itself (though this is how it is ever more often depicted – when, typically, the correlation between criminality and immigration, the influx of strangers, of foreign races or cultures, is spied out or declared). It is, instead, the consumer society's own product, logically (if not legally) legitimate; and what is more – also an *inescapable* product. The higher the 'consumer demand' (that is, the more effective the market seduction), the more the consumer society is safe and prosperous. Yet, simultaneously, the wider and deeper is the gap between those who desire and those who can satisfy their desires, or between those who have been seduced and proceed to act in the way the state of being seduced prompts them to act, and those who have been seduced yet are unable to act in the way the seduced are expected to act. Market seduction is, simultaneously, the great equalizer and the great divider. Seductive impulses, to be effective, must be transmitted in all directions and addressed indiscriminately to everybody who will listen. But there are more of those who can listen than of those who can respond in the fashion which the seductive message was meant to elicit. Those who cannot act on the desires so induced are treated daily to the dazzling spectacle of those who can. Lavish consumption, they are told and shown, is the sign of success and a highway leading straight to public applause and fame. They also learn that possessing and consuming certain objects and practising certain life-styles is the necessary condition of happiness; perhaps even of human dignity.

If consumption is the measure of a successful life, of happiness and even of human decency, then the lid has been taken off the human desires; no amount of acquisitions and exciting sensations is ever likely to bring satisfaction in the way the 'keeping up to the standards' once promised: there are no standards to keep up to – the finishing line moves forward together with the runner; the goals keep forever distant as one tries to reach them. Far ahead, records keep being broken. Dazzled and baffled, people learn that in the newly privatized, and thus 'liberated', companies, which they remember as public institutions that were austere and constantly famished for cash, the present managers draw salaries measured in millions, while those sacked from their managerial chairs are indemnified, again in millions of pounds, for their botched and sloppy work. From all places, through all communication channels, the message comes loud and clear: there are no standards except those of *grabbing more*, and no rules, except the imperative of 'playing one's cards right'.

In no card game are hands even, so the advice to play one's cards right suggests one should use whatever resources one can muster. From the point of view of the casino owners some resources – those which they themselves allocate or circulate – are *legal* tender; all other resources, though – those beyond their control – are *prohibited*. The line dividing the fair from the unfair does not look the same, however, from the side of the *players*; and particularly from the side of the would-be, *aspiring* players; and most particularly, from the side of the *incapacitated* aspiring players, who do not have access to the legal tender. They must resort to the resources they do have, whether recognized as legal or declared illegal – or opt out of the game altogether. That latter move, however, has been made by the seductive force of the market all but impossible to contemplate.

The disarming, disempowering and suppressing of unfulfilled players is therefore an indispensable supplement of the integration-through-seduction in a market-led society of consumers. The impotent, indolent players are to be *kept outside the game*. They are the waste-product of the game, but a product the game cannot stop sedimenting without grinding to a halt and calling in the receivers. Also, the game would not benefit from halting the production of waste for another reason: those who stay in the game need to be shown the horrifying sights of (as they are told) the only alternative – in order to be able and willing to endure the hardships and the tensions which life lived as play gestates.

Given the nature of the game now played, the hardships and misery of those left out of it, once treated as a *collectively caused* blight which needs to be dealt with by *collective means*, can be only redefined as an *individual crime*. The 'dangerous classes' are thus redefined as *classes of criminals*. And so the prisons now fully and truly deputize for the fading welfare institutions.

The growing volume of behaviour classified as criminal is not an obstacle on the road to the fully fledged and all-embracing consumerist society; on the contrary, it is its natural accompaniment and prerequisite. This is so, admittedly, for a number of reasons; but I propose that the main reason among them is the fact that those 'left out of the game' (the *flawed consumers* – the unfulfilled consumers, those whose means do not measure up to the desires, and those refused the chance of winning while playing the game by its official rules) are precisely the embodiment of the 'inner demons' specific to the consumer life. Their ghettoization and criminalization, the severity of the sufferings administered to them, the cruelty of the fate visited upon them, are all – metaphorically speaking – the ways of exorcizing such inner demons and burning them in effigy. The criminalized margins serve as the sewers into which the inevitable, but excessive and poisonous, effluvia of consumerist seduction are consolingly channelled, so that such people as manage to stay in the game of consumerism may not worry about the state of their own health. If, however, this is, as I suggest it is, the prime stimulus of the present exuberance of what the great Norwegian criminologist Nils Christie called 'the prison industry', then the hope that the process can be slowed down, let alone halted or reversed, in a thoroughly deregulated and privatized society animated and run by a consumer market, are – to say the least – dim.

Nowhere is the connection exposed more fully than in the United States, where the unqualified rule of the consumer market reached, in the years of Reaganite free-for-all, further than in any other country. The years of deregulation and dismantling of the welfare provisions were also the years of rising criminality, of a growing police force and prison population. They were also years in which an ever more gory and spectacularly cruel lot needed to be reserved for those declared criminal to match the fast-growing fears and anxieties, nervousness and uncertainty, anger and fury of the 'silent' or not-so-silent majority of ostensibly successful consumers. The more powerful the 'inner demons' became, the more insatiable grew the desire of that majority to see 'crime punished' and 'justice apportioned'. The liberal Bill Clinton won the presidential election promising to multiply the ranks of the police and build new and more secure prisons; some observers (among them Peter Linebaugh of the University of Toledo, Ohio, the author of *The London Hanged*) believe that Clinton owes his election to the widely publicized execution of a retarded man, Ricky Ray Rector, whom he allowed to go to the electric chair when Governor of Arkansas. Recently Clinton's opponents of the radical right sections of the Republican Party swept the board in the congressional elections having convinced the electorate that Clinton had not done enough to fight criminality and that they would do more.

In 1972, just as the welfare era reached its summit and just before its fall began, the Supreme Court of the United States, mirroring the public mood of the time, ruled the death penalty to be arbitrary and capricious, and as such unfit to serve the cause of justice. Several other rulings later, the court in 1988 permitted the execution of sixteen-year-olds, in 1989 the execution of the mentally retarded, until finally in 1992 in the infamous case of Herrera vs. Collins it ruled that the accused may be innocent, but he could still be executed if his trial was properly conducted and constitutionally correct. The recent Crime Bill passed by the Senate and the House of Representatives extends the number of offences punishable by death to fifty-seven or even, according to certain interpretations, seventy. With high-profile publicity and much fanfare, a federal state-of-the-art execution chamber with a death row planned to hold 120 convicts was built at the US penitentiary in Terre Haute, Indiana. At the beginning of 1994, altogether 2,802 people were awaiting execution in American prisons. Of these, 1,102 were Afro-American, while thirty-three were sentenced to death when juveniles. The overwhelming majority of the death row inmates comes from the so-called 'underclass', that huge and growing warehouse where the failures and the rejects of consumer society are stored. As Linebaugh suggests, the spectacle of execution is 'cynically used by politicians to terrorize a growing underclass'. But in demanding the terrorization of the underclass, the silent American majority attempts to terrorize its own inner terrors . . .

The restoration of the death penalty is perhaps the most drastic, yet not the only symptom of the changing role of criminality – and the changed symbolic message it conveys. Blood, not just sweat, tends to be drawn from the incarcerated part of the 'underclass'. In *Dead Man Walking*, Sister Helen Prejean, Chairperson of the National Coalition against the Death Penalty, describes the 'plasma plant' run by Angola Prison, in which blood 'donations' were collected, with payments dropping by March 1994 from the original $12 to $4 per donation. Meanwhile, Dr Jack Kevorkian, the front-line advocate of euthanasia, campaigns for the inclusion of compulsory organ 'donations' in the execution procedure. These few facts signal the new casting of the poor in its new version of the 'underclass', or the 'class beyond the classes': no longer is it the 'reserve army of labour', but fully and truly the 'redundant population'. What is it good for? For the supply of spare parts to repair other human bodies?

Each year a million and a half Americans populate American prisons; about four and a half million American adults are under some form of judicial control. As Richard Freeman, an economist from Harvard, puts it, 'If the long-term unemployed in Europe are paid compensation – in the USA we put them in prisons.' Increasingly, *being poor* is seen as crime; *becoming poor*, as the product of criminal predispositions or intentions – abuse of alcohol, gambling, drugs, truancy and vagabondage. The poor, far from meriting care and assistance, deserve hate and condemnation –

as the very incarnation of sin. In this respect, there is little to distinguish between Bill Clinton and Newt Gingrich, vying as they are with each other to capture the mood of the 'silent majority'. As the *New York Herald Tribune* put it on 25 December 1994, the Americans – conservatives, moderate, Republican – consider it their right to blame the poor for their fate and simultaneously condemn millions of their children to poverty, hunger and despair.

'The Welfare State is dead', announced a leading spokesman of the American right which claims to be, and increasingly looks like, the American majority – one of the directors of the Progress and Freedom Foundation, established in 1993 to supply ideas for the Republican majority in the Congress. 'We need to pick up the corpse and bury it before the stench gets unbearable.' This turns out to be a self-fulfilling prophecy. Dismantling – not just of the welfare provision, but of everything that remained of the American New Deal – is today in full swing. On the one hand, the new congressional majority wants young single mothers to be deprived of their $377 of monthly benefit and have their children sent into orphanages – symbolically confirming the criminality and the social unfitness of the mothers. On the other, high on the agenda of legal reform is the abolition of the last constraints put on banking activities, the introduction of 'flexibility' into the anti-pollution laws, making appeal against company actions more difficult. The radical privatization of human fate goes along and apace with the radical deregulation of industry and finances.

I wonder what Willem Adriaan Bonger would make of this, had he not chosen death over life under the Nazis – those other, past promoters of 'radical solutions', who, as Klaus Dörner pointed out in his eye-opening book *Tödliche Mitleid*, should be also seen as *Bürger*, who like all ordinary folk before and after sought answers to whatever irritated them as 'social problems'. Unfortunately, Bonger is not here to tell us – he did not live long enough to see the birth of the Brave New World of deregulation, privatization, consumer choice – and of the criminalization of those unable to choose. We need to make sense of this world without his help.

I am not suggesting that here in Europe we have already found ourselves in the American situation. I am not suggesting either, that the present of the US necessarily displays the future of Europe. But I think that the signal it sends is clear enough: there is overwhelming evidence of the intimate link between the universal tendency towards a radical freedom of the market and the progressive dismantling of the Welfare State, as well as between the decomposition of the Welfare State and the tendency to criminalize poverty. I sincerely hope that the American evidence will serve us as a *warning*, not as an *example*. I wish, though, that my hopes were better founded. Ibrahim Warde of Berkeley wrote recently (*Le Monde diplomatique* of May 1995) of the advancing tyranny of the 'economically correct'. Indeed, gradually yet relentlessly it becomes an axiom of public discourse that whatever 'makes sense' economically does not need the support of any other sense and does not need to apologize for the absence of any other sense – political, social or downright human. In a world in which the principal actors are no longer democratically controlled nation states, but non-elected, unbound and radically disembedded financial conglomerates – the question of greater profitability and competitiveness invalidates and delegitimizes all other questions before one has the time and will to ask them . . . One dreads to think of what may happen in Europe, frightened by rising structural unemployment and the fast-growing 'unproductive' sector of the population, if the present trend in America continues unabated; and if it is recognized as 'economically correct' thanks to the advances in profits and competitive capacity . . .

(The text of the Willem Bonger Lecture, delivered at the University of Amsterdam in May 1995.)

4
Morality Begins at Home: or the Rocky Road to Justice

Levinas's moral world stretches between I and the Other. It is this space which Levinas visits again and again throughout his ethical writings, exploring it with an uncanny determination and patience. It is inside this space that he finds the birthplace of ethics and all the food the ethical self needs to stay alive: the silent challenge of the Other and my dedicated yet selfless responsibility. This is a *vast* space, as far as ethics goes: large enough to accommodate the ethical self in its full flight, scaling the highest peaks of saintliness, and all the underwater reefs of moral life, the traps that must be avoided by the self on its way to ethical life – to the assumption of uneasy responsibility for its responsibility. But this is a *narrow*, tightly circumscribed space as far as the human-being-in-the-world goes. It has room for no more than two actors. The moral drama is always played at the moral party of two: 'The Other' or 'The Face' are generic names, but in every moral encounter these names stand for just *one*, only one being – one Another, *one* Face; neither name may appear in the plural without losing its ethical status, its moral significance. This leaves aside most of the things that fill the daily life of every human: the pursuit of survival and self-aggrandizement, the rational consideration of ends and means, the calculation of gains and losses, pleasure seeking, power, politics, economics . . . Above all, entering this moral space means taking time off from daily business, leaving outside its mundane rules and conventions. At the moral party of two I and the Other arrive disrobed of our social trappings, stripped of status, social distinctions, handicaps, positions or roles, being neither rich nor poor, high or lowly, mighty or disempowered – reduced to the bare essentiality of our common humanity.

The moral self constituted inside such a space cannot but feel uncomfortable the moment the moral party of two is broken into by the Third. But can it survive such an intrusion? Does it not rather remind one of the deep-water fish which bursts when drawn out of its element and brought to the surface, its inner pressure no more bearable in the rarefied atmosphere of the 'average' and 'normal'?

It is not just the moral self which feels uncomfortable. So does its painter – Levinas himself. No better proof of his discomfort is needed than the obsessive, almost compulsive urgency with which he returns in his late writings and interviews to the 'problem of the Third' and the possibility of salvaging the validity of his life-long description of the ethical relationship in the 'presence of the Third party' – that is, under the conditions of ordinary mundane life. There is a remarkable similarity between this late Levinasian effort to bring back what he struggled, with such astonishing zeal and success, to exclude, and the ageing Husserl's attempts to return to intersubjectivity from the transcendental subjectivity he spent his life purifying of all 'inter-bound' contamination – never to anybody's, and above all to his own, satisfaction. We know what followed Husserl's eager, yet inconclusive, attempts: Heidegger's decision to cut the Gordian knot rather than to try in vain to untie it, his bold proclamation that *Sein* is *ursprünglich Mitsein*, 'being with', and thus the understanding of being and all its works cannot but start from this *Mitsein* (intersubjective, Husserl would say) condition. But this was the kind of solution to Husserl's troubles which all but invalidated, made null and void the significance of Husserl's 'purifying' effort for the understanding of understanding. The question is: is it necessary to cut the Gordian knot also in the case of Levinasian ethics? Can the ethics, born and grown in the greenhouse of the twosome encounter, withstand the assault by the Third party? And – more to the point – can the moral capacity made to the measure of the responsibility for the Other as the Face be strong enough, or potent enough, or vigorous enough to carry an entirely different burden of responsibility for the 'Other as such', the Other without a Face?

Before the strange world, inhospitable to ethics, that includes the Third had turned into his major, obsessive preoccupation, Levinas visited it but briefly and gingerly, without much curiosity or enthusiasm, and seldom on his own initiative unprompted by impatient interviewers. And once visiting it, he trod the ground hesitantly, as one tends to do in an unfamiliar landscape one suspects of being full of unspeakable, and above all unreadable, dangers. He did not stop long enough to count the trees in the forest. And his travel reports show that he felt out of his element there: premonitions of threats prevail over all other impressions.

In *Le Moi et la totalité* (1954) Levinas signals an essential discontinuity between the self's relation to the Other, made fully out of respect for the Other's freedom and integrity, and the relation towards the 'concept of the human being', so extended that it falls under the spell of impersonal reason. In that second case, the case of *totality*, the Other – now transformed into the Third – is 'a free being to whom I may do harm by violating his liberty'. 'Totality', sadly concludes Levinas, 'cannot consitute itself without injustice.' What is more, someone must ask me to account for my action, before I become aware of injustice done and visualize the possibility of justice. Very much in the Husserlian spirit, Levinas suggests that 'Justice does not result from the normal play of injustices. It comes from the outside, "through the door", from beyond the mêlée – it appears as a principle external to history.' It comes in defiance of the 'theories of justice which are forged in the course of social struggles, in which moral ideas express the needs of one society or one class'; it appeals to the 'ideal of justice', which requires that *all* needs – all of them, after all, but relative – are abandoned on 'approach to the absolute'. Justice comes, therefore, not out of history, but as a judgement pronounced on history: 'Human is the world in which it is possible to judge history' – which, in turn, is the world of 'rationalism'. In relation to daily charity and cruelty, those dual works of the self struggling toward responsible morality, justice able to conquer the inborn injustice of social totality may arrive only as *Deus ex machina*. Reason, first expelled from the primal moral scene, is called back from its exile to take care of humanity which the morality of the self is too slender and finespun to carry.

Almost thirty years later, in *La Souffrance inutile* (1982), the last motif is repeated: 'Interhumanity in the proper sense lies in one's non-indifference towards the others, one's reponsibility for the others, but before the reciprocity of such responsibility is inscribed into the impersonal law.' For this reason, 'the interhuman perspective may survive, but may be also lost in the political order of the City or in the Law which establishes mutual obligations of the citizens'. There are – so it seems – two mutually independent, perhaps even unconnected orders, political and ethical.

> Political order – whether pre- or post-ethical – which inaugurates the 'social contract' is neither the sufficient condition nor the necessary outcome of ethics. In the ethical position 'I' is distinct from the citizen and from that individual who, in his natural selfishness, precedes all order, yet from whom political philosophy, from Hobbes on, tried to derive – or derived – the social and political order of the City.

Such a philosophical strategy is declared mistaken and therefore vain; but what is there to replace it, given the separation and, indeed, virtual absence of communication between the two orders?

In the same year (1982) an interview with Levinas appeared under the title *Philosophie, justice et amour*. Pressed by the questions put to him by R. Fornet and A. Gómez, Levinas allows for a certain mutual dependency between the political and the ethical order. Without the order of justice, says Levinas here, there would be no limit to my responsibility and thus cohabitation with Others as generalized citizens would not be possible. But – he insists immediately – 'only departing from my relation to the Face, from me in front of the Other, one may speak of the State's legitimacy or illegitimacy'. The principle of justice does not come after all, contrary to what he suggested thirty years before, from a cause 'external to ethics', from reason; it is the ethics that now claims the right to pass judgement on the politically construed justice, that demands the obedience of the State to its own, ethical, rules. And then, in response to the straightforward question 'Do you think that such a (just) State is possible?', comes equally the straighforward answer: 'Yes, an agreement between the ethics and the State is possible. The just State will be the work of just people and the saints, rather than of propaganda and preaching . . . Charity is impossible without justice, but justice without charity is deformed.'

De l'unicité appeared in 1986. Here an attempt is made to represent the difference between the ethical and the 'formal', the legal, in a systematic way – focusing the story on the radical dissolution of the uniqueness of the ethical Other in the commonality/similarity of the individual as citizen. This dissolution – the loss of uniqueness – is a foregone conclusion since the appearance of 'the Third' – other than the one close to me (*mon prochain*), but at the same time close to the one close to me and moreover close to me in his own right – an '*also* close'. Now there are 'they'. They, those various others, do things to each other, may harm each other, make each other suffer. 'This is the hour of justice.' The uniqueness of the Other, incomparable when constituted by moral responsibility, will not help much now; one needs to appeal to a force one could do without before, to Reason – that allows one, first, to 'compare the incomparable', and – second – to 'impose a measure upon the extravagance of the infinite generosity of the "for the Other" '. And yet this recourse to Reason feels necessary precisely thanks to the memory of the 'uniqueness' of the Other, which was originally experienced in the ethical relationship; it is because each of the 'multiple others' is unique in his challenge to my responsibility, in its claim on my 'being for', that it 'postulates judgement and thus objectivity, objectivation, thematization, synthesis. One needs arbitrating institutions and political power that sustains them. Justice requires the foundation of the State. In this lies the necessity of the reduction of human uniqueness to the particularity of a human individual, to the condition of the citizen.' That latter particularity reduces, impoverishes, dissolves, waters down the splendour of ethically formed uniqueness; but without that already ethically experienced uniqueness it would itself be inconceivable; it would never come to pass . . .

Justice is in many ways disloyal to its ethical origins, unable to preserve its heritage in all its inner richness – but it cannot forget its origins without ceasing to be itself, justice. 'It cannot abandon that uniqueness to political history, which finds itself subjected to the determinism of power, reason of the State and seduction of the totalitarian temptations.' It must, instead, measure itself over and over again by the standards of original uniqueness, however unattainable such standards may be among the multiplicity of citizens. Hence the indelible trait of all justice is its dissatisfaction with itself: 'Justice means constant revision of justice, expectation of a better justice.' Justice, one may say, must exist perpetually in a condition of *noch nicht geworden*, setting itself standards higher than those already practised.

The same themes return at length in the extensive conversations with François Poirié (*Emmanuel Lévinas: Qui êtes-vous?* (Lyon: Éditions la Manufacture, 1987)). In the presence of the Third, says Levinas, 'we leave what I call the order of ethics, or the order of saintliness or the order of mercy, or the order of love, or the order of charity – where the other human concerns me regardless the place he occupies in the multitude of humans, and even regardless our shared quality of individuals of the human species; he concerns me as one close to me, as the first to come. He is unique.' Beyond this order stretches the realm of choice, proportion, judgement – and comparison. Comparison already entails the first act of violence: the defiance of uniqueness. This violence cannot be avoided, since among the multiplicity of others certain divisions (assignment to classes, to categories) are necessary – they are 'justified divisions'. Ethics demands, one may say, a certain self-limitation; so that the ethical demand may be fulfilled, certain sacred axioms of ethics must be sacrificed . . . The liberal state, says Levinas – the state grounded on the principle of human rights, is the implementation, and conspicuous manifestation, of that contradiction. Its function is nothing less than to 'limit the original mercy from which justice originated'. But 'the internal contradiction' of the liberal state finds its expression in perceiving, 'above and beyond all justice already incorporated in the regime, a justice more just . . .' 'Justice in the liberal state is never definitive.' 'Justice is awakened by charity – such charity which is before justice but also after it.' 'Concern with human rights is not the function of the State. It is a non-state institution inside the State – an appeal to humanity which the State has not accomplished yet.' The concern with human rights is an appeal to the 'surplus of charity'. One may say: to something larger than any letter of Law, than anything that the State has done so far. State-administered justice is born of charity gestated and groomed within the primary ethical situation; yet justice may be administered only if it never

stops being prompted by its original *spiritus movens*; if it knows of itself
as of a never ending chase of a forever elusive goal – the re-creation
among the individuals/citizens of the uniqueness of the Other as
Face . . . If it knows that it *cannot* 'match the kindness which gave it birth
and keeps it alive' (*L'Autre, Utopie et justice*, 1988) – but that it cannot
ever *stop trying* to do just that.

Just what can one learn from Levinas's exploration of the 'world of the
Third', the 'world of the multiplicity of others' – the social world? One
can learn, to put it in a nutshell, that this world of the social is,
simultaneously, the legitimate offspring and a distortion of the moral
world. The idea of justice is conceived at the moment of encounter
between the experience of uniqueness (as given in the moral responsibility for the Other) and the experience of multiplicity of others (as given
in social life). It cannot be conceived under any other circumstances;
it needs both parents and to both it is genetically related, even if the
genes, though being complementary, contain also contradictory genetic
messages.

*If it were not for the memory of the uniqueness of the Face, there would
be no idea of generalized, 'impersonal' justice.* And this is the case in
spite of the fact that impersonality means the defiance and the denial of
personhood – of the selfsame value which is to be cherished and
groomed and defended and preserved in moral relationship. (Moral
responsibility is taken up in the name of exactly such a preservation.)
Thus, paradoxically, morality is the school of justice – even if the
category of justice is alien to it and redundant within the moral relationship. (Justice comes into its own together with comparison, but there is
nothing to compare when the Other is encountered as unique.) The
'primal scene' of ethics is thereby also the primal, ancestral scene of
social justice.

Another paradox: justice becomes necessary when the moral impulse,
quite self-sufficient inside the moral party of two, is found to be a poor
guide once it ventures beyond the boundaries of that party. The infinity
of the moral responsibility, the unlimitedness (even the silence!) of the
moral demand simply cannot be sustained when 'the Other' appears in
the plural. (One may say that there is an inverse ratio between the
infinity of 'being for' and the infinity of the others.) But it is that moral
impulse which makes justice necessary: it resorts to justice in the name
of self-preservation, though while doing it it risks being cut down,
trimmed, maimed or diluted . . . In the *Dialogue sur le penser-à-l'Autre*
(1987) the interviewer asked Levinas:

> As far as I am an ethical subject, I am responsible for everything in
> everybody; my responsibility is infinite. Is not it so that such a situation is

unlivable for me, and for the other, whom I risk terrorizing with my ethical voluntarism? Does not it follow that ethics is impotent in its will to do good?

To which Levinas gave the following answer:

> I do not know whether such a situation is unlivable. Certainly, such a situation is not what one would call agreeable, pleasant to live with, but it is good. What is extremely important – and I can assert this without being myself a saint, and without pretending to be a saint – is to be able to say that a human truly deserving that name, in its European sense, derived from the Greeks and the Bible, is a human being who considers saintliness the ultimate value, an unassailable value.

This value is not surrendered once the stern, uncompromising ethical requirement of 'being-for' is replaced by a somewhat diluted and less stressful code of justice. It remains what it was – the ultimate value, reserving to itself the right to invigilate, monitor and censure all deals entered into in the name of justice. Constant tension and never calmed suspicion rule in the relationship between ethics and the just State, its never sufficiently industrious plenipotentiary. Ethics is not a derivative of the State; the ethical authority does not derive from the State's powers to legislate and to enforce the Law. It precedes the State, it is the sole source of the State's legitimacy and the ultimate judge of that legitimacy. The State, one may say, is justifiable only as a vehicle or instrument of ethics.

Levinas's view of the ethical origins of justice and the State itself as an instrument of justice (and, obliquely, of the ethics itself) can be interpreted as a phenomenological insight into the meaning of justice – or as a non-neutral (indeed, per-locutionary in the Austinian sense) 'etiological myth', setting the stage for the subordination of the State to ethical principles and subjecting it to the ethical criteria of evaluation, as well as setting limits to the State's freedom of ethical manœuvre. It can hardly be seen, though, as a comprehensive account of the complex and convoluted process through which ethical responsibility for the other comes (or does not come, as the case may be) to be implemented on a generalized scale through the works of the State and its institution. It certainly goes a long way towards explaining the growing concern with the plight of the 'generalized other' – the far-away Other, the Other distant in space and time; but it says little about the ways and means through which that concern may bring practical effects, and even less about the reasons for such effects falling so saliently short of needs and expectations, or not being visible at all.

Levinas's writings offer rich inspiration for the analysis of the endemic aporia of moral responsibility. They offer nothing comparable for the scrutiny of the aporetic nature of justice. They do not confront the possibility that – just as in the case of assuming moral responsibility for the Other – the work of the institutions which Levinas wishes to be dedicated to the promotion of justice may have consequences detrimental to the moral values. Neither do they allow for the possibility that such detrimental consequences may be more than just a side-effect of mistakes and neglect, being rooted instead in the very way such institutions can – must – operate to remain viable.

Quite a few insights into the latter issue can be found in the work of another great ethical philosopher of our times – Hans Jonas. Unlike Levinas, Jonas puts our present moral quandary in historical perspective, representing it as an event in time, rather than an extemporal, metaphysical predicament. According to Jonas, for the greater part of human history the gap between 'micro' and 'macro' ethics did not present a problem; the short reach of the moral drive was not fraught with terminal dangers for the simple reason that the consequences of human deeds (given the technologically determined scale of human action) were equally limited. What has happened in quite recent times is the tremendous growth of the possible consequentiality of human acts unmatched by a similar expansion of human moral capacity. What we can do now may have effects on distant lands and distant generations; effects as profound and radical as they are unpredictable, transcending the power of the always time-bound and place-bound human imagination, and morally uncontrollable, stepping far beyond the issues with which human moral capacity became used to cope. Yet the awareness of responsibility for all this did not make much progress. Quite the contrary: the same development which put in the hands of humankind powers, tools and weapons of unprecedented magnitude, requiring close normative regulation, 'eroded the foundations from which norms could be derived; it has destroyed the very idea of norm as such' (*The Imperative of Responsibility* (University of Chicago Press, 1984)). Both departures are the work of science which suffers no boundary to what humans can do, but neither takes gladly the argument that not all that could be done should be done; the ability of doing something is, for science and for technology, its executive arm, all the reason ever needed for doing it, be what may. New powers need new ethics, and need them badly – as a matter of our collective life and death. But the new powers undermine the very possibility of satisfying that need, by denying in theory and in practice the right of ethical consideration to interfere with, let alone arrest, their own endless and self-propelling growth.

This blind tendency must be reversed, Jonas demands. A new ethics must be called into being, made to the measure of the new human powers. A sort of a new categorical imperative – like 'Act so that the effects of your action are compatible with the permanence of genuine human life.' This is not easy, though. First, violating such an imperative mark two, unlike in the case of the original Kantian version, entails no rational contradiction, and thus is deprived of the sole *ratio* to which the logic of science would accord a self-imposing and unquestionable authority. Second, it is notoriously difficult, nay impossible, to know for sure which deeds of technoscience are, and which are not, 'compatible with the permanence of genuine human life' – at least before the damage, often irreparable, has been done. Even in the unlikely case of the new categorical imperative having been awarded normative authority, the vexing question of its application would still remain open: how to argue convincingly that a controversial development should be stopped, if its effects cannot be measured in advance with such a degree of precision, with that near-algorithmic certainty, which scientific reason would be inclined to respect? If a truly algorithmic calculation of the looming dangers is not on the cards, Jonas suggests, we should settle for its second-best substitute, '*heuristics* of fear': to try our best to visualize the most awesome and the most durable among the consequences of a given technological action. Above all, we need to apply the 'principle of uncertainty': 'The prophecy of doom is to be given greater heed than the prophecy of bliss.' We need, one could say, an ethics of systematic pessimism, so that we may err, if at all, solely on the side of caution.

Kant's trust in the grip of ethical law rested on the conviction that there are arguments of reason which every reasonable person, being a reasonable person, must accept; the passage from ethical law to ethical action led through rational thought, and to smooth the passage one needed only to take care of the non-contradictory rationality of the law, counting for the rest on the endemic rational faculties of moral actors. In this respect Jonas stays faithful to Kant – though he is the first to admit that nothing as uncontroversial as Kant's categorical imperative (that is, no principle which cannot be violated without violating simultaneously the logical law of contradiction) can be articulated in relation to the new challenge to human ethical faculties. For Jonas, as for Kant, the crux of the issue is the capacity of legislative reason; and the promotion, as well as the eventual universality, of ethical conduct is ultimately a philosophical problem and the task of philosophers. For Jonas, as for Kant, the fate of ethics is fully and truly in the hands of Reason and its *alter ago* – *ur*-reason. In this scheme of things there is no room left for the possibility that reason may, even if only on occasion, militate against what is, in its name, promoted as ethical principles.

In other words, there is no room left for the logic of human interests, and the logic of social institutions – those organized interests whose function is, in practice if not by design, to make the by-passing of ethical restrictions feasible and ethical considerations irrelevant to the action. Neither is there room left for the otherwise trivial sociological observation that for the arguments to be accepted they need to accord with interests in addition to (or instead of) being rationally flawless. There is no room either for another equally trivial phenomenon of 'unanticipated consequences' of human action – of deeds bringing results left out of account, or unthought of at the time the action was undertaken. Nor is there room for the relatively simple guess that when interests are many and at odds with each other, any hope that a certain set of principles will eventually prevail and will be universally obeyed must seek support in a sober analysis of social and political forces capable of securing its victory.

I suggest that a mixture of all those factors – overlooked or ignored and left out of account in Jonas's search for the new ethics – can be blamed for the present plight of the world, in which the growing awareness of the dangers ahead goes hand in hand with a growing impotence in preventing them or alleviating the gravity of their impact. In theory, we seem to know better and better that if catastrophe is to be averted the presently unruly forces must be kept in check and controlled by factors other than endemically dispersed and diffuse, as well as short-sighted, interests. In practice, however, the consequences of human actions rebound with a blind, elemental force more reminiscent of earthquakes, floods and tornadoes than of a model of rational and self-monitored behaviour. As Danièle Sallenave has recently reminded us ('L'alibi de la compassion', in *Le Monde diplomatique* of July 1995), Jean-Paul Sartre could aver, just a few decades ago, that 'there are no such things as natural disasters'; but today natural disasters have turned into the prototype and model of all the miseries that afflict the world, and one could as well reverse Sartre's statement and say that 'there are no other than natural catastrophes'. Not just the dramatic changes in the degree of livability of our natural habitat (pollution of air and water, global warming, ozone holes, acid rain, salination or desiccation of the soil, etc.), but also the thoroughly human aspects of global conditions (wars, demographic explosion, mass migrations and displacements, social exclusion of large categories of the population) come unannounced, catch us unawares and seem utterly oblivious to the anguished cries for help and to the most frantic efforts to design, let alone to provide, the remedy.

Obviously, these are not results one can account for by following Jonas's ethical strategy. The dearth of ethical knowledge and understanding can hardly be blamed for what is happening. No one except lunatic fringes certified as lunatic fringes would seriously aver that it is good and beneficial to pollute the atmosphere, to pierce the ozone layer, or for that matter to wage wars, to overpopulate the land or to make people into homeless vagabonds. Yet all this happens despite its consensual, well-nigh universal and vociferous condemnation. Some other factors than ethical ignorance must be at work if the grinding, systemic consistency of the global damage more than matches the cohesion of ethical indignation. One may sensibly surmise that those other factors are entrenched in such aspects of social reality as are either left unaffected by ethical philosophy, or are able successfully to withstand or by-pass its pressures; or better still, render ethical demands inaudible. Among such factors, the increasingly deregulated market forces, exempt from all effective political control and guided solely by the pressures of competitiveness, must be awarded pride of place. The sheer size of the main players in global markets today far exceeds the interfering capacity of most, if not all, elected state governments – those forces amenable, at least in principle, to ethical persuasion. General Motors had in 1992 an annual turnover of $132.4 billion, Exxon of $155.7 billion, Royal Dutch/Shell of $99.6 billion, against the Gross National Product of $123.5 billion of Denmark, $112.9 billion of Norway, $83.8 billion of Poland and $33.5 billion of Egypt . . . The five biggest 'non-national' companies had a joint turnover just twice as big as the whole of sub-Saharan Africa.

This is what Jonas's problem is about: the globally disastrous long-distance and long-term effects of the growing human potential to do things and remake the world. This is undoubtedly one of the crucial problems with which any macro-ethical reasoning must come to grips. But it is not the only problem; moreover, not the one with which Levinas was concerned with in the first place. For Levinas, the macro-ethical extension of moral responsibility for the Other reaches further than the defence against shared dangers. His postulates addressed to macro-ethics are therefore more demanding yet than everything which Jonas's 'heuristics of fear' may require. Let us recall that for Levinas the macro equivalent of moral responsibility is nothing less than *justice* – a quality of human existence which obviously needs the prevention of global disasters as its preliminary condition, but on no account can be reduced to it, and which need not be provided for and satisfied even if that prevention was somehow made effective.

Unlike the disasters which can be *universally* recognized as detrimental and undesirable since they hit *at random* and pay no heed to earned or inherited privileges, justice is a notoriously *contentious* issue. Rarely has human ingenuity and imagination been stretched as much and as painfully as when devising the arguments meant to depict as 'justice being done' the state of affairs which some other people considered unjust and thus a legitimate reason for rebellion. One can sensibly expect that in a divided society, and above all a modern society, which is – simultaneously! – sharply unequal *and* dedicated to the promotion of equality as a supreme value, the contents of justice will forever remain a matter of controversy. (Levinas admitted as much, though from a somewhat different angle, when pointing out that the fate of a just society is to remain forever dissatisfied with the level of justice achieved.) Above all, the agreement as to when to assume that the postulate of justice has been satisfied, if such agreement were at all attainable, would hardly be reached through philosophical argument alone – appealing as it must to extraterritorial and extemporal joint human essence, while neglecting on the whole the time- and space-bound social, cultural and political circumstances gestating the experience of injustice.

We know from the thorough and perceptive historical analysis conducted by Barrington Moore Jr that while 'the masses' (more generally, the non-philosophical part of the population) have no idea, or at best a vague one, of the abstract notion of 'justice as such', they tend to recognize unerringly a case of *injustice*. In opposition to what the logic of the vocabulary suggests, 'injustice' is the 'positive' notion, while 'justice' is the 'negative' one; it is *injustice* that seems to be the prime notion of popular ethics, 'justice' being the marked, a derivative, unit in the opposition. Justice makes sense here solely as the enemy (and postulated conqueror) of injustice, the latter being the sole 'datum' given in experience; justice means redemption, recuperation of losses, making good the damage, compensation for the suffered ills – repairing the distortion caused by the act of *injustice*. In the light of Barrington Moore Jr's findings it is difficult to say under what conditions the popular perception of the human condition as just and proper will tend to grow, and it is doubtful whether such a growth, if it occurs, will be subject to any ascertainable and generalizable rules. On the other hand, one can reasonably assume that the perception of the state of affairs as *unjust* will tend to spread and deepen together with the intensification of the hardships already condemned as unjust and the appearance of new hardships not experienced before (whatever the starting point used to be and however well or badly it fared from the point of view of any abstract models of justice).

If this is the case, then the last three or four decades did little to enhance the perception of the world as 'just'. Quite to the contrary: virtually all indices of welfare and quality of life pointed towards growing inequality and, indeed, a rampant polarization both on the global scale and inside almost every social/political unit taken apart: fast enrichment on the one side made all the more salient and offensive by rapid impoverishment on the other. The visibility of the process, and the likelihood of its condemnation as unjust, has been further increased by the fact that during the same period, between 1960 and 1992, literacy in the world grew from 46 to 69 per cent and life expectancy from 46.2 years to 63. The first factor, coupled with the formidable spread of worldwide communication (which made poverty, once a local plight and local 'problem', into a question of 'relative deprivation'), must have facilitated competent comparisons of jarringly unequal life standards, while the second factor must have to a large degree arrested the 'natural solutions' to the 'problems' of extreme deprivation and poverty among the 'surplus' or 'supernumerary', that is 'economically redundant', section of the population.

And the degree of polarization (and therefore also of the relative deprivation) has broken in these three decades all registered and remembered records. The top fifth of the world population was in 1960 thirty times richer than the bottom fifth; in 1991 it was already sixty-one times richer. Nothing points to the likelihood in the foreseeable future of this widening of the gap being slowed down or stopped, let alone reversed. The top fifth of the world enjoyed in 1991 84.7 per cent of the world's gross product, 84.2 per cent of global trade and 85.0 per cent of internal investment, against respectively the 1.4, 0.9 and 0.9 per cent which was the share of the bottom fifth. The top fifth consumed 70 per cent of world energy, 75 per cent of metals and 85 per cent of timber. On the other hand, the debt of the economically weak countries of the 'third world' was in 1970 more or less stable at around $200 billion; it has grown tenfold since then and is today fast approaching the mind-boggling figure of $2,000 billion (see United Nations *Programme for Development*, 1994 edition).

This picture of rapidly growing inequality on a global scale is replicated inside virtually every single 'national society'. The gap between the rich and the poor, whether measured on the scale of global markets or on a much smaller scale of whatever passes for 'national economies' (but what is increasingly little more than administratively circumscribed units of computations), is growing unstoppably, and the prevailing feeling is that the rich are likely to become richer still, but the poor will most certainly grow poorer. That feeling is likely to be reforged, at the receiving end, into the experience of a wrong having been done, of unfairness and injustice. It does not follow, though, that it will necessarily trigger a desire for collective vindication of wrongs. The shared plight may well be interpreted as an aggregate of individual mishaps, caused by personal indolence or inadequacy – and feed non-cumulative efforts of personal exit from misery and a dream of individual good luck.

That last probability is enhanced by the widely evident tendency to overlay the division between rich and poor by another division – that between the seduced and oppressed. While the rich (presumed satisfied) enjoy a high degree of personal freedom of choice, responding keenly and joyfully to the growing range of attractive market offers, it is all too easy to redefine those who do not respond in the way expected from proper (seducible) consumers as people unfit to put their freedom of choice to good use: people who are, in the last account, unfit to be free. Moreover, the poor of today (those hopelessly flawed consumers, immune from market blandishments and unlikely to contribute to the supply-clearing demand, however alluring that supply may be) are of no evident use to consumer-oriented markets, and increasingly also to state governments, acting more and more as local bailiffs and sheriffs on behalf of extraterritorial finance and commerce. The poor of today are no longer the 'exploited people' producing the surplus product later to be transformed into capital; nor are they the 'reserve army of labour', expected to be reintegrated into that capital-producing process at the next economic upturn. Economically speaking (and today also politically elected governments speak in the language of economy), they are fully and truly *redundant*, useless, disposable and there is no 'rational reason' for their continuing presence . . . The sole *rational* response to that presence is the systematic effort to exclude them from 'normal' society – that is, the society which reproduces itself through the play of consumer supply and consumer choice, mediated by allurement and seduction.

Short of being physically disposed of (pressure for such a 'solution' is manifested most conspicuously in the populist slogans demanding de-portation of foreigners, that 'drain on our resources', and closing the borders to migrants, *a priori* defined as parasites and spongers, not creators of wealth) – they need to be isolated, neutralized and disempowered, so that the chance of their massive, yet individually experienced, miseries and humiliations being condensed into collective (let alone effective) protest be further diminished, ideally reduced to nought. These results are sought through the two-pronged strategy of the criminalization of poverty and the brutalization of the poor.

Criminalization seems to be emerging as the consumer society's prime substitute for the fast disappearing welfare state provisions. The welfare state, that response to the poverty problem at a time when the poor were the 'reserve army of labour' and were expected to be groomed back into the productive process, is under these changed conditions no longer 'economically justifiable', and is increasingly seen as a 'luxury we cannot afford'. The 'problem' of the poor is recast as the question of law and order, and social funds once earmarked for the rehabilitation of people temporarily out of work (in economic terms, the recommodification of labour) are pumped over into the construction and technological updating of prisons and other punitive/surveillance outfits. The switch is most pronounced in the USA, where the prison population tripled between 1980 and 1993, reaching in June 1994 the number of 1,012,851 (the average growth was more than 65,000 a year), where the poorest, black part of the 'underclass' constitutes roughly half of those sentenced to one year of imprisonment and more, and where the systematic increase of expenditure on police and prisons goes hand in hand with systematic cuts of welfare funds and entitlements. Some observers suggest that massive incarceration, spine-chilling stories of the lengthening death-row queues and the systematic, deliberate deterioration of prison conditions (the progressive and widely advertised dehumanization of prisoners) are deployed as the principal means of 'terrorization' of the underclass, now presented to public opinion as – purely, simply and unambiguously – the enemy number one of public safety and a drain on public resources (though one may guess at another function as well – of a deterrent to the possible rebellion of the well-off against the tensions endemic to consumer life; the horrors of the alternative to the 'free consumer' life render palatable and endurable even the most vexing stresses for which that life is notorious). Europe as yet stays far behind the United States, but a similar trend, albeit on a much diminished scale, is in evidence here. According to statistics offered by the Council of Europe, between 1983 and 1992 the prison population has grown by more than 50 per cent in Greece, Spain, Portugal and the Netherlands, and by between 20 and 50 per cent in France, Switzerland, Ireland and Sweden; everywhere the trend was upwards.

Policing, and thereby obliquely criminalizing, the 'global poor' – that is, the areas of the world afflicted with, or allocated to, endemic poverty – is another necessary accompaniment of growing inequality, confronting the rich part of the world with a task no less urgent, yet much more complex. Police operations, military expeditions, long-term 'pacification' of troublesome areas are costly affairs, which the well-off taxpayer is the less willing to finance the more distant from home (and therefore less relevant to his own well-being) they appear to be. The task of keeping the 'global poor' at bay is thus the most suitable case for that deregulation, privatization and commercialization of punitive and surveillance activity, which is still applied only half-heartedly and gingerly in the domestic prison system. No excessive ingenuity is needed to move the task altogether from the 'debit' to the 'credit' side of the budget: supplying local chiefs and warlords of distant lands with sophisticated weapons may bring the double profit of financial gains and such a brutalization of life as is guaranteed to all but paralyse the protest potential of the poor. The endless, increasingly devastating and ever less ideologically motivated (or in any other way 'cause-oriented', for that matter) civil (or simply gang) wars are from the rich countries' point of view utterly effective, cheap and often profitable forms of policing and 'pacifying' the global poor. Beamed onto millions of TV screens for everybody to watch, they provide a vivid testimony of the savagery of the poor and the self-inflicted character of their misery, as well as convincing arguments for the pointlessness of aid, let alone any substantial redistribution of wealth.

The brutalization of the poor (not necessarily deliberately induced, but eagerly embraced once it appears, keenly transformed into a 'public concern number one' and beefed up and magnified by constantly spurred media attention) may also be seen as serving the task of policing the domestic scene. Made into the outcasts of a thriving society of seduced consumers, transformed into an underclass without a present or prospective place in society and deprived of the legally recognized tokens of access to the goods hailed as the uppermost values of the good life, the poor tend to resort to drugs, those poor man's (and illegal) substitutes for the rich man's (and legal) tools of consumer ecstasy. They also on occasion tend to initiate the politically neglected 'redistribution of wealth', attacking the nearest-to-hand private possessions and thus supplying the guardians of law and order with the most welcome statistical proof of the close link between being a ghetto-dweller and being a criminal, keenly used (the way all self-fulfilling prophecies normally are) in support of. the criminalization of poverty. From time to time the outcasts of the consumer society assume the role of its Luddites – going on the rampage, demolishing and burning down the shops, those outposts of consumerism scattered on the hostile, not-yet-conquered, perhaps unconquerable, territory; committing acts which are immediately represented as riots and thus supply a further proof, if a further proof was needed, that the question of the underclass is – first and foremost, perhaps even solely – the problem of law and order.

To conclude: the situation of the larger part of the present-day population, whether located in areas of the globe afflicted with endemic poverty, or placed inside relatively well-off societies boasting high GNP and a high 'average' level of consumption, is not just 'comparatively bad', but also quickly – and thus palpably – deteriorating. Under such conditions, one would expect a widespread feeling of *injustice*, with the potential to condense into a mass protest movement, if not an open rebellion against the system. The fact that this does not happen testifies perhaps to the effectiveness of the combined strategies of exclusion, criminalization and brutalization of potentially 'problematic' strata.

This, however, is not the problem most relevant to our main topic – to the question of 'macroethics' as essentially one of justice as the extension of that responsibility for the Other which is induced and trained inside the 'moral party of two'. Even if the experience of growing deprivation did lead to an effective protest of and by the poor – this would be, by and large, a case of a forceful *vindication* of claims, maybe a case of redistribution of inequalities – not necessarily heralding the rule of ethical principles in the world of economy and politics, and unlikely to promote the cause of 'ethical politics'. If justice is to be understood, as Levinas wants, as stretching out and generalizing the narrowly applied and selective responsibility for the singular or singled-out Other – then, like that responsibility, it needs to arise not from the demands of the Other, but from the moral impulse and concern of the moral self which assumes the responsibility for justice being done. *Demanding* is not by itself a moral act (only its recognition may be); awarding the right to demand, and even more the anticipation of a yet-unspoken-demand, is. Moral responsibilities are asymmetrical and non-reciprocal.

The *ethical* question, therefore, is not so much whether the new deprived and disprivileged stand up and are counted fighting for justice, which they can only understand as rectification of the injustice done to them, as whether the well-off and, by the same token, privileged, the new 'contented majority' of John Kenneth Galbraith, rise above their singular or group interests and consider themselves responsible for the humanity of the Others, the less fortunate. Whether, in other words, they are ready to endorse, in thought and in deed, and before they are forced to do so, and not out of the fear of being forced, such principles of justice as could not be satisfied unless the Others are awarded the same degree of practical, positive freedom they have been enjoying themselves.

That being ready to do exactly that is the condition *sine qua non* of such justice as may be properly considered the 'macro' equivalent of the 'micro' moral stance is a philosophical proposition. But whether the contented majority is likely to do it is a sociological and political question. More to the point: the factors which facilitate and the factors which hamper the chances of taking up the responsibility for admittedly weaker and less outspoken Others (precisely *because.*of their weakness and inaudibility) are not an issue which can be unpacked theoretically by philosophical analysis nor resolved practically by the normative/persuasive efforts of philosophers.

It goes without saying that the problem of justice cannot be as much as posited unless there is already in place a democratic regime of tolerance which guarantees in its constitution and political practice 'human rights' – that is, the right to retain one's identity and uniqueness without risking persecution. This tolerance is a necessary condition of all justice; the point is, though, that it is not its *sufficient* condition. By itself, the democratic regime does not promote (let alone guarantee) the transformation of tolerance into *solidarity* – that is, the recognition of other people's misery and sufferings as one's own responsibility, and the alleviation and eventually the removal of misery as one's own task. More often than not, given the present shape of political mechanism, democratic regimes translate tolerance as callousness and indifference.

Most democratic political systems move today from the parliamentary or party rule models towards the model of 'opinion poll rule', where the composition of political platforms and the making of decisions on controversial issues are guided by the advance consideration of the relative popularity of the intended move and careful calculation of the anticipated electoral gains and losses – the number of votes a given measure may attract and the number of electors it may repel. As has been noted by political scientists, this attitude leads in practice to the rule of the 'median voter' principle: no measure is likely to be undertaken by the government of the country which is not seen as being 'in the interest' of at least half the voters plus one . . . With the demise of the welfare state as all-inclusive, universal entitlement to collective insurance, and its replacement with a model of administered charity for the minority who fail the 'means test' (that is, are certified as 'subnormal'), the chance of the 'median voter' approving of the larger welfare provision (now experienced by him first and foremost as an increased burden of taxation) has shrunk radically. Hence the growing electoral approval for the demotion of the welfare state and for leaving the impecunious and the destitute to their own (nonexistent or inadequate) resources. Under present conditions it is not very hard, and certainly not fanciful, to imagine the majority of voters giving their democratic approval to the total and permanent removal of people dependent for state-administered redistribution of resources from the list of public concerns.

Democracy is also a necessary condition of the free public discussion of issues – and particularly of the issue of social justice and the ethical quality of public affairs. Without democracy, with its freedom of expression and open controversy, it is difficult to envisage a serious consideration of the shape of a good society, of the overall ends which political decision-making should promote and the principles by which its effects ought to be critically assessed, or the mature public awareness of the risks ahead and the chances of their prevention. And yet, once more, one finds that, being a necessary condition of public awareness, democracy is not the sufficient condition of a public action which such awareness would demand. Again and again one finds a growing gap, indeed a contradiction, between values promoted in the public discussion and those whose cause is served by political practice. Aversion to war, loathing of cruelty, abhorrence of massacre, rape and looting is today almost universal – yet wars and genocides on an ever growing scale are made possible by the saturation of present and prospective warring factions with modern weapons, the production and selling of which is keenly promoted by politicians and supported by their voters in the name of the national balance of payments and the defence of jobs. Pictures of famine and destitution arouse universal alarm and anger – yet the destruction of the economic self-sufficiency of the afflicted peoples in the name of free trade, open markets and favourable trade balances can count on the wide support of the democratic electorate. The progressive depletion of world resources and associated mortgaging of the life conditions of future generations is unanimously bewailed and protested against – yet politicians promising increased 'economic growth', that is a yet larger consumption of non-renewable resorces, can invariably count on electoral success.

Two books have appeared recently in France (*Les Conflits identitaires*, by François Thual, published by Ellipses/Iris, and *La Fin des territoires*, by Bertrand Badie, published by Fayard) which trace the contradictions of contemporary politics, and the resulting impossibility of meeting the ends which enjoy widespread, perhaps even universal, approval, to the principle of *territoriality* – the principle which was taken originally for the major tool in the modern struggle for the rule of law and order, but proved to be a major source of contemporary world disorder. The authors point to the present practical impotence of states, which, however, remain to this day the only sites and agencies for the articulation and execution of laws; devoid of all real executive power, not self-sufficient and unsustainable militarily, economically or culturally, those 'weak states', 'quasi-states', often 'imported states' (all Bertrand Badie's expressions) nevertheless claim territorial sovereignty – capitalizing on identity wars and appealing to, or rather whipping up, dormant tribal instincts. It might be seen that the kind of sovereignty which relies on tribal sentiments alone is a natural enemy of tolerance and civilized norms of cohabitation. But the territorial fragmentation of legislative and policing power with which it is intimately associated is also a major obstacle to an effective control over forces that truly matter, and which are all or almost all global, extraterritorial in their character.

Thual's and Badie's arguments carry a lot of conviction. And yet their analysis seems to stop short of unravelling the full complexity of the present plight. Contrary to what the authors suggest, the territorial principle of political organization does not stem from tribal instincts alone, natural or contrived, and its relation to the processes of economic and cultural globalization is not simply one of the 'spoke in the wheel' kind. In fact, there seems to be an intimate kinship, a mutual conditioning and reciprocal reinforcement between the 'globalization' and 'territorialization'. Global finance, trade and information industry depend for their liberty of movement and unconstrained freedom to pursue their ends on the political fragmentation of the world scene. They have all, one may say, developed vested interests in 'weak states' – that is, in such states as are *weak* but nevertheless remain *states*. Such states can easily be reduced to the (useful) role of local police stations, securing the modicum of order required for the conduct of business, but need not be feared as effective brakes on the global companies' freedom. It is not difficult to see that the replacement of territorial 'weak states' by some sort of global legislative and policing powers would be detrimental to the extra-territorial companies' interests. And so it is easy to suspect that far from being at war with each other, political 'tribalization' and economic 'globalization' are close allies and fellow conspirators. What they conspire against are the chances of justice being done and being seen to be done; but also the chances that neighbourhood responsibilities swell, stretch and eventually grow into the consistent care for global justice – and result in a politics effectively guided by ethical principles.

Immersed as we are in the 'primal scene of morality', in times which favour (though not necessarily guarantee) the 'remoralization' of primary human relations and the facing up to the question of responsibility for the Other (a responsibility which comes to the surface also in the act of its denial and abandonment) – we cannot help becoming increasingly morally sensitive, and as Levinas suggested, also prone to set ourselves ethical goals that reach beyond the narrow sphere of the 'moral party of two' – into the world ruled by the principles of justice, rather than by personal responsibility. It seems, however, that the social institutions which could conceivably serve as the vehicles of that extended ethical sensitivity bar in fact its translation into practical progress of justice. The road from the 'primal moral scene' to macro-ethics leads through political action. But is there any kind of political action in sight which may prove adequate to this task?

In a recent article ('Movements and Campaigns', *Dissent*, Winter 1995) Richard Rorty singles out 'movement politics' as the once dominant, and preferred, form of political action in modern times.

Membership in a movement requires the ability to see particular campaigns for particular goals as parts of something much bigger. This bigger thing is the course of human events described as a process of maturation . . . [P]olitics is no longer just politics, but rather the matrix out of which will emerge something like Paul's 'new being in Christ' or Mao's 'new socialist man' – the mature stage of humanity, the one which will put aside current childishness . . .

This kind of politics assumes that things must be changed utterly, so that a new kind of beauty may be born.

To this 'movement politics' Rorty opposes the 'campaign politics', which disposes of the ideas of 'maturation', 'growing rationality' and 'forward movement of history', without which movement politics would have had no legitimacy and would have been unable to accord sense to any of its undertakings. 'Campaigns for such goals as the unionization of migrant workers in the American Southwest, or banning big trucks from the Alps, or the overthrow (by votes or by force) of a corrupt government, or legal recognition of gay marriage, can stand on their own feet.' The turn away from the movements and toward the campaigns, Rorty suggests,

is a turn away from the transcendental question 'What are the conditions of possibility of this historical movement?' to the pragmatic question 'What are the causal conditions of replacing this present actuality with a better future actuality?' . . . The intellectuals of our century have been distracted from campaigns by the need to 'put events in perspective,' and by the urge to organize movements around something out of sight, something located at the impossibly distant end of this perspective. But this has made the best the enemy of the better.

It is better to concentrate on the better than to chase the best, implies Rorty. The alternative, as we know now only too well, never managed to reach the best, while it did manage to sacrifice a lot of the better in the bargain. Campaign politics looks attractive precisely as a substitution for the discredited movement politics, notorious for neglecting the real present for the sake of an imaginary future, only to neglect again today's future the moment it stops being imaginary. As a replacement for movement politics, campaign politics does indeed have advantages which can hardly be dismissed; it may bring a lot of succour and genuine improvement here and there, now and then, to these or those people. Whether it will improve on the 'totality' and drag mankind as a whole to a radically better condition is another matter. But doing this was neither its intention nor its promise. Its advantages over the alternative are thus indubitable. Its own virtues though – yet untried – are open to questioning.

What Rorty proposes here is a fragmented politics made to the measure of the fragmented world and fragmented human existence. His proposition squares and chimes well with the life-experience of many people with scattered, diffuse and always partial – fragmented – worries; with American experience better than with Serbian or Croatian, with the American Midwest better than with the American Southeast, with American Midwest academics better than with American Midwest unemployed and ghetto-dwellers. It also fits well the fleeting and flitting attention of the era of shrunk space and flattened time – the kind of attention notorious for its inability to concentrate, to stay put, to cling to any object for longer than the attraction of novelty lasts; an attention that uses itself up before it consumes its object, shifts perpetually in the search for new attractions, acquiring in the process remarkable skating and gliding skills but shunning all deep diving and digging.

Choosing political strategies also means taking sides in political/social divisions. Fragmented politics, a politics in which campaigns do not cumulate into movements and do not count the overall improvement of life among their ends, must look flawless – and, above all, as the sole politics needed – to those whose worries are fragmented, do not cumulate into experience of injustice and do not sum up into the desire of changing the rules of the game or the world in which the game is played. There are many such people; as Galbraith suggested, they constitute the 'contented majority', at least inside the 'contented minority' of well-to-do countries. Is not Rorty's proposition addressed primarily to them? Does not Rorty's proposition tell them what they wish to hear: that there is not much point in worrying about justice in the world, in assuming responsibility for the unfreedom and prospectless life of those whose worries are not scattered, unfocused and peripheral as our own? That these 'big issues' of justice are best served when split and fragmented just as their own problems are, and never confronted in their genuine or imaginary entirety, as the question of 'something being wrong with that world we all share'? And, above all, that those 'big issues' have nothing to do with the fragmentariness of our own affluent worries, and with our decision to settle for 'campaigns' instead of 'movements'?

These are perhaps the reasons for which Rorty's proposition rings true and proper to us, its intended addressees. They are unlikely to be received as good news by many others, who may well spy out a Pontius Pilate gesture in this recipe for 'deconstructing' the big issue (which we have decided that we can do nothing about) into a series of little ones (which we think we can do something about without sacrificing the big and little comforts we like so much about our life). This clash of perspectives and ensuing perceptions is, however, once more an essentially *political*, rather than ethical, issue. More directly relevant to our subject-matter, on the other hand, is the question of the *ethical* ramifications of Rorty's proposition. More particularly – what does it augur for the feasibility of the Levinasian passage from micro- to macro-ethics, from the 'self's responsibility for the Face' to 'commonly administered justice'?

To invoke Bakhtin's famous analysis of the function of the 'carnival' in reasserting the norms through the periodical yet strictly controlled visualization of their reversal, we may say that there is a pronounced tendency in the affluent part of the world to relegate charity, compassion and brotherly sentiments (which according to Levinas underlie our desire for justice) to the carnival events – reasserting thereby, legitimizing and 'normalizing' their absence from quotidianity. Moral impulses aroused by the sight of human misery are safely channelled into sporadic outbursts of charity in the form of Live Aid, Comic Aid or money collections for the most recent wave of refugees. Justice turns into a festive, holiday event; this helps to placate the moral conscience and to bear with the absence of justice during working days. Lack of justice becomes the norm and the daily routine. . . .

These seem to be valid objections and well-grounded suspicions. What they suggest is that Rorty's project of 'campaign politics' is unlikely to serve the cause of justice better than the 'movement politics' it is proposed to replace. Instead of smoothing the road from personal morality to public justice, for which movement politics is notorious, it substitutes new dangers for the old ones. The cause of justice, one may say, is not 'safe in its hands'. And yet such caveats do not invalidate Rorty's proposal. They would amount to the round condemnation of campaign politics only if the set of assumptions which sustained and validated movement politics were retained – if it was believed that the lifting of moral sentiments to the level of public justice had not been accomplished 'as yet' to full satisfaction solely because the right, reliable and fully effective lever had not been found, but that a perfect crane to do the lifting job without fail could be construed and constructed, that designing it was but a matter of time and that historical time 'runs towards' its construction. The point is, though, that those beliefs are ever more difficult to seriously entertain. For all that we know today, history does not seem to run towards 'just society', and all attempts to force it to run in this direction tend to add new injustices to the ones they are bent on repairing. It seems more and more likely that justice is a movement, rather than a goal or any describable 'end state'; that it manifests itself in the acts of spotting and fighting injustices – acts which do not necessarily add up to a linear process with a direction; and that its trademark is a perpetual self-deprecation and dissatisfaction with what has been achieved. Justice means always wanting more of itself.

And so it looks as if we need to reconcile ourselves to less-than-perfect, less than 'one hundred per cent effective' means; but it also looks as if such reconciliation is not necessarily bad news for the prospects of justice; that it may well be, on the contrary, more akin to the nature of justice – and thus, in the last account, better serve its cause. Rorty's proposal offers just what is needed: a salutary irony that pierces through the veil of the humourless, unctuous solemnity of the 'alternative world' movements – but an irony that is itself treated seriously, as all fate should be, if one wants to live it consciously, as a vocation. The weaknesses of campaign politics are simultaneously its strength. It is important not to entertain illusions and to know that partial, specific improvements are indeed partial and specific; that they settle problems, not resolve issues; that none of the improvements is likely to conclude the history of 'humanity's long march to justice' and bring the progress to its victorious end; that every improvement will leave justice as wanting and as unsatisfied as it was before, as pressing for further effort, and as militating against all slow-down and let-up. Only when we know all this is the desire for justice likely to be immune to the most awesome of dangers – that of self-contentment and of a conscience once and for all cleaned and clear.

In this crucial respect the realm of justice does not differ from the realm of moral responsibility; it retains all the essential features fully formed already at the 'primal moral scene'. Both realms are kingdoms of ambivalence; both are conspicuously short of patented solutions, cures free of side-effects and moves free of risks; both need that uncertainty, inconclusiveness, underdetermination and ambivalence to keep the moral impulse and the desire of justice forever alive, vigilant and – in their less-than-perfect, limited way – effective. Both have everything to gain and nothing to lose from knowing of their endemic and incurable ambivalence and refraining from an (in the end, suicidal) anti-ambivalence crusade. And so it is in its never conclusive, never truly satisfactory, chronically imperfect form, in its state of perpetual self-indignation, that justice seems best to answer Levinas's description as the projection of moral sentiments upon the wide screen of society.

Both morality and justice (or, as some would prefer, micro- and macro-ethics) are true to their name only as open-ended conditions and projects aware of their open-endedness. They are linked by this similarity much as they are linked genetically. Let me repeat that the primal moral scene, the moral party of two, is the breeding ground of all responsibility for the

Other, and the training ground for all the ambivalence the assumption of that responsibility necessarily contains. This being the case, it seems plausible that the key to a problem as large as social justice lies in a problem as (ostensibly) small-scale as the primal moral act of taking up responsibility for the Other nearby, within reach – for the Other as Face. It is here that moral sensitivity is born and gains strength, until it grows strong enough to carry the burden of responsibility for any instance of human suffering and misery, whatever the legal rules or empirical investigations may tell about their causal links and 'objective' allocation of guilt.

5

Parvenu and Pariah: the Heroes and Victims of Modernity

Socially, modernity is about standards, hope and guilt. Standards – beckoning, alluring, or prodding; but always stretching, always a step or two ahead of the pursuers, always forging onward just a little bit quicker than their chasers. And always promising that the morrow will be better than the now. And always keeping the promise fresh and unsullied, since the morrow will forever be a day after. And always mixing the hope of reaching the promised land with the guilt of not walking fast enough. The guilt protects the hope from frustration; the hope sees to it that the guilt never dries up. 'L'homme est coupable', observed Camus, that uniquely perspicacious correspondent from the land of modernity, 'mais il l'est de n'avoir su tirer de lui-même'.[1]

Psychically, modernity is about identity: about the truth of existence being not-yet-here, being a task, a mission, a responsibility. Like the rest of standards, identity stays stubbornly ahead: one needs to run breathlessly to reach it. And so one runs, pulled by hope and pushed by guilt, though the running, however fast, feels eerily like crawling. Surging ahead towards perpetually enticing and perpetually unfulfilled identity looks uncannily like recoiling from the flawed, illegitimate reality of the present.

Both socially and psychically, modernity is incurably self-critical: an endless, and in the end prospectless, exercise in self-cancelling and self-invalidating. Truly modern is not the *readiness* to delay gratification, but the *impossibility* of being gratified. All achievement is but a pale copy of its paragon. 'Today' is but an inchoate premonition of tomorrow; or, rather, its inferior, marred reflection. *What is* is cancelled in advance by *what is to come*. But it draws its significance and its meaning – its only meaning – from that cancellation.

In other words, modernity is the impossibility of staying put. To be modern means to be on the move. One does not necessarily choose to be on the move – as one does not choose to be modern. One is set on the move by being cast in the kind of world torn between the beauty of the vision and the ugliness of reality – reality having been made ugly by the beauty of the vision. In such a world, all residents are nomads; but nomads who wander in order to settle. Round the corner there is, there should be, there must be, a hospitable land in which to settle; but behind every corner new corners appear, with new frustrations and new, yet undashed hopes.

The habitat of nomads is the desert – that place-no-place of which Edmond Jabès wrote that in it 'there are no avenues, no boulevards, no blind alleys and no streets. Only – here and there – fragmentary imprints of steps, quickly effaced and denied'.[2] Effacing yesterday's footprints is all there is to the chimeric homeliness of the overnight stay; it makes the arrival feel, comfortingly, like being at home – that is, until it also turns into an imprint to be denied and effaced. The sight of tents pitched yesterday on the site of the overnight stay is reassuring: it fences off a plot of the desert so that it may feel like an oasis and give a sense of purpose to yesterday's wanderings. These tents pitched yesterday, being but tents, call, however, the bluff of self-congratulation. They prove, were proof needed, the self-deception of existence which wants to forget its nomadic past; it shows home to be but a point of arrival, and an arrival pregnant with new departure.

Wherever they come and dearly wish to stay, the nomads find themselves to be parvenus. Parvenu, *arriviste*; someone already *in*, but not quite *of*, the place; an aspiring resident without a residence permit. Someone reminding the older tenants of the past which they want to forget and the future they would rather wish away; someone who makes the older tenants run for shelter in hastily erected permit-issuing offices. The parvenu is told to carry the 'just arrived' label, so that all the others may trust their tents to be cut in rock. The parvenu's stay must be declared temporary, so that the stay of all the others may feel eternal.

The older tenants hate the parvenus for awaking the memories and premonitions they struggle hard to put to sleep. But they can hardly do without parvenus, without some of them being branded parvenu, set apart, charged with carrying the bacillus of restlessness in their bodies; it is thanks to such a branded part, and them only, that the whole may think that the bad dreams and the morbid premonitions are other people's tales and do not quite apply to themselves. The parvenu needs a parvenu in order not to feel a parvenu. And so nomads fight other nomads for the right to issue residence permits to each other. It is the only way they can make their own residence feel secure. The only way in which they can fix time which refuses to stay still is to mark the space and protect the marks against being effaced or moved. At least, such is their desperate hope.

In Robert Musil's incisive description, 'The train of events is a train unrolling its rails ahead of itself. The river of time is a river sweeping its banks along with it.'[3] It was the modern 'melting of solids and profaning the sacreds' that brought about such trains and such rivers. Premodern trains ran predictably and boringly in circles, much like children's toy trains do. And premodern rivers stayed in their beds for a time long enough to feel immemorial. As Wylie Sypher observed, 'in any society where the class structure is so closed that everyone has the place and knows it – and keeps it', there is no place for a parvenu nor is there a purpose a parvenu could conceivably serve; 'but the nineteenth century produced a horde of parvenus'.[4] Not that inordinately many people began to challenge their class-bound or otherwise-bound definitions and refused to heed their place; but the contours of places had been themselves washed up – the river banks having been swept along with the rivers, and uncertainty called *the new*, or *the better*, or *progress*, having become the only official destination of trains. Places and their names were now to be *made* (and, inevitably, re-made) 'as one goes'. In Hannah Arendt's memorable phrase, *man's autonomy turned into the tyranny of possibilities*. The small print of the great modern Act of Emancipation carried an injunction against the restfulness of certainty.

Definitions are *born with*; identities are *made*. Definitions tell you who you are, identities allure you by what you are not yet but may yet become. Parvenus were people in frantic search of identities. They chased identities because, from the start, they *had been denied* definitions. It was only too easy to conclude that it was their restlessness that put paid to definitions, and charge them with the criminal act of breaking the border-signposts. Once hurled in the vast expanse of unlimited possibilities, the parvenus were an easy prey: there were no fortified places in which to hide, no trusty definitions to wear as an armour. And from all places still protected by old ramparts, and from all places that strove to build new ones, poisonous arrows were showered.

Early in his life, Goethe's Wilhelm Meister found out that only young aristocrats can count on being taken for *what they are*; all others would be appraised or condemned for *what they do*. Wilhelm Meister drew the only logical conclusion to be drawn: he joined the theatre. On the stage, he took on and took off *roles*. This is what he was doomed to do in life anyway, but at least on stage – and only on stage – everyone expected roles to be but roles and to be played, and dropped, and replaced by other roles. In life, he would be expected to do the opposite or at least pretend that he was doing it: he would be expected to be *what he is*, though this is precisely what he was denied the right to.

Most parvenus cannot follow Meister's choice. *Life* is their stage, and in life, unlike in the theatre, skilful acting is called insincerity, not finesse; it is precisely to squeeze it out from the daily and the normal that acting as an honourable activity has been confined inside theatre walls. In life, roles must deny being roles and pretend to be identities, even if identities are not available in any other shape or form but that of roles. No one learns this truth better than the parvenu – living as they do under constant, relentless pressure (to quote Hannah Arendt) 'to have to adapt their taste, their lives, their desires'; who are 'denied the right to be themselves in anything and in any moment'. [5]

Having learned the rules of the game does not mean being wiser, though. Even less does it mean being successful. There is little the parvenus can do to change their plight, however strongly they desire to do so. 'One cannot modify one's image: neither the thought, nor freedom, lie, nausea, or disgust can help one to get out of one's proper skin.'[6] And yet getting out of one's proper skin is exactly what one is expected to do. The other-directed, other-monitored and other-evaluated parvenus are asked to prove the legality of their presence by being self-directed, self-monitored and self-evaluating, and *being seen* to be such. Wilhelm Meister has prudently *chosen* to be an actor: his modern successors are *forced* to be actors – though they risk condemnation and ridicule once they consent to their fate. A vicious circle, if there ever was one. And, as if to rub salt into the wound, there is that deafening silence, that overpowering indifference, that baffling aloofness, the 'I wash my hands' gesture of the Pontius Pilates who sit in judgement. As Kafka wrote in *The Trial*, 'The court wants nothing from you. It receives you when you come and dismisses you when you go.'

The silence of the court makes the defendant into his own judge: or rather it seems to be the case. With the prosecutor abstaining from censorious speeches and no judge to brief the jury, it is up to the defendants to prove their innocence. But innocence of what? Their guilt, after all, is nothing else but the very fact of having been charged, of standing in judgement. And this is one guilt they cannot deny, however smartly they argue their innocence, and however massive is the evidence they gather to support the argument.

By the whim of French legislature, the blacks of Martinique and Guadeloupe have been appointed Frenchmen, unlike the blacks of Sénégal or Côte d'Ivoire or the Arabs of Morocco. Whatever is said or written about the rights of Frenchmen extends to them; nothing remains to be proved and thus no court summonses have been issued or need to be issued. Yet the absence of a court does not mean innocence: it only means that no final judgement will be ever passed and that innocence will be never certified. The silence of the Law means the endlessness of trial. The blacks of Martinique and Guadeloupe have to prove that their Frenchness requires no proof . . . Not unlike Weber's Calvinists, they must live a life of virtue (a virtue which, in their case, is called 'the Frenchness') without the trust that the virtue will be rewarded and despite the agonizing suspicion that even if it were, they would not know it anyway. All around agree that they acquit themselves of the task admirably. They excel in schools. They are the most loyal and dedicated civil servants. Louder still than their co-citizens of a paler shade of skin they demand that the French borders be closed to those alien blacks of Chad or Cameroon 'who have no right to be here'. They even join Le Pen's National Front to promote the purification of La Patrie from the hordes of the parvenus bound to dilute the very Frenchhood they wish to embrace. By the most finical of fastidious standards, the blacks of Martinique and Guadeloupe are exemplary Frenchmen. To most exemplary Frenchmen this is exactly what they are – black Martinicans and Guadeloupians passing for exemplary Frenchmen. Well, it is precisely this earnest effort to be exemplary Frenchmen that makes them the blacks of Martinique or Guadeloupe . . . The more they do to turn into something else than they are, the more they are what they have been called not to be. Or have they indeed been called?

To the many versions of Abraham's answer to God's call, considered by Kierkegaard, Franz Kafka, the great spokesman for the parvenus of this world, added his own: another Abraham – 'who really does want to perform the sacrifice properly . . . but who cannot believe that he has been chosen, the repulsive old man and his dirty son'. 'Although he was afraid of being laughed at, and even more afraid of joining in the laughter, his greatest fear was that, if he were laughed at, he would look even older and even more repulsive, and his son even dirtier. An Abraham who comes uncalled!'

For the parvenus the game is unwinnable, at least as long as it goes on being played by the set rules, while the exit from the game means rebellion against the rules; indeed, a reversal of rules. Although, as Max Frisch put it, *always* and *for everybody* in our restless world of modernity 'identity means refusing to be what others want you to be', you are refused the right to refuse; you have no such right, not in *this* game, not as long as the umpires have their way. And so the frustrated dedication turns into mutiny. The myth of belonging is exploded, and the dazzling light of the explosion draws out of its exilic darkness the truth of the incompleteness, the until-further-noticeness of the wanderer's existence. Being in the world the way one is (or imagines oneself to be, or wants to be) at home, could be accomplished solely in another world, a world one can reach only through the act of *redemption*.

For parvenus like Lukács and Benjamin, as Ferenc Feher observed, 'the natural way of belonging, the desire for which never left either one, was blocked . . . neither could become assimilated or a nationalist.' The desire of belonging could only point towards the future, beyond the suffocating crampedness of the here and now. There was no belonging in sight except on the other side of redemption. And redemption 'can either come in the form of the Last Judgment, where there is one single yardstick to measure with, and the Supreme Authority sitting in court; or in the form of a conciliatory act of redeeming all those who shared in the community of endless human suffering'.[7] One could struggle for a new certitude to put paid to the uncomfortable pretensions of the present one; seek the as-yet-undiscredited authority hoped to proclaim and enforce new canons and new norms. Or one could part ways with certitudes old, new, and still to come – and follow Adorno's injunction, that only experiments are legitimate, when certitudes are no more. Both alternatives have been embraced and tried.

The parvenu Lukács spent his life searching for the authority bold and mighty enough to dismiss the judgements of today and proclaim its own judgement as if it were the Last – be it aesthetically perfect form or the distant alliance of proletarian sufferings with universal truth. In this he followed a long string of other parvenus, from Karl Marx – announcing the universality of belonging imminent once universal man is stripped of humiliating and degrading parochial liveries – through Karl Mannheim, struggling to reforge the homelessness of the itinerant sophist into the patent of judgement superior to all settled opinions – to Husserl, making the truth-bearing subjectivity transcendental, and thus entitled to brush off the admittedly false pretensions of this-worldly subjectivities.

Benjamin's world, on the other hand, was a series of historical moments pregnant with premonitions yet littered with the corpses of miscarried hopes; one moment, for that reason, is not particularly different from another. The twin dangers against which the life-work of Benjamin militates are, in Pierre V. Zima's words, 'la différence absolue et la disjonction idéologique (la *position* d'un des deux termes)' and 'le dépassement (hégélien, marxien) vers l'affirmation, vers la *position* d'un troisième terme sur un plan plus élevé'.[8] Under Benjamin's pen, ambivalence turns into the crow's nest from which the archipelago of strangled chances can be sighted; instead of a malady to be cured, ambivalence is now the value to be cherished and protected. The angels – Benjamin noted in his *Agesilaus Santander* (the anagram, deciphered by Scholem as *Der Angelus Satanus*) – 'new ones each moment in countless hosts, are created so that, after they have sung their hymn before God, they cease to exist and pass away into nothingness'. And Adorno commented:

Benjamin was one of the first to note that the 'individual who thinks becomes problematic to the core, yet without the existence of anything supra-individual in which the isolated subject could gain spiritual transcendence without being oppressed; it is this that he expressed in defining himself as one who left his class without, however, belonging to another'.[9] Well, like Lukács, Benjamin was not alone on the road he has chosen. Simmel, with his uncanny flair for decomposing any, however mighty, a structure, into a bunch of human, all-too-human thoughts and emotions, was there first; and many would follow, to mention but Lévi-Strauss debunking progressive history with a pointer as one more tribal myth, Foucault with the discourses that themselves spawn all the limits which stand to confine and channel their formation, or Derrida with realities dissembled into the texts embracing each other in the never ending quadrille of interpretations.

As in so many similar cases, the modern revolution ended in parricide – poetically intuited by Freud in his desperate effort to penetrate the mystery of culture. The most brilliant and most faithful children of modernity could not express their filial loyalty otherwise than by becoming its gravediggers. The more they were dedicated to the construction of the artifice which modernity set about to erect, having first dethroned and legally incapacitated nature – the more they sapped the foundations of the edifice. Modernity, one may say, was from the start pregnant with its own postmodern *Aufhebung*. Her children were genetically determined to be her detractors, and – ultimately – her demolition squad. Those cast as parvenus (those-who-have-arrived), yet refused the comfort of arrival, were bound sooner or later to decry the safety of *any* safe havens; in the end they were bound to question the arrival itself as a plausible or desirable end of the travel.

Hence the astonishing case of a culture engrossed in a tooth-and-nail struggle with the social reality it was supposed, as all cultures should, to reflect and serve. In this disarticulation and the ensuing enmity between culture and reified existence modernity stands perhaps alone among all known societal arrangements. One can confidently define modernity as a form of life marked by such disarticulation: as a social condition under which *culture cannot serve reality otherwise than through undermining it*.

But hence also the uniquely tragic – or is it schizophrenic? – character of modern culture, the culture that feels truly at home only in its homelessness. In that culture, desire is stained with fear, while horror bears attractions difficult to resist. That culture dreams of belonging yet fears locks and barred windows; it dreads the solitude called freedom yet still more than anything else resents oaths of loyalty. At whatever

direction it turns, that culture – like the hungry rats of Miller and
Dollard's maze – finds itself suspended at the point of ambivalence,
where the lines of falling allurement and rising repulsion cross. Walter
Benjamin reproached his friend in entrapment and adversary in the
search for escape, Gershon Scholem: 'I almost believe that you desire this
in-between state, yet you ought to welcome any means of ending it.' To
which Scholem replied: 'You are endangered more by your drive for
community . . . than by the horror of loneliness that speaks from so many
of your writings.'[10]

In the Indian caste system, the pariah was a member of the lowest
caste or *of no caste*. In an untouchable order of belonging, who could be
more untouchable than those who did not belong anywhere? Modernity
proclaimed no order untouchable, as all untouchable orders were to
be replaced with a new, artificial order where roads are built that lead
from the bottom to the top and so no one belongs anywhere forever.
Modernity was thus the hope of the pariah. But the pariah could stop
being a pariah only by becoming – struggling to become – a parvenu.
And the parvenu, having never washed out the stain of his origin,
laboured under a constant threat of deportation back to the land he tried
to escape. Deportation in case he failed; deportation in case he succeeded too spectacularly for the comfort of those around. Not for a
moment did the hero stop being a potential victim. Hero today, victim
tomorrow – the dividing wall between the two conditions was but
paper-thin. Being on the move meant belonging nowhere. And belonging nowhere meant not to count on anybody's protection: indeed, the
quintessence of the pariah existence was not to be able to count on
protection. The quicker you run, the faster you stay put. The greater
the frenzy with which you struggle to cut yourself off from the caste
of the pariah, the more you expose yourself as the pariah of non-
belonging.

It was the alluring image of a majestic artifice shimmering at the end
of the tunnel that set the pariah on his journey and transformed him into
the parvenu. It was the agony of the endless travel that dimmed the shine
of the artifice and dented its attraction: looking back on the road
travelled, the seekers of homes would dismiss their past hopes as a
mirage – and they would call their new frustrated sobriety the end of
utopia, the end of ideology, the end of modernity, or the advent of the
postmodern age.

And so they would say: artificial homelands are hallucinations at best,
vicious delusions at worst. No more revolutions to end all revolutions.
No more stretching oneself towards the sweet future that turns bitter the
moment it becomes the present. No more philosopher kings. No more
salvation by society. No more dreams about identities that are not –

dreams that spoil the enjoyment of the definitions that are. Travel has not brought redemption to the parvenu. Perhaps once there is nowhere to arrive, the sorry plight of the *arriviste* will be cancelled together with the travel?

With the setting of the universal sun, wrote the schoolboy Karl Marx, moths gather to the light of the domestic lamp. With the drying up of the hi-tech artificial lake of universality, yesteryear's putrescent bogs of parochiality glisten invitingly as the natural havens for all who need to swim safely. No more salvation by society – but perhaps *community* will make the salvation unnecessary? 'We should not look for skyhooks, but only for toeholds' is how Richard Rorty sums up the mood of the bereaved, and proceeds to praise the ethnocentrism and to advise us, rather than wasting our time in the vain search for objectivity and universal standpoints, to apply ourselves to the questions, 'With what communities should you identify?' and 'What should I do with my aloneness?'[11] Isaiah Berlin, on the other hand, tells his interviewers that there is nationalism which is rapacious, intolerant, cruel and bad in many other ways, but that there is also nationalism which is warm, cosy, at peace with nature and itself and therefore also, hopefully, with its neighbours: 'le doux nationalisme', as conscientious Frenchmen, baffled by the spectacular successes of Le Pen, and desperately trying to steal a march on the sinister adversary, call it. The tired wanderer sentenced to the life of a parvenu agony still wants to belong. But he gave up the hope that belonging can be attained through universality. He believes no more in long round-about routes. He dreams now of shortcuts. Or, better still, of arriving without travelling; coming home without really ever moving out.

Whatever used to be a virtue turned into vice. And the vices of yore have been (and one hopes: not posthumously) rehabilitated. The verdict has been quashed, those who passed it condemned or dismissed as incompetent judges. What modernity set to destroy, has its day of sweet vengeance. Community, tradition, the joy of being *chez soi*, the love of one's own, the sticking to one's kind, the pride of being so stuck, the roots, the blood, the soil, the nationhood – they no more stand con-demned; on the contrary, it is their critics and detractors, the prophets of universal humanity, who are now challenged to prove their case and of whom it is doubted that they ever will.

Perhaps we live in a postmodern age, perhaps not. But we do live in the age of tribes and tribalism. It is tribalism, miraculously reborn, that injects juice and vigour into the eulogy of community, the acclaim of belonging, the passionate search for tradition. In this sense at least, the long roundabout of modernity has brought us to where our ancestors once started. Or so it may seem.

The end of modernity? Not necessarily. In another respect, after all, modernity is very much with us. It is with us in the form of the most defining of its defining traits: that of hope, the hope of making things better than they are – since they are, thus far, not good enough. Vulgar preachers of unadorned tribalism and elegant philosophers of communally based forms of life alike teach us what they do in the name of changing things to the better. 'Whatever good the ideas of "objectivity" and "transcendence" have done for our culture can be attained equally well by the idea of community', says Rorty – and this is precisely which makes that latter idea attractive for yesterday's seekers of the universal roads to a world fit for human habitation. Rational designs of artificial perfection, and the revolutions meant to imprint them on the shape of the world all failed abominably to deliver on their promise. Perhaps communities, warm and hospitable, will deliver what they, the cold abstractions, could not deliver. We still want the work to be done; we just let drop the tools which have been proved useless and reach for others – which, who knows?, may still do the job. One may say that we still agree that marital happiness is a good thing; only we would no longer endorse Tolstoy's opinion that all happy marriages are happy in the same way.

We know quite well why we dislike the tools we have abandoned. For two centuries or so people deserving or demanding to be listened to with attention and respect told the story of a human habitat which curiously coincided with that of the political state and the realm of its legislative powers and ambitions. The human world was, in Parsons's memorable rendering, the 'principally co-ordinated' space – the realm upheld or about to be upheld by uniform principles maintained by the joint efforts of the legislators and the armed or unarmed executors of their will. It was such an artificial space that was represented as a habitat which 'fits naturally' human needs and – most importantly – fits the need to gratify the needs. The 'principally co-ordinated', possibly rationally designed and monitored, society was to be that good society modernity set about constructing. Two centuries is a long time – enough for all of us to learn what solitary great minds of Jeremy Bentham's type intuited from the start: that rationally designed 'principal co-ordination' fits equally well a school and a hospital as it fits a prison and a workhouse; and to find out that such a universality of application makes even the school and the hospital feel like a prison or a workhouse. That period has also shown that the wall separating the 'benign' brand of rational engineering from its malignant, genocidal variety is so rickety, slippery and porous that – to paraphrase Bertrand Russell – one does not know when one should start to cry . . .

As for the communities – those allegedly uncontrived, naturally growing organisms, toeholds instead of skyhooks – we do not yet know all
those things we know only too well about the Grand Artifice modernity
promised to build. But we may guess. We know that the modern zest for
designed perfection condensed the otherwise diffuse heterophobia, and
time and again channelled it, Stalin- or Hitler-style, towards genocidal
outlets. We may only surmise that the messy tribalism suspicious of
universal solutions would gravitate towards exilic, rather than genocidal,
outlets for heterophobia. Separation rather than subjugation, confinement or annihilation. As Le Pen put it, 'I adore North Africans. But their
place is in the Maghreb.' We know as well that the major conflict of the
modern setting grew from the inherent ambivalence of the assimilatory
pressures, which prodded towards effacing the differences in the name
of a universal human pattern, while simultaneously recoiling before the
success of the operation – but we may only hypothesize that a similarly
conflict-pregnant ambivalence will be disclosed in the postmodern acco-
lade of difference, which veers between the equally unpalatable and
indefensible extremes of 'wet liberalism', that meekly surrenders the right
to compare and evaluate the others, and rampant tribalism, denying the
others the right to compare and evaluate.

There is no certainty – not even a high probability – that in the
universe populated by communities no room will be left for the pariah.
What seems more plausible, however, is that the parvenu's route of
escape from the pariah status will be closed. Mixophilia may well be
replaced with mixophobia; tolerance of difference may well be wedded
to the flat refusal of solidarity; monologic discourse, rather than giving
way to a dialogic one, will split into a series of soliloquies, with the
speakers no more insisting on being heard, but refusing to listen into the
bargain.

These are real prospects, real enough to give pause to the joyful
chorus of sociologists welcoming the new soft world of communities.

Sociology has a long and distinguished record of sycophancy. Since its
birth, it established itself as the principal poet-laureate of the state-
centred and state-coordinated society, of the state bent on prohibiting
everything which has not been first made obligatory. With the state no
more interested in uniformity, losing interest in culture as a drilling
routine and gladly leaving the job of social integration to variety-loving
market forces, sociology is desperately seeking new courts where the
skills and experience of pensioned courtiers could be gainfully employed. For many, the endemically fissiparous mini-courts of imagined
communities, home ideologies and tribally invented traditions seem just
the thing they need. Once more, though in a strikingly different way

from before, one can flatter the practice with theoretical groundings by drawing elegant diagrams of messy reality. Once more one can herald a new ambivalence as a logical solution, and a definitive improvement on the old one. Courtiers' habits die hard.

In the course of the long, tortuous and convoluted march of modernity we should have learned our lesson: that the human existential predicament is ambivalent beyond cure, that good is always mixed with evil, that the line between the benign and the poisonous dose of medicine for our imperfections is impossible to draw safely. We should have learned this lesson. But we hardly did. Having discredited the medicine, we forget about the ailment it was meant to cure. Once more we announce, jubilantly, the discovery of a wonder-drug for human ills – only this time it is the old malady which has been proclaimed to be the medicine. Once more we try, confidently, to prescribe the right dose of the cure. There is a good, enabling, progressive form of belonging – we are told – and this is called ethnicity, cultural tradition, nationalism. People are different, and let them stay so. Well, there is also an ugly posturing called heterophobia, or xenophobia, or racism – a view and a practice of separating, banishing, exiling. But do the two have anything in common? Is not a small dose of the drug a foolproof antidote against its poisonous effects?

The orthodox consensus of sociology has been found guilty of aiding and abetting the all-too-often unwholesome practices of the nation-state. Some time will yet pass before the new 'communalistically orientated' sociology, now relishing its honeymoon period and blithely self-congratulating, stands charged of complicity in the unprepossessing effects of the present fashions in identity-building. This, presumably, will not happen (not by common agreement at any rate) before those fashions are found, as usual in retrospect, to be wrong choices and lost chances.

6

Tourists and Vagabonds: the Heroes and Victims of Postmodernity

Inviting me to give this lecture, Professor Hunter asked me to 'attempt to answer the question of how the fragmentation, deinstitutionalization, and subjectivism (among other processes) unfolding in contemporary social life are mediated within the frameworks of everyday life'. He also wished me 'to move beyond the abstractions and even obfuscations of "theory" . . . to the concrete and empirical experience of real human beings'. A challenging briefing, and a challenge I could not refuse, though I cannot be sure I can rise to it . . . After all, the philosophers' philosophies, the synthesizers' syntheses, the theorists' theories reveal their sense (providing they *have* sense) only if looked upon as attempts to order the disorderly, to simplify the complex, to detemporalize the temporary – the orderly and the simple and the extemporal being the 'theory', and the disorderly and the complex and the history-bound being the *experience* in which they, as the denizens of their time and place, are immersed. Theories tend to be shapely and shiny containers made to contain the oozy and muddy contents of experience. But to keep it there, their walls need to be hard; they also tend to be opaque. It is difficult to see the contents of experience through the walls of theory. Often one needs to pierce the walls – to 'deconstruct', to 'decompose' them – to see what do they hide inside.

There was one more reason why I found the challenge hard to refuse. Charlottesville is the home of Richard Rorty – the great philosopher, perhaps the greatest we have.

But what is a great philosopher? It used to be common to measure the greatness of philosophers by their dexterity in tying together loose ends, in winding up discussions, in pronouncing verdicts that exuded an air of finality and otherwise bringing philosophy to an end. The meaning of such greatness was derived from the Thanatos-driven philosophy, a philosophy which, like Heideggerian *Dasein*, lived-towards-death and carried its life rehearsing its own demise, sure that the end was its fulfilment. After the greatest of them all, after Aristotle or Hegel, one heard the anguished cries: philosophy did reach its end, everything worth saying has been said, nothing yet unsaid is worth saying, we have all the answers but no more questions . . .

I suggest that Richard Rorty is great philosopher in an altogether different sense. He is great in as far as that after Rorty one can no more philosophize the way one did before, even if what one philosophizes about is one's disagreement with Rorty's philosophy; though philosophize one must, because the impossibility to philosophize in the old fashion means precisely the impossibility of the kind of philosophy that lives-toward-death, the impossibility of philosophy ever coming to its end. Rorty's philosophical greatness is born of a different kind of philosophy – of the Eros-driven, libidinal philosophy, one that fulfils itself in its perpetual unfulfilment and in asking such questions as fear final answers more than they dread the prospect of remaining unanswered. In terms of such philosophy Rorty is a great philosopher. The greatness of Rorty, the philosopher, fulfils itself in helping such unfulfillable philosophy to be born.

Musing on the chances of some future inhabitants of the Sahara grasping the spirit of our modern way of life, Rorty observed that it would be more helpful if they took Dickens, rather than Heidegger, for their material witness; and this in spite of the fact that Heidegger spelled out in so many words what it means to be modern, while doing it never occurred to Dickens. In spite of? What Rorty really thinks about is *because.* The 'isness' of the society Dickens narrates is to be constantly indignant and deprecating about what it has been thus far and what it is likely to become – to be forever at war with itself and take no 'yes' for an answer – to be, as Bloch would have said, constantly *noch nicht geworden.* The 'isness' of the world Dickens narrates is the impossibility of 'isness'. And this is, Rorty says, more true about modernity than any, however refined and sophisticated, formula which the great synthesizers may put together. This does not mean that Dickens is wiser than Heidegger (even if we had a yardstick with which to measure and compare the two so distinct kinds of wisdom). But this does mean that Dickens, being a novelist, not an academic philosopher, and so trying as he did to remain faithful to the convoluted, contorted and confused experience of his contemporaries, rather than to the vocation of correcting it, straightening up and streamlining – was in a better position to tell the true story of that experience which was indeed the experience of convolution, contortion and confusion.

What Richard Rorty does not say, and where I take exception to his way of telling the story, is that it took quite a lot of *history* to assign more truth-value to the Dickens style of story-telling than to that of Habermas or Heidegger, and that therefore his own discovery (or, rather, his own choice of priority) is itself *an event in history*. Rorty refuses to locate himself and his thought *in history*. And in this refusal he drifts danger-ously close to that author/actor of the orthodox philosophy whom he did more than anyone else to disavow and disempower – to that 'ascetic priest' whom he spies out so skilfully in Heidegger. To that ascetic priest who believed that the truth has lain in wait since the day of creation and that it is but a matter of his priestly skills and wits to force it out of its hiding.

But *what* are we doing, when we say that the truth of the novelist is better than the truth of the philosopher? Are we stating a fact that has thus far avoided the eye of modern philosophers? A fact which they could have seen were they not, foolishly, averting their eyes? Or are we rather spotting something new, that was not there before? Or something which, if it was there, was too marginal, feeble, taciturn, or otherwise negligible to meet the eye? In other words: are we talking about a change in *philosophy*, or in the *life experience* we philosophize about?

In their traditional role as the healers of, and the legislators for, common sense, philosophers had to slice off and separate their own practices from the practices of the common man, so that the two could be set against each other. From this operation the practices of the non-philosophers emerged, naturally, as non-philosophical ones. The divi-sion was neat and tidy. On one side was philosophy, unpolluted by freak and flickery practices: on the other, raw practices unpolluted by thought – a primal stuff not unlike the blips on the accelerator screen waiting to be given meaning by the nuclear physicists. But this division was a by-product, or a waste-product, of the self-constitution of philosophy in the certain role it had chosen, or *was* chosen to play throughout the modern era. The absence of philosophy in living practices was trivially evident but for the decision to ignore its presence and/or deny its credentials.

It is trivially evident today that common experience is not at all as modern philosophy (and sociology, for that matter) painted it: not the void waiting to be filled with meaning, not the formless plasma to be given shape by professionals armed with hermeneutical know-how. That experience is rather from the start meaningful, interpreted, understood by those steeped in it – that meaningfulness, interpretation, comprehen-sion being *its mode of being*. Now, making trivially evident today the very opposite of what was trivially evident yesterday is, no doubt, a philo-sophical accomplishment. But the Owl of Minerva does indeed spread its wings only at dusk . . . A lot must have happened in the long day of life which modern men and women experience, for the philosophers to recognize, as the evening came, the evidence – to accept the evidence as evidence.

It is quite likely, but largely beside the point, that human experience bore at all times the character which we see as evident today. The problem, though, is that only under certain conditions do things, even the most ubiquitous and stubbornly present ones, become 'evident'. (It is evident to us, for instance, that already Cro-Magnon men and the Neanderthals 'must have had a culture'; but only in the second half of the eighteenth century could the concept of culture be coined, and they would hardly be the Cro-Magnons or Neanderthals they were if they were aware that they had a culture.) And it is under special conditions that lay perceptions, interpretations and ensuing life strategies may be recognized as knowledge – a *valid* knowledge – rather than manifestations of the endemically flawed, prejudiced and otherwise erroneous 'common sense'; that understanding might have been recognized as the ongoing, ever repeated and never final accomplishment of daily life, rather than the product of a sophisticated methodology accessible to the experts only and moving relentlessly toward the ultimate, conclusive resolution.

Much could be said about such special conditions, this special kind of common life experience, which made 'evident' these things which could be perhaps true also before, but certainly were not previously *considered* evident. I would like, however, to bring to your attention but one momentous change in life circumstances – namely, the *detemporalization of social space.*

The projection of spatial, contemporaneous difference upon the continuum of time, re-presentation of heterogeneity as ascending series of time stages, was perhaps the most salient, and possibly also the most seminal, feature of the modern mind. But metaphors transform both sides that enter the metaphorical relationship. The projection of space upon time furnished time with certain traits which only space possesses 'naturally': modern time had direction, just like any itinerary in space. Time progressed from the obsolete to the up-to-date, and the up-to-date was from the start the future obsolescence. Time had its 'front' and its 'behind'; one was goaded and boosted to move 'forward with time'. The boisterous, self-congratulating town elders who built Leeds Town Hall in the middle of the nineteenth century as the monument to their own miraculous rise-in-time, have engraved their moral principles around the walls of its assembly hall. Alongside other commandments there is one most striking by its self-confident brevity – 'Forward!' Those who designed the Town Hall had no doubts as to where 'forwards' was.

And so the modern men and women lived in a time-space with *structure*; a solid, tough, durable time-space – just the right benchmark against which to plot and monitor the capriciousness and volatility of human will – but also a hard container in which human actions could feel sensible and secure. In that structured world one could be lost, but one could also find one's way and arrive exactly where one aimed to be. The difference between getting lost and arriving was made of knowledge and determination: the knowledge of the time-space structure and the determination to follow, be what may, the chosen itinerary. Under those circumstances, freedom was indeed the known necessity – plus the resolve to act on that knowledge.

The structure was in its place before any human deed began, and lasted long enough, unshaken and unchanged, to see the deed through. It preceded all human accomplishment, but it also made the accomplishment possible: it transformed one's life struggle from an aimless tussle into a consistent accomplishment. One could add one achievement to another, follow the road step by step, each step leading, thanks to the road, to another; one could build one's accomplishment from the bottom up, from the foundations to the roof. That was the world of life-long pilgrimage, of vocation, or – as the Owl of Minerva was to pronounce later on through Jean-Paul Sartre's lips – of the 'life project'. David Copperfield and Buddenbrooks alike were wrestling with indomitable standards – commanding yet slippery, obligatory yet well-nigh impossible to reach. And so they knew from the start where to seek success and knew right away if they failed. Our life struggles dissolve, on the contrary, in that *unbearable lightness of being* . . . We never know for sure when to laugh and when to cry. And there is hardly a moment in life to say without dark premonitions: 'I have arrived.'

Let me make myself clear. I am not saying that modern men and women spoke of all this in so many words, that they thought about it, reasoned and argued when going through their life business. I am saying rather that we, men and women of the late twentieth century, the late-modern, 'surmodern' or postmodern men and women, have to impute to them such a vision of the world whenever we want to make sense of what we know of their lives and try to comprehend the kind of experience which made that life possible while having been made possible by it. I am not saying that *they* lived daily with the knowledge of tightly structured time-space and the solidity and durability of the world – but that *we* live daily with the growing awareness that we cannot trust either. I am talking therefore above all about the present shock, not the past tranquillity. That past experience, as we tend to reconstruct it now, retrospectively, has come to be known to us mainly through its disappearance. What we think the past had – is what we know we do not have.

And what we know we do not have is the facility to set apart the

structure of the world from the action of the humans; the rock-steady
solidity of the world out there from the pliability of human will. Not that
the world has suddenly become submissive and obedient to human
desire; as before, it all too often makes light of human intention and
effort and easily twists and bends the effects of human labours. But this
world out there more and more reminds one of another player in the
game, rather than of the indomitable rule-setter and a no-appeal-allow-
ing umpire; and as a player in a game in which the rules are made and
remade in the course of playing. The experience of living in such a world
(or is it, rather, the experience of living that world?) is the experience of
a player, and in the experience of the player there is no way of telling
necessity from accident, determination from contingency: there are but
the moves of the players, the art of playing one's hand well and the skill
of making the most of one's cards.

Human action has not become less frail and erratic; it is the world it
tries to inscribe itself in and orient itself by that seems to have become
more so. How can one live one's life as pilgrimage if the shrines and
sanctuaries are moved around, profaned, made sacrosanct and then
unholy again in a stretch of time much shorter than the journey to reach
them would take? How can one invest in a lifelong achievement, if today
values are bound to be devalued and inflated tomorrow? How can one
groom oneself for life's vocation, if skills laboriously acquired become
liabilities the day after they became assets? When professions and jobs
disappear without notice and yesterday's specialisms are today's blinkers? And how can one mark and fence off one's place in the world if all
acquired rights are but until-further-notice, when the withdrawal-at-will
clause is written into every contract of partnership, when – as Anthony
Giddens aptly put it – all relationship is but a 'pure' relationship, that is
a relationship without strings attached and with no obligations earned,
and all love is but 'confluent' love, lasting no longer than the satisfaction
derived?

The meaning of identity, as the late Christopher Lasch pointed out,
refers both to persons and to things. Both have lost their solidity in
modern society, their definiteness and continuity. The world construed
of durable objects has been replaced with disposable products designed
for immediate obsolescence. In such a world, identities can be adopted
and discarded like a change of costume. The horror of the new situation
is that all diligent work of construction may prove to be in vain; the
allurement of the new situation, on the other hand, lies in the fact of not
being bound by past trials, of never being irrevocably defeated, always
'keeping the options open'. But the horror and the allurement alike make
life-as-pilgrimage hardly feasible as a strategy and unlikely to be chosen

as one. Not by many, anyway. And not with a great chance of success.

In the life-game of postmodern men and women the rules of the game keep changing in the course of playing. The sensible strategy is therefore to keep each game short – so that a sensibly played game of life calls for the splitting of one big all-embracing game with huge and costly stakes into a series of brief and narrow games with small, not-too-precious ones. To quote Christopher Lasch again – determination to live one day at a time and depicting daily life as a succession of minor emergencies become the guiding principles of all rational life strategy.

To keep the game short means to beware long-term commitments. To refuse to be 'fixed' one way or the other. Not to get tied to one place, however pleasurable the present stopover may feel. Not to wed one's life to one vocation only. Not to swear consistency and loyalty to anything or anybody. Not to *control* the future, but *refuse to mortgage it*: to take care that the consequences of the game do not outlive the game itself, and to renounce responsibility for such consequences as do. To forbid the past to bear on the present. In short, to cut the present off at both ends, to sever the present from history. To abolish time in any other form but of a loose assembly, or an arbitrary sequence, of present moments; to flatten the flow of time into a *continuous present*.

Once dissembled and no more a vector, no more an arrow with a pointer or a flow with a direction – time no more structures the space. On the ground, there is no more 'forward' and 'backward'; it is just the ability to move and not to stand still that counts. *Fitness* – the capacity to move swiftly where the action is and be ready to take in experiences as they come – takes precedence over *health*, that idea of the standard of normalcy and of keeping that standard stable and unscathed. All delay, also 'delay of gratification', loses its meaning: there is no arrow-like time left to measure it.

And so the snag is no more how to discover, invent, construct, assemble (even buy) an identity, but how to prevent it from being too tight – and from sticking too fast to the body. Well-sewn and durable identity is no more an asset; increasingly and ever more evidently, it becomes a liability. *The hub of postmodern life strategy is not making identity stand – but the avoidance of being fixed.*

The figure of the tourist is the epitome of such avoidance. Indeed, tourists worth their salt are the masters supreme of the art of melting the solids and unfixing the fixed. First and foremost, they perform the feat of not belonging to the place they might be visiting; theirs is the miracle of being in and out of place at the same time. The tourists keep their distance, and bar the distance from shrinking into proximity. It is as if each of them was enclosed in a bubble with tightly controlled osmosis;

only such things as the occupant of the bubble admits may leak in, only such things as he or she allows to go, may seep out. Inside the bubble the tourist may feel safe; whatever the pulling power of the outside, however sticky or voracious the world outside may be, the tourist is protected. Travelling lightly, with just a few belongings necessary to insure against the inclemency of alien places, the tourists may set out on the road again at a moment's notice, as soon as things threaten to get out of control, or as their potential of amusement seems to have been exhausted, or as still more exciting adventures beckon from afar. Mobility is the name of the game: one must be able to move when the needs push or the dreams call. This ability the tourists call freedom, autonomy or independence, and they cherish it more than anything else, since it is the *conditio sine qua non* of everything else that their hearts desire. This is also the meaning of their most often heard demand: 'I need more space.' That is: no one shall be allowed to question my right to go out of the space I am presently locked in.

In the tourist life, the length of stay in any place is hardly ever planned in advance; neither is the next destination. The point of tourist life is to be on the move, not to arrive; unlike those of their predecessors, the pilgrims, the tourists' successive stopovers are not stations on the road, since there is no goal beckoning at the end of life's travels which could make them into stations. If the successive addresses add up into an itinerary, it happens only retrospectively, when a logic is discovered or imputed which did not guide the wanderer at the time of his wandering. When still on the move, no image of the future state is at hand to fill the present experience with meaning; each successive present, like works of contemporary art, must explain itself in its own terms and provide its own key to read out its sense.

The stopovers are campings, not domiciles; however long each respite in the travel may prove in the end, it is lived at each moment as an overnight stay. Only the shallowest of roots, if any, are struck. Only skin-deep relations, if any, are entered with the locals. Above all, there is no mortgaging of the future, no incurring of long-term obligations, no allowing something that happens today to bind the tomorrow. The locals are not, after all, the keepers of half-way inns, which pilgrims had to visit again and again on each pilgrimage; the locals the tourists come across are literally 'bumped into' incidentally, as a side-effect of yesterday's impulse, which the day before yesterday was not yet imagined or anticipated and which could easily be different from what it was and bring the tourist to some other place. Their company has been born of one impulse and will die with the next. True – that company is the consequence of the move, but it is an unanticipated consequence; it was not part of the bargain, and it has no claim on the wanderer's loyalty.

All this offers the tourist the gratifying feeling of 'being in control'. This is not, to be sure, control in the now old-fashioned and outdated, heroic sense of engraving one's shape on the world, remaking the world in one's own image or liking, and keeping it like that. This is but what can be called the 'situational control' – the ability to choose where and with what parts of the world to 'interface' and when to switch off the connection. Switching on and off does not leave on the world any lasting imprint; as a matter of fact, thanks to the facility with which the switches are operated, the world (as the tourist knows it) seems infinitely pliable, soft and friable; it is unlikely to hold any shape for long. Sightings replace shapes: it is now the tourist's wandering interests, his shifting attention and the mobile angle of view that gives the world its 'structure' – as fluid and as 'until further notice' as the gaze that brought it to be. Shaping the world in this way is effortless, but it is also, for the world at least, inconsequential.

An event which in principle has no consequences outlasting its own duration is called an episode; like the tourists themselves, the episode – so says Milan Kundera – breaks into the story without being part of it. The episode is a self-enclosed event. Each new episode is, so to speak, an absolute beginning, but equally absolute is its ending: 'not to be continued' is the last sentence of the story (even if, to make the plight of the unwary yet more bitter, it is written in invisible ink). The problem is, though – as Kundera hastens to add – that the decision about the finality of the ending is itself never final. One would never know whether the episode is truly over and done with. All the effort to prevent it notwithstanding, past events may return to haunt the future presents. The better-to-be-forgotten partners of past intercourse may turn up again, inside entirely different episodes, brandishing the sores left by the encounters of yore. Pruning the episodes, nipping in the bud the seedlings of future consequences, therefore takes a constant effort, and a constantly inconclusive effort with that. This is a nasty fly in the otherwise tasty ointment of a life lived at every moment as an episode; or perhaps this is a hole, through which the world out there breaks time and again into the tightly controlled space – thereby calling the bluff of the tourist's control. This is why the tourist's life is not all roses. There is a price to be paid for the pleasures it brings. The tourist's way of doing away with uncertainties brings about uncertainties of its own.

The tourists embark on their travels by choice – or so, at least, they think. They set off because they find home boring or not attractive enough, too familiar and holding too few surprises; or because they hope to find elsewhere more exciting adventure and deeper sensations than the homely routine is ever likely to deliver. The decision to leave the home behind in order to explore foreign parts is all the easier to make for the comforting feeling that one can always return, if need be. The discomforts of hotel rooms may indeed make one homesick; and it is gratifying and consoling to remember that there is a home – somewhere – a retreat from the hurly-burly where one could shelter, where one could be unambiguously, unproblematically *chez soi* – draw the curtains, close the eyes and plug the ears to new sensations, shut the door to new adventures . . . Well, the point is that such a prospect stays gratifying and consoling as long as it remains a *prospect*. The 'home', as in 'homesickness', is none of the real buildings of brick and mortar, timber or stone. The moment the door is shut from the outside, home becomes a *dream*. The moment the door is shut from inside, it turns into *prison*. The tourist has acquired the taste for vaster, and above all open, spaces.

The tourists become wanderers and put the dreams of homesickness above the realities of home – because they want to, because they consider it the most reasonable life-strategy 'under the circumstances', or because they have been seduced by the true or imaginary pleasures of a sensation-gatherer's life. But not all wanderers are on the move because they prefer being on the move to staying put. Many would perhaps refuse to embark on a life of wandering were they asked, but they had not been asked in the first place. If they are on the move, it is because they have been pushed from behind – having been first uprooted by a force too powerful, and often too mysterious, to resist. They see their plight as anything but the manifestation of freedom. Freedom, autonomy, independence – if they appear in their vocabulary at all – invariably come in the future tense. For them, to be free means *not to have to* wander around. To have a home and to be allowed to stay inside. These are the *vagabonds*; dark moons reflecting the shine of bright suns; the mutants of postmodern evolution, the unfit rejects of the brave new species. The vagabonds are the waste of the world which has dedicated itself to tourists' services.

The tourists stay or move at their hearts' desire. They abandon the site when new untried opportunities beckon elsewhere. The vagabonds, however, know that they won't stay for long, however strongly they wish to, since nowhere they stop are they welcome: if the tourists move because they find the world irresistibly *attractive*, the vagabonds move because they find the world unbearably *inhospitable*. They take to the roads not when they have squeezed out the last drop of amusement the locals could offer, but when the locals lose patience and refuse to put up with their alien presence. The tourists travel because they *want to*; the vagabonds – because they have *no other choice*. The vagabonds are, one may say, involuntary tourists; but the notion of 'involuntary tourist' is a contradiction in terms. However much the tourist strategy may be a necessity in a world marked by shifting walls and mobile roads, freedom of choice is the tourist's flesh and blood. Take it away, and the attraction, the poetry and, indeed, the liveability of the tourist's life are all but gone.

A word of warning: tourists and vagabonds are the *metaphors* of contemporary life. One can be (and often is) a tourist or a vagabond without ever travelling physically far – just as Max Weber's Puritans were pilgrims-through-life even if they hardly ever looked beyond the border of their home town, and were too busy pursuing their vocations ever to take time off and visit the seaside. Having this in mind, I suggest to you that in our postmodern society, we are all – to one extent or another, in body or thought, here and now or in the anticipated future, willingly or unwillingly – on the move; none of us can be certain that he or she has gained the right to any place once for all and no one thinks that his or her staying in one place forever is a likely prospect; wherever we happen to stop, we are at least in part displaced or out of place. But here the commonality of our plight ends and the differences begin.

I suggest to you that the opposition between the tourists and the vagabonds is the major, principal division of the postmodern society. We are all plotted on a continuum stretched between the poles of the 'perfect tourist' and the 'vagabond beyond remedy' – and our respective places between the poles are plotted according to the degree of freedom we possess in choosing our life itineraries. Freedom of choice, I put to you, is in postmodern society by far the most seminal among the stratifying factors. The more freedom of choice one has, the higher is one's rank in the postmodern social hierarchy. Postmodern social differences are made of the width and narrowness of the range of realistic options.

But the vagabond is the tourist's *alter ego* – just as the destitute is the *alter ego* of the rich, the savage the *alter ego* of the civilized, or the stranger the *alter ego* of the native. Being an *alter ego* means to serve as a rubbish bin into which all ineffable premonitions, unspoken fears, secret self-deprecations and guilts too awesome to be thought of are dumped; to be an *alter ego* means to serve as a public exposition of the innermost private, as an inner demon to be publicly exorcized, an effigy in which all that which cannot be suppressed may be burnt. The *alter ego* is the dark and sinister backcloth against which the purified ego may shine.

No wonder that the tourist half of postmodern society is in two minds as far as the other, the vagabond, half is concerned. The vagabonds mock the tourist style, and mocking means ridicule. The vagabonds are the caricature which reveals the ugliness hidden underneath the beauty of makeup. Their presence is irksome and infuriating; there is no evident use they may be put to; for all one knows, they may be disposed of to no one's – not even their own – loss or regret.

But remember – the vagabonds are the rubbish bins for the tourist filth; dismantle the waste-disposal system, and the healthy ones of this world will suffocate and poison amidst their own refuse . . . More importantly yet, the vagabonds – remember that – are the dark background against which the sun of the tourist shines so brightly that the spots are hardly seen. The darker the background, the brighter the shine. The more repulsive and abhorrent the lot of the vagabond, the more bearable are the minor discomforts and major risks of the tourist life. One can live with the ambiguities of *uncertainty* which saturate the tourist life only because the *certainties* of vagabondage are so unambiguously loathsome and repugnant. The tourist needs an alternative too dreadful to contemplate to keep repeating, at the hour of stress, that 'there is no alternative'.

The vagabonds, the victims of the world which made the tourists into its heroes, have their uses, after all; as the sociologists love to say – they are 'functional'. It is difficult to live in their neighbourhood, but it is unthinkable to live without them. It is their all-too-blatant hardships that reduce one's own worries to marginal inconveniences. It is their evident unhappiness that inspires the rest to thank God daily for having made them tourists.

(Lecture delivered at the University of Virginia in October 1995.)

7

Postmodern Art, or the Impossibility of the Avant-garde

Literally, 'avant-garde' means the vanguard, an advance post, a spearhead or the first line of a moving army: a detachment which moves in front of the main body of the armed forces – but remains ahead only to pave the way for the rest of the army. A platoon, say, which has captured a foothold in the territory still controlled by the enemy, will be followed by battalions, regiments and divisions. The avant-garde gives the distance which separates it from the bulk a temporal dimension: what is being done *at present* by a small advance unit will be repeated *later* by all. The guard is seen as 'advanced' on the assumption that 'the rest will follow suit'. It goes without saying that we know for sure on which side is the front and where is the rear, where is 'before' and where 'behind'. (We know too that the stretch between them does not stand still – the front line itself is on the move.) The concept of the avant-garde conveys the idea of an essentially orderly space and time, and of an essential co-ordination of the two orders. In a world in which one can speak of the avant-garde, 'forward' and 'backward' have, simultaneously, spatial and temporal dimensions.

For this reason it does not make much sense to speak of the avant-garde in the postmodern world. Surely, the postmodern world is anything but immobile – everything in that world is on the move; but the moves seem random, dispersed and devoid of clear-cut direction (first and foremost a cumulative direction). It is difficult, perhaps impossible, to judge their 'advanced' or 'retrograde' nature, since the past co-ordination between spatial and temporal dimensions has all but fallen apart, while space and time themselves display repeatedly the absence of an orderly, intrinsically differentiated structure. We do not know for sure (and we do not know how to be sure that we know it) where is 'forward' and where 'backward', and so we cannot say with certainty which move is 'progressive' and which 'regressive'. Already in 1967 Leonard B. Meyer suggested that the contemporary arts had reached a changeable-steady state, a sort of mobile stagnation (he called that condition 'stasis'): every single unit is on the move, but there is little logic in this to-ing and fro-ing; fragmentary changes do not add up to a unified current; and the totality would not budge – the effect known to every schoolchild under the name of Brownian motion.

We may say that what is absent today is the front line which allowed us once to decide which is the forward movement and which is the retreat. Instead of a regular army, the scattered battles are fought now by guerrilla units; instead of a condensed offensive action with a determined strategic goal, endless local skirmishes take place, devoid of an overall purpose; no one paves the way for others, no one expects that the others will follow. Using Iuri Lotman's metaphor (more apt than the notorious 'rhyzomic' trope of Deleuze and Guattari), we can visualize the difference as one between the concentrated energy of a powerful river – which burrows a crevice in the rocky ground as it surges towards the sea, so that in the future all waters will feed into the same riverbed – and the dispersed energy of a minefield – in which from time to time, here and there, explosions occur, but no one can say with certainty when and where the next mine will explode.

If the turn-of-the-century arts experienced their own restlessness and innovations as an avant-garde action, they did it thanks to the perspective of *modernism* – the intellectual movement fed by disgust and impatience with the slothful, sluggish pace of change which modernity taught people to hope for and promised to accomplish. Modernism was a protest against broken promises and dashed hopes, but also a testimony to the seriousness with which the promises and the hopes were treated. The modernists swallowed – hook, line and sinker, and perhaps with a greater gusto than all the rest of modern men and women – the values, which modern mentality hallowed and modern society swore to serve; they also firmly believed in the vector-like nature of time, convinced that the time-flow has a direction, that whatever comes later is (must be, ought to be) also better, while everything receding into the past is also worse – backward, retrograde, inferior. The modernists did not wage their war against the reality they found in the name of alternative values and a different world-vision, but in the name of acceleration: on their battle standards they wrote Hiç Rhodos, hic salta (You promised, you keep your word). They could declare and wage the war against the found reality of modern life only because they accepted in full its premises: they trusted the progressive nature of history and thus believed that the appearance of the new makes the extant, the bequeathed and the inherited redundant, turning them into relics and depriving them of the right to persist. The modernists wished to spur trotting modernity into a gallop; to add fire to the engine of history.

Stefan Morawski, the great Polish philosopher of art, put together the exhaustive inventory of traits which united all, otherwise starkly distinct sections of the artistic avant-garde: all of them were imbued with pioneering spirit, all gazed at the extant state of the arts with disgust and aversion, all were critical about the role currently allotted to the arts in society, all derided the past and ridiculed the canons it cherished, all keenly theorized about their own ways and means, imputing a deeper historic sense to their artistic accomplishments; all of them followed the pattern of revolutionary movements, preferred to act collectively, created and joined sect-like brotherhoods, hotly discussed common programmes and wrote manifestos; all looked far beyond the realm of the arts proper, viewing the arts and the artists as the advance troops of the army of progress, a collective harbinger of the times yet to come, a preliminary blueprint of tomorrow's universal pattern – and sometimes a ram meant to pulverize the hurdles piled up in history's way.

It follows from the above description that the modernists were *plus moderne que la modernité elle-même*; they acted in the name of modernity, by its inspiration and permission. Just like modernity itself, only perhaps more so, they lived at the front line; just like modernity as a whole, though perhaps more dogmatically still, they believed that the sole use of tradition is that one knows what needs to be broken, and the frontiers are there to be transgressed. Most of them took hints and courage (and the self-assurance allowing them to allot praise or condemnation) from science and technology, those most defiant, adventurous and irreverent stormtroopers of modern tradition-bashing: impressionists from the anti-Newtonian optics, the cubists from the anti-Cartesian relativity theory, surrealists from psychoanalysis, the futurists from combustion engines and assembly lines. Without modernity and all its works, the modernists would be unthinkable. They wanted to serve modernity; it was not their fault that they had to impose themselves with their offer upon a reluctant or indifferent society. They laid the guilt at the door of the many who stuck to the canons already left behind: people with outdated taste (that is, in the modernist language, tasteless people), unable or unwilling to catch up with the insights of the avant-garde. They construed such atrocious and contemptible people into a collective image of the *bourgeois*, labelled them philistines, decried them as vulgar, coarse, uncultured or dilettantish. They refused the so-construed enemy the right to artistic judgement – an enemy in such case can be nothing but outdated, an expression of the past which has forfeited its right to exist, not to mention the right to speak with such authority as may bind the present.

Those seen as immature, not fully developed, retarded, the modernists wished to show the light, to teach, to educate and to convert; the modernists could, after all, remain in the avant-garde position only when treating the others as-not-yet-fulfilled, sunk in darkness, waiting for enlightenment. Occasionally they felt overwhelmed with anger – perplexed and embarrassed (as most teachers happen to be at one point or another) by the evident obtuseness or mental stupor of their assumed wards. As a rule, the pupils (as long as they remain pupils) cannot catch up with the skills of their teachers, while the proselytes (as long as they have not been initiated yet) cannot match the faith of the missionaries – and so there was a constant supply of reasons to be angry. But truly appalled and horrified the modernists felt on such (rare) occasions when the lessons appeared to be too easy and undemanding, since their propositions met with common approval and their works acquired popularity; the very distinction between teachers and pupils, avant-garde and the rest, fell then under the threat of erasure. If those in the process of being educated joyfully applauded the educators instead of resisting their efforts, if they failed to feel shocked and perplexed, this might have been the outcome of insufficient radicalism, loss of vigilance, unforgivable compromise with the taste (or, rather, tastelessness) that should have been fought to the death. Whatever the reason, the avant-gardist identity of the avant-garde would be questionable – together with its entitlement to spiritual leadership, to revile the priggish, to assume the missionary stance.

The paradox of the avant-garde, therefore, is that it took success for the sign of failure, while defeat meant to it a confirmation of being in the right. The avant-garde suffered when public recognition was denied – but it felt tormented even more when dreamt-of acclaim and applause finally arrived. The rightness of its own reasons and the progressiveness of the steps it took, the avant-garde measured by the depth of its own isolation and the power of resistance of all those whom it set out to convert. The more vituperated and spat at it was, the more it was assured that the cause was right. Goaded by the horror of popular approval, the avant-garde sought feverishly ever more difficult (thus possibly ever less digestible) artistic forms. What was to be but a means to an end and a temporary condition was thereby imperceptibly transformed into the ultimate goal and a state of permanence. In the result and in a jarring opposition to the modernist outspoken declarations, it looks (as John Carey recently observed in his *Intellectuals and the Masses*, prompting a unanimous outcry among his learned readers fond of the avant-garde mantle) as if the most advanced detachments of the European intellectual classes undertook a concerted effort to exclude the masses from culture; as if the essential function of modern art was to divide the public into two classes – those who can understand and those who cannot. There were no other stakes, so Carey suggests (unwittingly endorsing unquoted Bourdieu's findings), except keeping the distance and reasserting the superiority of the learned and the creative: the significance of the minority was reckoned to be directly proportionate to its ability to outrage and puzzle the masses.

In this paradox was laid the seed of perdition (it was with good reason that Benjamin wrote of modernity that it was born under the sign of suicide). The ruin was to come, simultaneously, from two sides.

To start with, acceleration did not help: however hard the avant-garde tried, it could not cut itself clean from 'the populace', which it feared and tried to enlighten at the same time. The market quickly sniffed out the huge stratifying potential which the 'incomprehensible arts' carried. It soon became known that whoever wished to inform his peers of his own progress in the world and had adequate means to back up his wish, could do so easily by adorning his residence with the latest inventions of the front-line arts which baffled and frightened ordinary, unrefined mortals; by the same token, one could simultaneously prove one's own good taste and demonstrate one's own distance from the uncultured and tasteless rest. In Peter Bürger's opinion it was its astounding commercial success which delivered the mortal blow to the avant-garde art, now 'incorporated' by the 'artistic market'. Due to its endemic controversiality, that art came to signify social distinction: it was in this capacity that avant-garde art found eager customers among the up-and-coming, *arriviste* middle-class, unsure of their social position and keen to arm themselves with the foolproof symbols of prestige. In its primary, aesthetic capacity, avant-garde art could as before put off its viewers, shock and stupefy; in its other, stratifying, distinction-bestowing capacity, it attracted ever growing numbers of uncritical admirers and, most importantly, purchasers. The applause the avant-garde simultaneously desired and feared did finally arrive (not just applause – a pious adoration and worship) – but, unexpectedly, through the back door: it materialized not so much as the coveted triumph of the modernizing mission, not as a tangible manifestation of successful conversion, but as an unanticipated consequence of the feverish search for portable and purchasable tokens of superior position in a world which uprooted inherited identities and made the construction of identity the task of the uprooted. Avant-garde art was absorbed and assimilated not by those who (under its ennobling influence) came round to the creed it taught, but by such people as wished to bask in the reflected glory of the recondite, the exclusive and the élitist.

On the other hand, it appeared gradually that the escape from the trap of popular consent and acceptance had its limits. Sooner or later, one had to reach the wall: the supply of frontiers for transgression and patterns for breaking was anything but infinite. Following Umberto Eco's suggestion, we may say that the natural limit of the avant-garde adventure was reached in the blank or charred canvas, the erased Rauschenberg drawings, the empty New York gallery at Yves Klein's private viewing, the hole dug up by Walter de Maria in Kassel, Cage's silent piano composition, Robert Barry's 'telepathetic exhibition', empty pages of unwritten poems. The limit of arts lived as a permanent revolution was self-destruction. A moment arrived when there was nowhere to go.

The end came, therefore, both from the outside and the inside of avant-garde art. The world of the mundane refused to be kept at a distance; but the supply of sites for ever new other-worldly shelters was finally exhausted. We may say that the avant-garde arts proved to be *modern in their intention, yet postmodern in their consequences* (their unanticipated, yet inescapable, consequences).

In the present-day postmodern setting, speaking of an avant-garde does not make sense. One artist or another may now assume an attitude remembered from the *Sturm und Drang* times of high modernity – but under the present circumstances this would be more a pose than a posture. Stripped of the past meaning, auguring nothing and carrying no obligations – a sign of panache rather than rebelliousness, and certainly not of spiritual fortitude. The phrase 'postmodern avant-garde' is a contradiction in terms.

The multitude of styles and genres is no longer a projection of the time arrow upon the space of cohabitation. Styles do not divide into progressive and retrograde, forward-looking and outdated. New artistic inventions are not meant to chase out and replace extant ones, but to join the others, finding some elbow room for themselves on the notoriously overcrowded artistic stage. In a setting where synchrony replaces diachrony, co-presence takes the place of the succession and the perpetual present replaces history – competition takes over from the crusades. No more talk of missions, of advocacy, prophesying, of the one and only truth bound to strangle all pseudo-truths. All styles, old and new alike, must prove their right to survival applying the same strategy, since they all submit to the same laws that rule all cultural creation, calculated – in George Steiner's memorable phrase – for maximal impact and instant obsolescence. (In an over-supplied market the most urgent task is to attract the attention of the customer; a close second comes the task of vacating the surface of the market stall for fast-coming new products.) And when competition rules, there is little room or time left for group actions, brotherhoods of ideas, disciplined and disciplining schools – all that 'joining forces and closing ranks' so typical of the time of holy wars. There is little room therefore for collectively negotiated and collectively proclaimed rules and canons. Every work of art starts from square one and thinks little of creating family, forgetful of Baudelaire's injunction that modern inventions ought to be the classics *in spe*.

Such concepts as philistinism, priggishness, vulgarity sound strange and foreign amidst the present-day cacophony of commercial publicity. How to draw the dividing line, if novelty is no more connected to revolution, innovations are no tantamount to progress, and rejection of novelty does not necessarily tie up with obscurantism and reaction? The vision of progress, if universally accepted, allowed seemingly objective answers to the questions like 'What is, and what is not, art?' or 'What is good, and what is bad, art?' – and lent unshakeable authority to the judgements pronounced in its name. Once the vision is rejected or cast in doubt one is doomed (as, for instance, Howard Becker or Marcia Eaton suspect) to rely in one's judgements on hints as blatantly non-objective as the relative prestige of galleries or concert halls and the relative prices of the works they sell. (All too often the two criteria merge into one.) The stratifying power belongs now not so much to the artistic creations, as to the site in which they are viewed or purchased and the price they command. In this respect, though, works of art do not differ from other marketable commodities. Where to look, therefore, for the distinctiveness of arts in the postmodern, post-avant-garde universe?

The legacy of the avant-garde era (and, more generally, of the times of modernist movements) is the image of the arts and the artists as the stormtroopers of advancing history. The artistic avant-garde lived its labours as a revolutionary activity. (The intense sympathy and presumption of spiritual kinship and identity of purpose felt by most avant-garde artists for revolutionary politics of the left and the right alike, the deeper and more enthusiastic the more radical, even totalitarian, a given politics was – is well documented and known. That sympathy, though, appears in retrospect to be a story of unrequited love: political revolutionaries were naturally suspicious of everyone who put principles and canons above the demand of party discipline; moreover, the élitist predispositions of the artists could only jeopardize the politicians' bid for massive support, more akin to the praise of the 'popular taste' which the avant-garde swore to demolish.) Art was hoped to force social reality into a mould which, by itself and unaided, reality was unlikely to assume.

The present-day arts, on the contrary, care next to nothing about the shape of social reality. More precisely, they have elevated themselves into *sui generis* reality, and a self-sufficient reality at that. In this respect the arts share the plight of postmodern culture as a whole – which, as Jean Baudrillard put it, is a culture of *simulacrum*, not *representation*. Art is now one of many alternative realities (and, conversely, so-called social reality is one of many alternative arts), and each reality has its own set of tacit assumptions and openly proclaimed procedures and mechanisms for their self-assertion and authentication. It is increasingly difficult to ask, and even more difficult to decide, which of the many realities is 'more real', which is primary and which is secondary, which is to serve as the reference point and criterion of correctness or adequacy for the rest. Even if questions like these keep being asked by force of habit, it is not clear where to start the search for an answer. (Simulation, as Baudrillard insists, is not faking or false pretence; it is rather akin to psychosomatic disease, where the patient's pains are quite real and the question whether his illness is also real does not make much sense.)

The postmodern arts have reached a degree of independence from the non-artistic reality of which their modernist predecessors could only dream. But there is a price to be paid for this unprecedented freedom: the price is the renunciation of the ambition to blaze the new trails for the world. This is not the question of the arts losing their 'social utility', genuine or putative. Schoenberg had radicalized Gautier's slogan 'art for the art's sake', asserting that nothing useful can be art – but even in this radical form the statement does not fully grasp the situation of the arts in the postmodern setting, in which the very notion of 'useful arts' is devoid of obvious sense, since in the realm of arts it is unclear how the presence or absence of utility could be ascertained; while the issue of usefulness versus harmfulness in respect of non-artistic reality has become highly contentious.

In other words, freedom of the type won by the arts in the postmodern setting is hardly a fulfilment of Gautier's postulate. Independence does not necessarily mean autonomy, while the slogan 'art for the art's sake' demanded precisely autonomy: the right to self-government and self-assertion, not cutting the ties with social life and surrendering the right to influence its course. As Baudrillard suggest, the importance of the work of art is measured today by publicity and notoriety (the bigger the audience, the greater the work of art). It is not the power of the image or carrying power of the voice that decide about the 'greatness' of creation, but the efficiency of reproductive and copying machines – factors outside the artists' control. Andy Warhol made this situation an integral part of his own work – inventing techniques which put paid to the very idea of the 'original' and produced but copies from the beginning. What counts, after all, is the number of copies sold, not what is being copied.

The avant-garde would not recognize in all this the fulfilment of its thoughts; but a sociologist might recognize in it the consequence (unanticipated consequence, to be sure) of its deeds.

8

The Meaning of Art and the
Art of Meaning

Two remarkable analysts and practitioners of contemporary culture, Michel Foucault and Pierre Boulez, met in 1983 to discuss the sense of new music and its public reception.[1] Said Foucault:

> One cannot speak of a single relation of contemporary culture to music in general, but of a tolerance, more or less benevolent, with respect to a plurality of musics. Each is granted the 'right' to existence, and this right is perceived as an equality of worth.

Boulez admitted that indeed, the present-day reticence to take a stand, the unqualified acceptance of pluralism and a certain liberal generosity which characterize our time create a situation in which 'Everything is good, nothing is bad; there aren't any values, but everyone is happy.' And yet, he said, 'This discourse, as liberating as it may wish to be, reinforces, on the contrary, the ghettos, comforts one's clear conscience for being in a ghetto, especially if from time to time one tours the ghettos of others.' Intolerance may kill, but tolerance, even if admittedly less cruel, isolates: one kind of music from another, one artist from another, music and the artist from their audience.

Whatever meaning the new music may convey, it is not easily grasped by those who listen. And Boulez explains why this is the case:

> In classical and romantic music ... there are schemas which one obeys, which one can follow independently of the work itself ... They have the efficacy and security of signals; they recur from one piece to another, always assuming the same appearance and the same functions. Progressively, these reassuring elements have disappeared from 'serious' music ... Musical works have tended to become unique events, which ... are not reducible to any guiding schema admitted, *a priori*, by all.

Boulez goes on to suggest that musical training – which, let us note, is always a training in rule-following and pattern-recognizing – is a handicap, rather than an asset, to understanding; one could speak here of a phenomenon similar to the 'trained incapacity', observed in the practice of big organizations, notorious for the promotion of regular patterns of conduct. Paradoxically (or not that paradoxically after all) it is the newcomers, 'foreigners' to music, amateurs, who find themselves less inhibited and thus more capable of listening attentively . . . Foucault agreed with this explanation:

> [E]ach hearing presents itself as an event . . . There are no cues which permit [the listener] to expect it and recognize it. He listens to it happen. This is a very difficult mode of attention, one which is in contradiction to the familiarities woven by repeated hearing of classical music.

Admittedly, new 'serious' music presents the most extreme and radical case of the 'channel noise' – the difficulty encountered in passing the message; but its case only sharpens and makes more protruding the widely recognized trouble of contemporary art in general. Ludwig Wittgenstein has demonstrated convincingly the impossibility of a 'private language'. It is the social acceptance of necessary connections between certain signs and certain meanings which makes a language. But contemporary art seems to be preoccupied more than anything else with challenging, defying and overturning everything which social acceptance, learning and training have solidified into schemas of 'necessary' connection; it is as if every artist, and every work of art, struggled to construe a new private language, hoping against hope to turn it into a genuine, consensual language, that is into a vehicle of communication – but recoiled in panic into a new wilderness, not yet domesticated by comprehension, at the moment when the dream comes near its fulfilment . . . As François Lyotard put it, if since the beginning of modernity arts sought the ways of representing the 'sublime', that which by its nature defies representation – the modern artists' search for the sublime formed a 'nostalgic aesthetics'; they posited the non-representable as an 'absent content' only. Postmodern artists, on the other hand, struggle to incorporate the non-representable into the presentation itself. But this effort has its consequences:

> A postmodern artist or writer is in a situation of a philosopher: the text he writes, the work he performs are not in principle governed by already established rules, and they cannot be subjected to a determined judgment by applying known categories. It is these rules and these categories which the text or the work seeks. The artist and the writer work therefore without rules, in order to establish the rules of what *will have been done*. Hence the work and the text have the quality of an event; they arrive too late for their authors, or – what amounts to the same – their realization begins always too early. The postmodern needs to be understood through the paradox of the future anterior tense.[2]

The rules by which the work has been constructed can be found, if at all, only *ex post facto*, at the end of the act of creation, but also at the end of reading or examining – since each act of creation is unique and unprecedented, and refers to no antecedents except by citing them, that is, tearing quotations out of their original site and thus ruining, instead of reasserting, their original meaning. The rules are perpetually in the making, being sought and found, each time in a similarly unique form and as a similarly unique event, in each successive encounter with the eyes and ears and the mind of the reader, viewer, listener. None of the form in which such rules happen to be found has been determined in advance by the extant norms or habits, authoritatively sanctioned or learned to be recognized as correct. Neither will such rules, once found or composed *ad hoc*, become binding for future readings. The creation and the reception alike are the processes of perpetual discovery, and a discovery never likely to discover all there is to be discovered, or discover it in a form that precludes the possibility of an entirely different discovery . . . The work of the postmodern artist is a heroic effort to give voice to the ineffable, and a tangible shape to the invisible – but it is also (obliquely, through the refusal to reassert the socially legitimized canons of meanings and their expressions) a demonstration that more than one voice or shape is possible, and thus a standing invitation to join in the unending process of interpretation which is also the process of meaning-making. As Maaretta Jaukkuri aptly put it a few months ago at the Bødo seminar, the meaning of the work of art resides in the space between the artist and the viewer.

One may trace back this new interpretative freedom, which present-day paintings or sculptures dangle before the eyes of their viewers, to the cutting of the umbilical cord tying the visual arts to the 'reality' they were supposed to represent – or, more precisely, tying them to the set of conventional rules and symbols which, when observed, assured the 'representational' status of artistic creation. Granted – modern art from its birth played havoc with inherited rules and symbols, insolently rejecting the authority of all tradition, discrediting the bequeathed tools of representation, relentlessly seeking new codes and new techniques, challenging the conventional/habitualized way of seeing the world – and forging new links between the object and whatever ought to be recognized as its image. What it did not do, however, was to question the value of representation as such; whatever modern artists did was done under the auspices of a representation-better-than-before, and motivated by the urge to come ever closer to 'the truth', only belied or temporarily hidden by the extant conventions. Each successive breakthrough in the era of the permanent revolution triggered a flurry of shrill and strident manifestos and declarations of faith, all proclaimimg the discovery and the imminent rule of new truth and new principles which from now on will guide the truth-seeker. Contemporary art, on the other hand, is no longer concerned with 'representing'; it assumes no more that the truth which needs to be captured by the work of art lies in hiding 'out there' – in the non-artistic and pre-artistic reality – waiting to be found and given artistic expression. Having been thus 'liberated' from the authority of 'reality' as the genuine or putative, but always supreme, judge of truth-value, the artistic image claims (and enjoys!), in the ongoing bustle of meaning-making, the same status as the rest of the human world. Instead of reflecting life, contemporary art adds to its contents. As Jean Baudrillard put it – 'there is no privileged object . . . [T]he work of art creates its own space.' Images do not represent, but *simulate* – and 'simulation refers to the world without reference, from which all reference has disappeared'. Art creates not just the images, but their meanings as well – it 'gives a meaning or a sense of identity to something which is meaningless, which has no identity'.[3]

Thus art and non-artistic reality operate on the same footing, as meaning-creators and meaning-holders, in a world notorious for being blessed/plagued simultaneously by the paucity and excess of meanings. No longer is there a vantage point, towering above the entire territory of life experience, from which the whole of that experience could be sighted, charted, and patterned, so that some meanings may be vouch-safed as real and others unmasked as erroneous or phantom-like. In such a world, all meanings are suggestions, standing invitations to discussion and argument, to interpretation and reinterpretation; no meanings are made definitely, and none is definite once made. One may say that in this world of ours signs float in search of meanings, meanings drift in search of signs, while the marriage-registration offices have been dis-banded and the marrying magistrate's functions deregulated. Under such circumstances, both marriage and divorce rates have reached unheard-of proportions. And the role of the marriage-broker in uniting signs and meanings in their – no longer holy – matrimony needs to be assessed anew.

An acute Polish analyst and interpreter of contemporary, postmodern, art, Anna Jamroziak, has the following apposite suggestion: artistic images, she says,

> ready to absorb senses and meanings, confront the contemporary viewer as phantoms: intriguing and intense, puzzling and seductive by what they are themselves and by bonds in which they may be placed and in which they appear thanks to their creators and interpretatively inclined recipients . . .

The author of postmodern images is an animator or performer, rather than creator . . . The authorship consists in the act of setting the process in motion, while the process thus originated does not aim at some point of final objectivation in a reified form, running instead in a free, unbridled fashion, through many paths – and stays incomplete and open . . .[4]

The meaning of postmodern art, we may say, is to stimulate the process of meaning-making and guard it against the danger of ever grinding to a halt; to alert to the inherent polyphony of meaning and to the intricacy of all intepretation; to act as a sort of intellectual and emotional antifreeze, which prevents solidification of any half-way finding into an icy canon arresting the flow of possibilities. Instead of reasserting reality as a graveyard of untested possibilities, postmodern art brings into the open the perpetual incompleteness of meanings and thus the essential inexhaustibility of the realm of the possible. One may even go a step further, and suggest that the meaning of postmodern art is deconstruction of meaning; more exactly, revealing the secret of meaning, the secret which modern theoretical practice tried hard to hide or belie – that meaning 'exists' solely in the process of interpretation and critique, and dies together with it.

It is this which makes postmodern art into a subversive force – contrary to the frequently voiced (notably by Habermas) charges of conservatism. Such charges hark to the modern, Thanatos-guided conception of progression as, essentially, the introduction of a higher-degree order, as an authoritative selection of possibilities and foreclosure of the others, deselected, as reaching towards a state in which all further change is either frowned upon or illegal. In the light of that conception, postmodern art, which stoutly refuses commitment to any authoritative solution and insists on building noise into the very design of each channel of communication, may be seen as conservative; it is, after all, flouting all hope to close down discord and to secure the rule of consensus where polyphony and the infinity of possibilities once lived and continue to live. But conservatism, one is tempted to say, exists solely in the eye of that conception . . .

Once freedom replaces order and consensus as the measure of life's quality, postmodern art scores very high indeed. It enhances freedom through keeping the imagination awake, and thus keeping the possibilities alive and young. It also enhances freedom by keeping creeds liquid, so they would not petrify into dead and blinding certainties. Drawing from the experience of contemporary art, Piotr Kawiecki, the Polish aesthetic philosopher, includes the challenge to habitual wisdom in the very definition of artistic activity:

Undoubtedly, into the realm of artistic culture enters that fragment, whose creations cannot be sensibly comprehended in terms of the current aesthetic-symbolic awareness, and it is for that fragment that the name of 'art' is reserved. By so deciding, we accept that the whole of art constitutes precisely that fragment of artistic culture whose meaning is for the common aesthetic perception obscure.[5]

Kawiecki develops here Hans Gadamer's observation that it is incriminating for an art object to simply evoke in the viewers the canons of their aesthetic education, or remind them of other artists, instead of confronting them with novel and original 'spiritual ordering energy' which challenges both the canons they learned and the memorized habits of seeing. Of René Magritte, the painter whom she rightly calls 'the precursor' (he anticipated, as she points out, 'the problems that will preoccupy successive generations'), Susan Gablik says that to him,

all the possible acts of mind . . . are indifferent unless they directly evoke mystery. Painting manifests that moment of lucidity, or genius, when the power of the mind declares itself by revealing the mystery of things that appear, until that moment, familiar. This moment of lucidity is something which, according to Magritte, no method can bring about.[6]

Not just the absence of schemas to be reproduced and reasserted, of the paths already laid by other artists which one can safely follow, or the habitualized conventions of expressing meanings and reading them – but, in addition, no accepted and reliable methods of arriving at new meanings and the fashions of expressing them. Postmodern artists are doomed to live, one may say, on credit; the practice which is brought forth by their works does not exist yet as a 'social fact', let alone 'aesthetic value', and there is no way of deciding in advance that it will ever become such. One can trust the future, after all, only if the past is endowed with authority which the present is obliged to obey. This not being the case, the artists are left with one possibility only: that of *experimenting*.

The experiment which is their destiny, however – as Anna Zeidler-Janiszewska, a leading Polish philosopher of art, has shown admirably – shares the fate of meanings, ways of expressions, and methods: it defies and turns upside down the inherited, institutionalized idea of experimenting. Traditionally, experiments were construed under the guidance of a theory which they were expected to test; they served the purpose of confirming or correcting that theory, and were therefore well incorporated and necessary stages of continuous and collective action; no more nor less than steps followed by the many, along the road clearly marked by signposts legible to all of them. What is today meant by experimenting is an altogether different activity. The experimenting artist acts in the dark, drafting maps for a territory not yet certified to exist and not guaranteed to emerge out of the map now drafted. Experimenting means risk-taking, and taking risks in the state of solitude, on one's own responsibility, counting solely on the power of one's own vision as the only chance of the artistic possibility ever getting hold on aesthetic reality. In Zeidler-Janiszewska's own words, it is still the task of postmodern art, as it was the task of modern artists,

> to resist the outer world, to break the consensus and to widen, through experimenting, the possibilities which instrumentalized, linguistic-informational reason together with the 'cultural policy' made to its measure cannot anticipate, [But] the hope of future consensus is replaced by the praise of the final and irreducible differentiation; justice towards the difference can be fulfilled only negatively, and thus is bound to do without the vision of totality; culture emancipated from the prison of metaphysics and its ideological extensions, themselves would-be prisons.[7]

The task remains as formidable as it has been through the modernism-and-avant-garde era, but now it calls for yet more courage and determination on the part of the artist. The acts of lonely dissent need to be undertaken without hope of being rewarded by new collectivity. Postmodern artists are, like their predecessors, an 'avant-garde', but in a sense quite different from how the modernists thought of their role and from how they wanted that role to be seen. To put it in a nutshell, one can say that if the modernist avant-garde was about blazing trails leading to a 'new and improved' consensus, the postmodern avant-gardism consists in not just challenging and sapping the extant and admittedly transitory form of consensus, but undermining the very possibility of any future universal, and thus strangling, agreement.

Michel Foucault distinguished two kinds of critical, and potentially emancipatory strategy: 'One may opt for a critical philosophy that will present itself as an analytical philosophy of truth in general, or one may opt for a critical thought that will take a form of an ontology of ourselves, an ontology of the present.'[8] I wish to propose that postmodern artists, by force of the cultural situation, if not necessarily by their own deliberate choice, find themselves involved in both critical strategies simultaneously. Their work is situated at the point of convergence where the questioning of truth and the questioning of the subjectively lived present meet, inform and reinforce each other.

Let me offer a few examples, all drawn from the wonderful *Artscape* initiative undertaken by Maaretta Jaukkuri and executed by her, her friends, and the artists she commissioned, in Nørland, Norway.

Take first the huge boulders of rock thrown among the rugged, craggy landscape of the Bødo bay by Tony Cragg. Each rock has been drilled in many criss-crossing directions with drills of different diameters; look inside the rock, into any one of the pathways left as the combined effects of drilling, and you will see the most breath-taking landscapes, with mountain chains, valleys, peaks and gorges. Landscape inside, landscape all around . . . Art in landscape, landscape in art? How is a landscape known to be a landscape? Is the work of the human eye that different in its logic from the work of the human hand? The ontology of the truth and the ontology of ourselves are here brought together. Two questions merge into one, none can be tackled without facing the other. The truth of the world and the work of its dweller (or is it its carrier? conjuror?) blend; they also demand to be confronted in their indivisible unity.

Or take the huge, heavy, immovable *Protractor* of Kristjan Gudmundsson, which proudly dominates the lake and the hills of Skjerstad. A protractor, as very child knows, is an instrument to measure the angles between the lines, the surfaces, the ascents and declines of things in the world 'out there'; each act of using the protractor confirms that things have their qualities, that the qualities are inalienable attributes of things, and that the one task left to us, the users of protractors, is to find out what they are. The Skjerstad protractor performs all those tasks, and with the solid, imposing authority of the stone in which it has been cut. But look – there is a narrow duct drilled through the base of the protractor, so tiny that it can accommodate just one human eye. If you look through it, you see that a picture is called into being by your look, preselected and preshaped by your sight and the attention that follows it . . . So where from the qualities of things you look at does it come? True, not much room has been left for your eye's expeditions, what with the stifling and impenetrable heaviness of the stony protractor; and yet a small hole pierced through that heaviness is enough to cast doubt on its sovereignty, ridicule its regality, throw the whole question of authority and authorship back into the melting pot . . . Again, the ontology of truth leads to the ontology of the subject. Of their encounter, critical insight is born.

Or take Gediminas Urbonas's *Four Expositions*, dug into a hillslope near Saltdal. Four containers have been placed a few dozen feet above road level. Cars stop, intrigued drivers climb the hill to see what is inside them. They find objects inside three – a deliberately made *objet d'art*, a ready-made and a found object; the fourth container is empty. The puzzled explorers spend most time contemplating the empty one. Obviously, there is nothing inside it, but that nothing is overflowing with meaning, with a meaning perhaps more profound and eye-opening than the meaning of the other containers: it questions, re-values, re-vises the other meanings. One knows now that the other things, just like the emptiness of the fourth container, owe their meanings to the fact of being an exposition; you know that you would not penetrate their meanings if you forgot about acts of making them into expositions and contemplating them as expositions. The ontology of truth and the ontology of human motive and will wink to each other, embrace each other, and in this embrace none of them feels safe . . .

Let me repeat: postmodern art is a critical and emancipatory force in as far as it compels the artist, now bereaved of binding schemas and foolproof methods, and the viewer/listener, now left without canons of seeing and the comforting uniformity of taste, to engage in the process of understanding/interpreting/meaning-making which inevitably brings together the questions of objective truth and the subjective grounds of reality. By so doing, it liberates the possibilities of life, which are infinite, from the tyranny of consensus, which is – must be, cannot but be – foreclosing and incapacitating. The meaning of postmodern art, I propose, is to open wide the gate to the arts of meaning.

Let me finish these comments by quoting Foucault once more:

> A critique is not a matter of saying that things are not right as they are. It is a matter of pointing out on what kinds of assumptions, what kinds of familiar, unchallenged, unconsidered modes of thought the practices that we accept rest . . .
> Criticism is a matter of flushing out that thought and trying to change it: to show that things are not as self-evident as one believed, to see that what is accepted as self-evident will no longer be accepted as such. Practicing criticism is a matter of making facile gestures difficult.[9]

About forty years before these words of Foucault were written, Magritte noted in his autobiographical sketch, published in April 1940 by the Belgian magazine *L'Invention collective*:

> This contradictory and disorderly world of ours hangs more or less together by dint of very roundabout explanations, both complex and ingenious by turns, which appear to justify it and excuse those who thrive wretchedly on it . . .
> That pictorial experience which puts the real world on trial, gives me belief in the infinity of possibilities as yet unknown to life. I know I am not alone in affirming that their conquest is the sole aim and the sole valid reason for the existence of man.

This is, I guess, why Suzi Gablik wrote about René Magritte, the Precursor. And why it sounds so true and obvious once she has written it.

9

On Truth, Fiction and Uncertainty

As William James put it in 1912,[1] the true is 'only an expedient in our way of thinking'. In Richard Rorty's rendition, the role which James ascribed to that 'expedient' consisted in praising – and through praise, endorsing – the beliefs held. By this view, one that I share, the word 'truth' stands in our usages for a certain attitude we take, but above all wish or expect others to take, to what is said or believed – rather than a relation between what is said and certain non-verbal reality (as Locke first suggested – between ideas and the objects which they well or poorly *represent*). It needs to be pointed out, however, that the particular form of endorsement accomplished by the 'expedient of truth' consists precisely in asserting that there is more to certain beliefs than our approval – this 'more' being, in most cases, the supposed identity between what the beliefs assert and that something they tell us about, or an exemplary cohesion between the belief in question and other beliefs currently undisputed; that there are, in other words, grounds for approval more solid and reliable than the fickle and erratic agreement between the believers – so that the beliefs in question may not just be *approved*, but *approved with trust and confidence*, and embraced firmly enough to *reject* other, alternative or downright contrary views on the subject.

In this commentary on James, Rorty adds other uses of the truth concept: apart from the endorsing use, a cautionary use and a disquotational use are named.[2] And yet, however enriched, Rorty's list of the truth concept's uses is still short of one function which, I suggest, underlies, conditions and endorses all other uses, the 'endorsement use' among them – namely, the *disputational* use.

The idea of truth belongs to the rhetoric of power. It makes no sense unless in the context of opposition – it comes into its own only in the situation of disagreement: when different people hold to different views and when it becomes the matter of dispute *who is in the right and who in the wrong* – and when for certain reasons it is important to some or all adversaries to demonstrate or insinuate that it is *the other side* which is in the wrong. Whenever the veracity of a belief is asserted, it is because the acceptance of that belief is contested or anticipated to be contestable. The dispute about the veracity or falsity of certain beliefs is always simultaneously the contest about the right of some to *speak with the authority* which some others should *obey*; the dispute is about the establishment or reassertion of the relations of superiority and inferiority, of domination and submission, between holders of beliefs.

The *theory* of truth, by this reckoning, is about establishing systematic and thus *constant and secure* superiority of certain kinds of beliefs, on the ground that they have been arrived at thanks to a certain procedure which may be trusted, or is vouched for by the kind of people who may be trusted to follow it. One needs a theory of truth in one of two situations: either the positions of various active, assumed or potential participants of the debate are unequal and their inequality must be justified in order to be defended and preserved, or the domination is to be yet established and the competence of certain agents claiming at present to speak with authority must be for this purpose questioned and discredited.

Theorizing about truth has been developed into a fine art and the life-vocation of thinkers labelled by Nietzsche as *ascetic priests* – engrossed in their search of 'some purificatory procedure which can render them fit for the intercourse with something Wholly Other' and thus pursuing 'a language entirely disengaged from the business of the tribe'.[3] If there is some substance in Whitehead's claim that philosophers keep writing footnotes to Plato, it certainly applies to the truth-theorists, who go on struggling to get out from Plato's dark smoke-filled cave, populated by ordinary mortals, into the wholly other universe of pure and well-lit ideas. No less important than forcing one's way through to that wholly other universe is that the trail blazed is not wide and comfortable enough to accommodate the many – and so remains accessible only to the chosen few; each theory of truth follows Plato's pattern, in being a theory why and how the chosen few *can* emerge from the cave and see things as they truly are, but also, and perhaps above all, a theory of why all the others *cannot* follow suit unguided and why they are inclined to resist the guidance and stay inside the cave rather than exploring what is visible only in the sunlight outside. If the truth-theorists develop a comprehensive recipe for getting out of the cave (as they put it, the way to seek the truth methodologically, the *methodology* of truth-reaching) they hasten to add, as Husserl did in the case of his transcendental reduction and εποχη, that the questions they ask are not the kind of questions that would emerge from the experience of ordinary mortals – and they raise the stakes and the price of the exit tickets sufficiently high to make sure that the ordinary mortals abide by that verdict.

In this they follow Kant's fateful decision to establish reason in the role of a 'tribunal' which 'pronounces against all baseless ambitions and pretensions', to announce 'the duty of philosophy to destroy the illusions which had their origin in misconceptions' – and to proclaim the *opinion* – defined as a view bearing no stamp of reason – as 'perfectly inadmissible'. 'It is only the principles of reason which can give to concordant phenomena the validity of laws.' To deny the positive advantage to the service rendered by reason, Kant pointed out, 'would be as absurd as to maintain that the system of police is productive of no positive benefit, since its main business is to prevent the violence which citizen has to apprehend from citizen . . .'. 'The supreme office of censor which it occupies, assures to [philosophy] the highest authority and importance.'[4] From the verdicts of reason whose laws Kant sought to explore, there would and could be no appeal: 'Metaphysics, as here represented, is the only science which admits of completion . . . so that nothing will be left to future generations except the task of illustrating and applying it *didactically.*'[5]

Admittedly, Kant's vision of philosophical truth, conceived at the threshold of the modern era, was democratic: this had to be a kind of truth which could be appropriated and operated by any being endowed with rational faculties – and most humans indeed are such beings. 'The idea of [the philosopher's] legislative power resides in the mind of every man', and in this respect metaphysics is aimed at the 'completion of the *culture* of human reason'. Once more we hear of 'completion': the inquiry into the laws of reason is a one-off effort; once brought to its end, its fruits will be recognized for their exquisite value, absorbed and digested by all rational beings, and nothing except a police force, a censorship office and their spokesmen or PR officers will be needed then to bring into the fold the occasional stray sheep. In its finally discovered form metaphysics is bound soon to work itself out of a job, abolishing its own necessity: not only will philosophy emerge victorious from the war of attrition waged against 'mere opinions', but it will eventually replace them in the role of universal common sense.

At the other end of the modern era not much is left of Kant's sanguine self-confidence. The youthful ambition of modern philosophy to conquer and seduce non-philosophical minds with its own rationality and to do away with raw and fickle common sense altogether, gave way to sad and sober reflection on the deafness of the common mind or the ordinary consciousness to the voice of universal philosophical reason and their staunch resistance to reform. Philosophy may still be after certainty, but one certainty it conspicuously and inexorably lacks is that of winning the argument. The stakes, if anything, have been reversed. And so Martin Heidegger asks:

Is not the question of essence [of the truth] the most inessential and superfluous that could be asked? . . . No one can evade the evident certainty of these considerations. None can lightly neglect their compelling serious-ness. But what is it that speaks in these considerations? 'Sound' common sense. It harps on the demand for palpable utility and inveighs against knowledge of the essence of beings, which essential knowledge has long been called 'philosophy' . . .

[P]hilosophy can never refute common sense, for the latter is deaf to the language of philosophy. Nor may it even wish to do so, since common sense is blind to what philosophy sets before its essential vision.[6]

This is the case, because the pastime of daily life – the disclosure of beings (*des Seiende*), of each being separately and in its own right – is always, and simultaneously, the concealment of 'being as a whole' (*Sein*). To the Dasein immersed in its daily pursuits, 'being as a whole' stays concealed; it is only the effort of the philosopher, freed from the slavery of quotidianity, that may allow the piercing through of that concealment to reach the self-disclosing *Sein*. 'Man's flight from the mystery toward what is readily available, onward from one current thing to the next, passing the mystery by – this is *erring* (*irren*).' And the 'situated and attuned man', the only man that there is, cannot but err in such a way. 'Man errs. Man does not merely stray into errancy. He is always astray in errancy, because as ex-sistent he in-sits and so already is caught in errancy . . . [E]rrancy belongs to the inner constitution of the Dasein into which historical man is admitted.' And errancy being 'the essential counter-essence to the primordial essence of truth',[7] common sense and philosophy are doomed to speak from two separate and contradictory essences, in languages incomprehensible and impenetrable to each other, hardly ever meeting in conversation and seldom as much as waving to each other in passing.

So what is there for the truth-theorist to do? Once the kind of error previously presented as the target of philosophical barrage under the code-name of common sense is seen as beyond the reach of philosophi-cal argument and beyond the bounds of the legitimate domain of philosophical ascendancy, it is increasingly *other philosophers' theories of truth* that supply the cause to sharpen one's own knives and refine one's own rhetorical armoury. That other front line is not necessarily new; modern truth-theorists hardly ever forgot to fortify that other frontier and deploy part of their troops there – though mostly, as in the case of Kant, out of their concern about the off-putting effects the unseemly quarrels between philosophers may have on the οι πολλοι whom philosophy was meant to convert – 'to prevent the scandal which metaphysical contro-versies are sure, sooner or later, to cause even to the masses'. If the pulling of the masses out of the quagmire of error remained at the top

of the philosophical agenda, Kant never forgot to point out that he
developed his critique of reason also to

> strike a blow at·the root of Materialism, Fatalism, Atheism, Free-thinking,
> Fanaticism and Superstition – as well as of Idealism and Scepticism . . .
> We must not be supposed to lend any countenance to the loquacious
> shallowness which arrogates to itself the name of popularity, nor yet to
> scepticism, which makes short work with the whole science of metaphys-
> ics . . .
> Those who reject . . . the method of the *Critique of Pure Reason can have
> no other aim but to shake off the fetters of science*, to change labour into
> sport, certainty into opinion, and philosophy into philodoxy.[8]

As the hopes and determination to convert the masses to the philosophers' creed receded, the preoccupation with in-house quarrels moved
slowly yet relentlessly into the centre of the philosophers' attention. It
never stayed far from the centre for long – but now it could draw ever
more office time, vacated by the fading interest in the reform of common
sense (now ennobled with pleasant-sounding and opprobrium-free
names like δοχα or φρονεσις, not to mention the highly positively charged
denominations of 'tradition' or 'communal identity'). One seldom hears
nowadays philosophers announcing their intention to correct the errors
of the common man or woman. One hears them, though, proclaiming
loudly each other's errors and the urgency of repairing them. The most
ferocious battles are waged today along the inter-university and inter-
departmental front lines.

There is a subtle yet seminal shift in the stakes of the battles. If the
loathing and anger against other truth-theories continue unabated – and
many a philosopher would repeat Kant's warning about the dire consequences of ignoring his own propositions – the same can no longer be
said about the ferocity with which philosophically unendorsed, self-
formed beliefs used to be condemned and sentenced to capital punishment. One may say that philosophers struggle today – paradoxically, if
one thinks of it – not so much about the one and true (one *because* true)
theory of truth, but about the true, and therefore one and only, theory of
truths (in the plural); and, because the plurality of truths ceased to be
seen as a temporary irritant soon bound to be left behind and because
the possibility that different beliefs may be not only simultaneously
deemed to be true, but be indeed simultaneously *true* – the theory of
truths now in the centre of philosophers' attention seems to forfeit much
of its disputational function regarding the status of non-philosophical
knowledge.

The task of philosophical reason seems to be shifting from legislating
about the correct way of separating truth from untruth to legislating

about the correct way of translating between separate languages, each generating and sustaining its own truths. Thus Hilary Putnam[9] develops his theory from the assumption of the impossibility of obtaining by human means a 'God's-eye view' from which the one and only meaning of phenomena could be contemplated; while Donald Davidson speaks of the truth in terms of 'native beliefs', views the practice of ethnographers as the royal road to the discovery of meanings and sets about answering the question, 'How, given that we "cannot get outside our beliefs and our language so as to find some test other than coherence" we nevertheless can have knowledge and talk about an objective public world which is not of our making?'[10]

Please note that the impossibility of getting 'outside our beliefs and language' is here taken for granted, as a 'given'; that the possibility of 'talking about', rather than 'attaining the truth of' the 'objective public world', is spelled out as the aim of philosophical inquiry and the realm of philosophical arbitration; that the qualifier 'public' appears beside the attribute of 'objectivity' when the 'world' as the object of cognition and talk is spoken about – thus hinting at the contrived, made-up, belief-mediated nature of that world; and that the *ontological* 'objectivity' is neither taken here for the sufficient condition of (let alone tanta-mount to) epistemological objectivity, nor does it any more guarantee its practical availability.

Richard Rorty's work may be read as a powerful statement to the effect that the 'whig vision of history' (that picture of history as the unstoppable march from errancy to truth and from folly and superstition to the rule of reason, the picture which used to be explicitly or implicitly embraced and put into operation by all modern philosophers, regardless of their enthusiasm or despair about it) was painted with the 'ascetic priest's' brushes. Borrowing from Milan Kundera, Rorty speaks of the 'tapestries' woven by the theologians, philosophers and learned men in order to cover up the unreadable mess of the human predicament with a clean and clear likeness of sense. This habit of tapestry-weaving was shared alike by such modern philosophers as sided with the utopia of progress and by their outspoken opponents, who wrote of sinister modern dystopias. It found its expression in Horkheimer and Adorno's weaving Candide and Auschwitz into the same pattern of Enlightenment's legacy, but it surfaced as well in Heidegger's reduction of the history of civiliza-tion to the ascent of technology – propelled by the lust for power, and resulting in the unstoppable growth of desiccated and arid wasteland, where the 'what' is torn apart from the 'that', and where essence and accident, reality and appearance, objective and subjective, rational and irrational, scientific and unscientific have parted their ways forever.

Against this ascetic-priestly urge to clean up and simplify the story of Western civilization Rorty raises another, more complex vision of Western life which would be well within its rights if repeating, after Goethe: 'Zwei Seelen wohnen Ach! in meiner Brust, die eine will sich von der anderen trennen . . .' Yes, there were all those things which the ascetic-priestly philosophers have noticed in the modern adventure, but they were not the only things that could be spotted there. Yes, there was the technology-induced lifelessness of the desert trodden by emaciated and enframed beings, yet there was also the moral protest, the hope of freedom and equality – and the latter were and still remain, so Rorty avers, 'the West's most important legacy'. Yes, Western culture has been justly rebuked for being racist, sexist and imperialist; but it is also 'a culture which is very *worried* about being racist, sexist, and imperialist, as well as about being ethnocentric, parochial, and intellectually intolerant'. It is precisely this other legacy, or part of a complex legacy, which comes today increasingly to the fore, while the part of which the ascetic priests proclaimed themselves guardians and executors is censured and refuted. We are inclined today 'to give up the last traces of the ascetic priest's attempt to see us as actors in a drama already written before we came on the scene'. We seem to be acquiring the ability 'to be comfortable with a variety of different sorts of people', and moving towards a togetherness in which 'nobody dreams of thinking that God, or the Truth, or the Nature of Things, is on their side'.[11]

This is one part of Western legacy, so Rorty tells us, which the ascetic-priestly philosophers did their best to play down or downgrade. Exiled from philosophical discourse, it needed, to survive, another shelter. Taking his cue from Kundera, Rorty suggests that it did find another shelter: in that great Western invention – the *novel*, the *work of fiction*. If this is the case, then one of the great paradoxes of a civilization bent on the extermination of paradoxes is that the *truth* of the West, the truth of modernity, found its home in the self-same work of *fiction* which it fought tooth and nail.

The self-inflicted sight-impairment of Western philosophy derived from the priestly asceticism of the philosophers who sought the scientists' mantle as the most exquisite reward for their self-sacrifice and viewed self-immolation as the surest way to earn it. They represented the reality they described – the reality of their description – by *mimicry*: they declared war on irreverence and spontaneity, they refused domiciliary rights to anything that could not or would not prove the properly certified grounds for its presence, and they plugged their ears tightly to the sound of laughter reverberating in the bawdy, shady or indecorous artistic quarters. They were legal representatives of the half-truth that strove to prove its ownership title to the whole and the only truth there is. The other half, however, survived the trial, and retained its vigour well after the litigation lost its energy and ran out of course. As Kundera put it,

> The art inspired by God's laughter does not by nature serve ideological certitudes, it contradicts them. Like Penelope, it undoes each night the tapestry that the theologians, philosophers and learned men have woven the day before . . .
>   The eighteenth century is not only the century of Rousseau, of Voltaire, of Holbach; it is also (perhaps above all!) the age of Fielding, Sterne, Goethe, Laclos.[12]

It follows from Kundera's description of art's labours, one that Rorty endorses, that it was – and is – the vocation of artistic fiction to serve as the ironic, irreverent counter-culture to the technological-scientific culture of modernity, that culture of ordering passion, neat divisions and taut discipline. In the world that swore to seek and to achieve certainty and leans over backwards to make the word into flesh, the artistically conceived fiction of alternative worlds prevents the designs from being shut up in cages and the contrived structures from ossifying into dead skeletons. In a world dominated by the mortal fear of everything contingent, opaque and inexplicable, artistic fiction is a continuous training session for living with the ambivalent and the mysterious; it rehearses tolerance and equanimity towards the wayward, the contingent, the not-wholly-determined, the not-wholly-understood and the not-wholly-predictable; it promotes reconciliation with contingency of life and the polyphony of truths.

But consider another, quite different, indeed opposite, description of artistic fiction – one offered by another redoubtable literary practitioner, Umberto Eco.[13] We read novels, says Eco, because they offer us the pleasant impression of inhabiting worlds in which the notion of truth is unshakeable; by comparison, the real world appears to be an awfully uncertain and treacherous land . . .

One can enjoy an unclouded comfort of certainty regarding the fact that Scarlett O'Hara married Rhett Butler – a certainty of a magnitude and a degree of imperturbability seldom attainable in the 'real world'. Whether I accept the truth of the novel, or the truth of the real world, I do it – as Willard Van Orman Quine would point out – because in both cases I have already accepted (knowingly or unknowingly – simply by refraining from questioning) a total, comprehensive set of interlocking assumptions. The assumptions I need to accept in order to agree that the marriage between Scarlett and Rhett did take place are few and conveniently simple and uncontested: suspension of disbelief, trusting Margaret Mitchell's sole and undivided authority over the destiny of her characters, will do nicely. The reasons for which I trust the historians who tell me that Napoleon died in 1821 are by comparison much more complex and cumbersome, says Eco. In order to find out what in the real world is true, and what is false, I must take quite a few difficult and never really foolproof decisions concerning the trust I would invest in some communities but deny to others – directly or indirectly, by saying so explicitly or through tacitly endorsing the assumptions which validate their opinions as true and so vouchsafe for the correctness of the belief in question. It is in fiction, says Eco, that we seek the kind of certainty and intellectual security which the real world cannot offer . . . We read novels in order to locate a shape in the shapeless heap of worldly experiences; we play a game, but we play it in order to instil sense in the disorderly multitude of worldly phenomena – we seek shelter from the *Angst*, that deep anxiety which haunts us whenever we wish to say something about the world with certainty.

It follows from Eco's propositions that the scores of the real and the fictional worlds in the game of certainty are inversely related: the deeper the uncertainty which rankles in the real world, the higher the certainty value of fiction, spelled out by Umberto Eco. We may assume that the opposite is also the case: the more the real world sways under the indomitable pressure of genuine or putative certainties, the more poignant and attractive becomes that other aspect of the contrived, fictional reality of the novel, which has been brought in focus by Milan Kundera – the unweaving of the real-world tapestries or their exposure for what they are: just tapestries, woven tissues, something that can be unravelled as easily or perhaps still more easily than if it had been sewn together.

It is tempting to explain the difference of emphasis in Kundera's and Eco's treatments of the same topic not by philosophical schools, but by the generational differences between them. Through Kundera's theory of the novel speaks the experience of the generation which grew up in the shadow of the totalitarian state – that most radical and therefore the most sinister embodiment of the modern dream of pure order and orderly purity. It was that state, intolerant of all difference and all contingency, that saturated the fable of the novel with emancipating and liberating power for the sole reason of its being *contingent* and portraying a *difference*. Eco, on the other hand, speaks for a generation that grew up in the increasingly deregulated, polyphonic world of postmodernity. The novel can hardly add freedom to a world already bewildered by the boundlessness of possibilities in which it itself dangles; but it may, on the contrary, offer a foothold for legs seeking in vain support in the quicksand of changing fashions, of identities that do not survive their own construction and of stories with no past and no consequence.

Contrary to some descriptions of the postmodern scene, it is not just the stubborn company of difference, nor the continuous, perhaps even permanent, cohabitation of various forms of life, that lies at the roots of the postmodern challenge to understanding – to the certainty, as Ludwig Wittgenstein put it, of 'how to go on' – and so to the characteristically postmodern form of anxiety. There is nothing new about living amidst difference, facing difference daily and being forced to accept its permanence. Neither the modern nor pre-modern world were homogeneous, and it is not even clear whether the plurality of forms of life known and experienced by pre-modern and modern men and women was less poignant or quantitatively more limited than the one lived through daily by postmodern humans. But the pre-modern and modern men and women found and practised their own (different from ours) ways of coping with the challenges that plurality posited.

José Ortega y Gasset found in the chronicle of the Spanish town of Briviesca a colourful description of the welcome which the residents prepared for the Doña Blanca of Navarra, travelling through the streets of Briviesca to her wedding with the son of King Juan II. Guild after craftsmen's guild filed in front of princess, each one adorned in the distinctive uniforms of its trade, carrying the banners of their corporations – and behind them marched the Jews carrying their holy scrolls and the Arabs with the Koran. For the inhabitants of fifteenth-century Spain, says Ortega y Gasset, 'All beings had the right and the duty to be what they were – dignified or humble, blessed or accursed. The Jew or the Moor was for fifteenth-century people a reality, endowed with the right to be, with a rank of its own and its own place in the hierarchical plurality of the world.' Not much later, already at the threshold of the next century, the Jews and Moors of Briviesca and other Spanish towns were forced out of the realm ruled by the Spanish king; but that was already, Ortega y Gasset suggests, the accomplishment of 'the first modern generation. Indeed, it is the modern man who thinks that it is possible to exclude certain realities and build a world according to its own preferences in the likeness of a certain preconceived idea.'[14]

Pre-modern men and women were trained to view the difference with equanimity and to accept the preordained plurality of beings as the integral part of God's creation. Looked at from our present perspective, they seem to have been tolerant of difference – but this was the sort of tolerance that expressed itself mostly in wishing and prompting everybody to 'stick to his own kind', in keeping one's distance, reducing the encounter between the kinds to strictly institutionalized and ritualized patterns, and otherwise suppressing all morbid curiosity about other, however starkly different, forms of humanity. But let us note that such an attitude could be upheld only as long as there remained more or less clearly defined kinds one could 'stick to'. With the advent of modern turmoil, the breaking up of traditions and communities, setting the once stiff categories afloat and 'disembedding' the individual identities, the pre-modern solution to the problem of plurality soon proved inadequate to avert or mollify the resulting anxiety born of confusion.

To the pre-modern man or woman, truth and reality, rolled into one, was the product of God's intention, as embodied once for all in the shape of God's Creation. It had been given since the moment of creation and thus called for nothing more than respectful contemplation, at best a diligent study. The givenness, obviousness, the ascribed and immutable nature of every man's or woman's place in the chain of being, all suggested such an understanding of the world – as the fulfilment of a supra-human, divine intention. Not so in the modern world of the 'permanent creation' (Ilya Prigogine's term).[15] With a place in the world turning into the individual's task, into something to be earned, conquered, fortified and defended, it was increasingly difficult to view reality as given, as emerged once and for all from the supra-human intention; what used to be authenticated in advance by the shape of the created world, was now to be subjected to the process of authentication in the course of world-creation. The legitimacy of found differences 'between kinds' – differences no more binding the 'disembedded' modern individuals and so experienced daily as flexible and malleable – was not now automatically assured; and new differences were plotted in ever increasing volume, as the conceived designs of a homogenous order kept to be superimposed upon the messy, heterogenous reality. Destruction of difference was now the condition of order: this was the new, modern variety of destruction – a *creative destruction*, destruction indistinguishable from the positive effort of order-building. In his edict of expulsion, King Ferdinand of Spain pioneered a strategy which was to be applied with greater or lesser zeal and bigger or smaller success throughout modern history and in all parts of the globe affected by the 'process of modernization'.

Whatever the fate of the battles, the modern war against difference and plurality has been, so far at least, by and large lost. Modern history resulted, and the modern practice goes on resulting, in the multiplication of divisions and differences; far from coalescing into a global uniformity, the local and partial orders which modern practice gained the unique expertise in conjuring up add to the overall plurality. As long as the modern way of life continues, the modern practice does not seem to lose its bearings and is unlikely to grind to a halt; the modern method of dealing with the ambivalence brought about by the difference resistant to the designed order will probably continue unabated, though in a deregulated, localized fashion, rather than in the form of a condensed effort to implement grand, total and totalistic blueprints. Yet there is something about the contemporary form of difference and plurality which neither pre-modern nor modern practice confronted; none was therefore given the chance of forging and sharpening the weapons meant to repel the confusion which such aspects of heterogeneity may spawn.

The new, characteristically postmodern and possibly unprecedented aspect of present-day diversity is the weak, slack and underpowered institutionalization of differences, and their resulting elusiveness, pliability and short life-span. If since the time of 'disembeddedment', and throughout the modern era of 'life projects', the 'problem of identity' was the question how to *build* one's identity, how to build it consistently and how to give it a universally recognizable form – today the problem of identity arises mostly from the difficulty of holding to any identity for long, from the virtual impossibility of finding such a form of identity-expression as stands a good chance of lifelong recognition, and the resulting need not to embrace any identity too tightly, in order to be able to abandon it at short notice if need be. It is not so much the co-presence of many kinds that is the source of confusion and anxiety, but their fluidity, the notorious difficulty in pinpointing them and defining – all this harking back to the central and most painful of anxieties: one that is related to the instability of one's own identity and the absence of lasting, trustworthy and reliable reference points which would help to render the identity more stable and secure.

But let us note that the evident 'made-up' nature of characters, their conditionality and conventional status, their in-built contingency, are defining features of the art work in general, of artistic fiction in particular; one may say therefore that under the postmodern condition the 'world out there', the 'real world', acquires in ever greater measure the traits traditionally reserved for the fictional world of art. The world 'out there' appears to the individual as a game, or rather a series of finite, episodic games, with no definite sequence and with consequences not necessarily binding the games that follow; and a game in which the world itself is one of the players rather than the ultimate law-giver or umpire, and a player who, just like the rest of the players, keeps his cards close to his chest and adores the surprise moves. Life is lived by its users (Georges Perec's memorable phrase) as a flow of events neither inevitable nor quite accidental. The outcome depends solely on the strength of the received hand and the skill or cunning displayed in the next move. The world feels like an ongoing interaction between variously skilful and variously clever artists of the game of life.

In such a world, daily experienced as both conventional and contingent, a world populated by the artists of the life-game – the novelist's exposure of the immanent fragility and underdetermination of human fate comes hardly as a revelation and thus loses much of the emancipatory and redeeming power ascribed to it by Kundera. That power was an outcome of the kind of world that is no more experienced by postmodern men and women – the world of hard, harsh and ostensibly unshakable laws leaving to the individual solely the duty of self-adjustment and adaptation. In that world, the art of the novel provided the outlet for pains and anxieties of the kind described by Freud in the book called *Das Unbehagen in der Kultur*: for the discontents typical of a kind of society which offered to individuals some security at the expense of some of their freedom. *Das Unbehagen in der Postmoderne* – the discontents, pains and anxieties typical of the postmodern world – arise from the kind of society which offers ever more individual freedom at the price of ever less security. Postmodern discontents are born of freedom rather than of oppression. It is the other qualities of artistic fiction, those spelled out by Umberto Eco – the ability to simplify the baffling complexity, to select a finite set of acts and characters out of the endless multitude, to cut the infinite chaos of reality down to an intellectually manageable, comprehensible and apparently logical size, to present the discordant flow of happenings as a story with a readable plot – that seem cut to the measure of postmodern discontents: of the pains and sufferings of postmodern men and women, bewildered by the paucity of sense, porousness of borders, inconsistency of sequences, capriciousness of logic and frailty of authorities.

In the modern world, the fiction of the novel laid bare the absurd contingency hidden under the surface of orderly reality; in the postmodern world it strings together cohesive and consistent, 'sensible' chains, out of the shapeless mass of scattered events. The status of fiction and of the 'real world' have, in the postmodern universe, been reversed. The more the 'real world' acquires the attributes relegated by modernity to the domain of art, the more artistic fiction turns into the shelter – or is it, rather, the factory? – of truth. But – let it be emphasized as strongly as possible – the truth admitted from its exile has, apart from its name, little resemblance to the one forced to emigrate. This truth has no endorsing function and little disputational use – and, moreover, it is conscious of its limitations and not at all worried. The truths of art are born in a company of other truths and used from the start to enjoy such company. They do not view the presence of other meanings/interpretations as an offence, a challenge, a threat to their own sense. They rejoice in adding to their multitude.

'In the work of art', says Heidegger, 'the truth of being has set itself to work.'[16] For Heidegger, as we know, the truth of being is being *unconcealed*; '*Seiende*' is the cover-up, the concealment of *Sein*, ever anew accomplished in existence – and it is up to the art, and in art's power only, to tear up the cover and put on display that which has been hidden. In the world of existence, 'a being appears, but it presents itself as other than it is. This concealment is dissembling . . . That a being should be able to deceive as semblance is the condition for our being able to be deceived, not conversely.' 'Beauty is one way in which truth essentially occurs as unconcealedness.' 'Art breaks open an open space, in whose openness everything is other than usual.' Take the work of architectural art, the temple, as an example: 'It is not a portrait whose purpose is to make easier to realize how the god looks; rather, it is a work that lets the god himself be present and thus *is* the god himself. The same holds for the linguistic work.' 'Projective saying is saying which, in preparing the sayable, simultaneously brings the unsayable as such into the world.'

Now, what is that unsayable that the arts give voice to? What is that truth (or, rather, the truths) of Being, that the work of art throws open, unconceals?

As Jean Baudrillard aptly pointed out, to the resident of the postmodern world all beings appear in the modality of *simulacra*. The simulacrum is the work of simulation, but simulation is not to be confused with feigning, with pretending that some attributes are present which in fact are not (as in the case of a healthy man, who, to avoid an unpleasant duty, pretends to be ill). 'Feigning or dissimulating leaves the reality principle intact: the difference is always clear, it is only masked; whereas simulation threatens the difference between "true" and "false", between "real" and "imaginary".' Simulation is rather like a psychosomatic disease; since the patient produces and experiences all the expected symptoms of the illness – 'Is he or she ill or not?'[17]

One may say, using Heideggerian language, that the specifically postmodern form of 'concealment' consists not so much in hiding the truth of Being behind the falsity of beings, but in blurring or washing away altogether the distinction between truth and falsity inside the being themselves, and so making the issues of the 'heart of the matter', of sense and of meaning senseless and meaningless. It is reality itself which now needs the 'suspension of disbelief', once the preserve of art, in order to be grasped and treated and lived as reality. Reality itself is now 'make-believe', although – just like the psychosomatic ailment – it does its best to cover up the traces.

As before, it is the fate of the arts to oppose reality and by this opposition to compensate life for what reality deprived it of; and so, obliquely, to make reality liveable, protecting it against the consequences of its self-inflicted blindness. But the meaning of the opposition has now changed, the battle-lines have been redrawn. It is left now to the work of fiction to unconceal this particularly postmodern variety of conceal-ment, to put on display what socially produced reality tries hard to hide – those mechanisms which take the separation of truth and falsity off the agenda, render the pursuit of sense irrelevant, unproductive and increas-ingly less attractive. In a world shot through with irony, it is the turn of art to become serious, to defend that seriousness which the socially produced world made all but laughable. Once debunking the solemn and unctuous pretences of the modern legislators of truth, the artistic fiction, that great school of imagination, empathy and experiment, may now render priceless service to the solitary, often confused and bewil-dered, postmodern interpreters of meaning and sense. Banished from reality, truths may only hope to find their exilic 'second home' in the house of art. Wiser after the bitter experience of the modern adventures, rejecting the baneful heritage of their 'one and only' ancestor, fully aware of their own contingency and so free of the immodest panache which made their ancestor so suitable to be deployed as the weapon of modern totalitarian instinct, no longer aiming at monopoly as its ideal fulfilment and no more seeking consensus as the measure and ultimate confirma-tion of its validity – the truths born in and through the work of artistic fiction may – just may – fill the gap in human existence left by the kind of reality which does everything possible to render the search for meaning redundant and irrelevant to its own self-perpetuation as well as a goal unworthy of life-efforts.

10

Culture as Consumer Co-operative

As they grow and mature, concepts begin to move on their own and sometimes they reach territories fairly remote from the place of their birth. They wander into the past, which was unaware of them at the time it was still the present. Or make a foray into the future, which – who knows? – may be similarly unaware of them when it arrives, since it will not find them useful. It looks as if concepts were born as plants, firmly rooted in the soil and sucking in its juices – but, as time passed, they cut themselves loose from the ground, grew legs and embarked on the search for more ample or varied food.

In the early, plant-like phase of their life concepts are what the soil and the circumstances of sprouting allowed them to be; they soak with the contents of the soil from which they sprouted. (The experts would have no difficulty determining exactly the site of their origin: they will find in their tissue the minerals typical of the spot, or the lasting traces of the climatic conditions under which the germination took place.) Once the concepts grow up, the direction and the extent of their travel depends on other things altogether; and yet wherever they go, they will carry their birthmarks with them. After all, they could see the light only once and in one place only: at no other place and no other time could they have been born.

What for the plant are the mineral contents, moisture and insulation of the soil, is for the concept *the experience* of the human beings in whose heads is was conceived and in whose conversations it took on a shape recognizable to all. By 'experience' we do not mean just the events which came to pass during the lifetime of the people in question – but also (or, rather, first and foremost) how those people lived through such events, how they stood up to their challenge, what sort of means they chose to cope with them. And this includes the ways and means they had available or knew of at the time, and to which they were naturally inclined to resort in order to grasp their own particular nettle. To put it in a nutshell, even the most *universal* of notions are born and acquire shape in the *particular* experience of people tied to specific place and time.

The notion of *culture*, born and given shape in the third quarter of the eighteenth century (in the seminal years branded by Kosseleck 'the mountain pass' – when the philosophy of history, anthropology and aesthetics, all in unison rearranging the world vision around human ideas and activities, were born as well) in the countries that stood then at the threshold of modernity, was not an exception to that general rule. Bound for a universal career, it was nevertheless conceived out of a particular experience of particular people who happened to live in particular times.

The French *civilisation*, German *Bildung*, English *refinement* (the three discursive currents destined to flow jointly into the riverbed of the supra-national cultural discourse) were all names of *activities* (and *purposeful* activities at that). They informed about what has been done and what should have been done or shall be done: they spoke of a civilizing effort, of education, moral improvement or ennoblement of taste. All three terms conveyed the sense of anxiety and the urge to do something about its causes. All three terms carried the same, overt or hidden, message: if we leave things to their fate and refrain from interfering with what people do when left to themselves, things too horrifying to contemplate will occur; but if we approach things with reason and subject people to the right kind of processing, we have all the chances to build a world of excellence, never known before to humans. (As Diderot, the theorist, summed it up: to teach people means to civilize them; take knowledge away and you will reduce the people to the state of primitive barbarity. And as Saint-Just, the practitioner, put it pithily: people are children forever.) One must do something, right away, without delay – and one must keep doing it all along – not for a single moment may vigilance take a nap. Action, a concerted and goal-conscious action, is the only breakwater protecting people against the tide of chaos. Only through the 'civilizing action' can one tame the beast in man, make people different from what they are in their present inferior state and what they would have become in case their inborn instinctual predispositions were not trimmed or kept at bay – if they were neither instructed nor trained to behave differently than they do.

The ideas of such action, its urgency and the determination to undertake it, all merged in the notion of *culture* (to make salient again the 'actionist' sense of the term, sharp at the time when the term was coined but now largely blunted and glossed over, it would be better to speak today of 'cultivation', 'husbandry' or 'breeding'; the term 'culture' entered modern language through Cicero's comparison of *cultura animi* with *agricultura*). The outer necessity of action and internal determination to act provided jointly the frame in which the world was perceived. The frame bisected the world vision, dividing humans into those who do and those who 'are done', the sculptors and the sculpted, teachers and pupils, the trainers and the trained, the guides and the guided. Such a division constituted 'the people', alternatively, as the savage mob goaded by vile instincts and unable to control itself, being for that reason both helpless and dangerous, or as uncut diamond waiting for the skilful hands of the expert cutter, a base ore from which the teacher is yet to smelt the precious metal it contains. The same division constituted the thinkers, the enlightened, the knowledgeable as teachers, educators and moral mentors – simultaneously the tamers of wild animals and masterful goldsmiths. Finally, it constituted the world as the stage of their encounter: the realm of socialization, education, teaching and learning.

Life as the learning of rules and the doing of homework; the world as a school. As Michel Foucault has shown, however, only by its named function, and not by its organization, structure and assumed values, did the school (in its modern form) differ from the factory, jail, military barracks, poorhouse, corrective institution, workhouse or hospital. All these modern inventions, regardless of their named functions, were also (and perhaps above all) *factories of order*, industrial plants producing situations in which the rule replaces accident and the norm takes place of spontaneity; situations, in which some events are highly probable, while some others are virtually impossible; to put it briefly, they were the factories of *predictable*, and therefore *controllable*, situations. All these modern inventions, moreover, went about the task of order-making in much the same fashion: all of them put the wards within the sight of the warden/supervisor, expected to punish the wrong-doings and reward the right ones; all of them exposed their wards to carefully selected pressures and stimuli while trying hard to neutralize all other influences, unplanned and disruptive; all of them therefore took care of the coherence and cohesion of the conditions, hoping that the unity of circumstances would result in the uniformity of the wards' conduct.

We can therefore broaden further our suggestion: the notion of culture was coined after the pattern of the *factory of order*. As in the case of any other order factory, the ultimate state culture was envisaged as attaining was that of a *system*, in which every element has a function to perform, in which nothing is left to chance, no element is left alone, but dovetails, gears and co-operates with the other; in which a clash between the elements may come solely from an error in design or build, from neglect or deficiency; and which has room solely for such rules of conduct as perform a useful function in supporting the envisaged model of order. The need has here the unquestioned priority: first comes the need, then the prescription; it is possible, therefore, at least in principle, to select the rules (i.e. the cultural norms and patterns) in a way best serving the needs already given and named. It is possible, moreover, to improve on the existing rules, given the improving knowledge of the teachers.

These were the overt contents of the notion of culture at the time it was coined, and the tacit yet unquestionable assumptions which endowed them with sense. Not every item of the above inventory passed the test of time unscathed. Relatively early fell by the board the assumption that from 'savagery' to 'the civilized condition' leads only one gate and a single track. The original *hierarchical* concept of culture (satisfaction of human needs may be improved in one fashion only; human history is the story of that improvement; the term 'culture' must therefore be used in the singular only) has not yet fallen out of use altogether, but it appears now in the company of another, *differential* concept (similar human needs may be satisfied in different fashions, one not necessarily intrinsically better than others; each culture is to some extent a product of the arbitrary choice among many possibilities; one needs therefore to employ the term 'culture' in the plural.) On the other hand, though, what proved to be radically immune to the passage of time were not so much the outspoken assertions, as the silent assumptions which underpinned them. In particular:

- that culture (in the sense of cultivation, acculturation) is an order-making entity or process;
- that, therefore, the norms promoted and installed through culture are (or at least ought to be) coherent and non-contradictory, just like the order itself; if it happens that they are not – this is an abnormal and unhealthy situation needing remedy and rectification;
- that culture being a coherent system of prescriptions and proscriptions, only such norms and cultural artefacts may belong to the system as are indispensable for the self-reproduction of the system; if we come across a norm or an artefact, we are thus entitled to ask what role it plays in the system, what need it satisfies; if we fail to pinpoint a function, we must assume that the norm or the artefact in question is a residue of a past state of the system, now useless and bound to die down – or an alien insert disruptive of the system's works;
- that cultural system has a 'structure', being an impersonal variety of the structure found in all 'factories of order': similarly to the controlling desk or the 'purposes of the organization', there must be a 'central value system' at the top of the cultural system – and everything in the system, all the way down, ought to be seen as the particularization and application of such values.

This is how we are inclined to think of culture to this very day: as of an anti-randomness device, an effort to introduce and maintain an order; as of an ongoing war against randomness and that chaos which randomness brings about. In the eternal struggle between order and chaos, the place of culture is unambiguously in order's camp. When facing the incoherence of norms, the state of behavioural ambivalence, the multitude of cultural products without obvious use 'for the system', we think either of a *conflict* between cultures, or of a cultural *crisis*. In either case we consider the situation abnormal or diseased; we are alarmed and expect a morbid turn of events.

It is ever more difficult, though, to think of culture in this fashion. As long as we cling to the inherited notions, crisis appears to be an everyday condition, abnormality turns into a norm, disease becomes chronic. Thomas Kuhn would say that the cultural discourse bears today all the symptoms of the 'paradigm crisis' – a situation in which the concepts which order our perceptions prompt us to treat the most typical and frequent occurrences as exceptions, making the 'norm' an ever more nebulous notion . . . He would also perhaps say that this is a situation typically pregnant with revolution: first a premonition, then a conviction are likely to take hold, that the error does not lie in our observations or the way we have them recorded, but in our tacit assumptions, which tell us to expect something different from what we actually see. We begin to suspect that the notions which convey such assumptions do not explain what is going on, but on the contrary: they block the vision and make the undertanding more difficult, if not impossible; that such notions are more a liability than a cognitive asset; and that we are not likely to go far if we do not get rid of the ballast they have become. In other words, the time has arrived to dispose of the old paradigm and find a new one, which will restore 'normality' to what appears in the light of the old paradigm abnormal and exceptional, so that what is truly exceptional will once more be marginal, and marginal phenomena will once more become exceptions only . . .

It is not unambiguously clear from where this 'paradigm crisis' has emerged. Did cultural phenomena change so drastically since the times when the concept of culture was coined, that the old notion does not apply to them any more? Or should the blame be rather assigned to the changes in our own way of looking at the world, in the observation tower built of our new concerns and experiences, in the foothold of everyday life from which we begin our exploratory travels? Or perhaps the collapse of the *cognitive* ordering power of the orthodox notions followed in the wake of the fall of their *practical* ordering potency, since the suggestions how to order the *knowledge* of the world bear no authority if they are not backed by the powers to order the *world* itself? It may be guessed that all three causes played some role in the present paradigmatical crisis. But it may be as well that it only seems to us that the three factors are separate from each other, each being endowed with its own logic.

The ordinary, the everyday, the familiar, the 'world within reach', the 'pre-reflexive knowledge' – all that which does not puzzle and does not call for questioning and scrutiny – is simultaneously the starting point and the safe haven of all understanding. 'To understand' means to match the perception of the experienced phenomena to that homely world which is understood without the effort to understand it and without the effort to understand what it means to understand. Hence the cognitive role of the metaphor: it juxtaposes the unclear with the obvious; it suggests thereby an affinity (always elective!) between the two; it points out that in some respects 'there' is not unlike 'here', and thus allows us to deploy language meant for the transparent 'here' (one that makes that 'here' transparent) to narrate the opaque and previously ineffable 'there'. To the orthodox notion of culture, such 'metaphorical boost' was given by the familiar images of a factory, school or other similar (always systemic in their intentions) order-producing plants. Another – perhaps crucial – metaphor was supplied by the modern state with its programme of a homogeneous national culture, one national language, one national history curriculum, a unified calendar of festivities and commemorations. (In orthodox sociological narrative the images of 'society' and 'culture' alike were enclosed overtly or surreptitiously within the framework of the territory subjected to the sovereign power of the state; their 'wholeness' was but a reflection of the integrity of such power.) One can quarrel endlessly about whether at the time when orthodox notions ruled virtually unchallenged all thinking about culture the connected metaphors were properly selected and thus directed the gaze towards truly crucial and decisive things, or whether they always, from the start, diverted eyes away from what was the real nature of cultural phenomena. Much more important, however, than this fruitless dispute is to take note that the traditional metaphors have lost now (or are fast losing) much of their original cognitive capacity; and this because the phenomena to which they refer occupy in contemporary experience an ever shrinking and more marginal place.

It could be argued that the first signals of the imminent rebellion against the orthodox 'order-building' paradigm of culture appeared in the work of Claude Lévi-Strauss. (The real, truly revolutionary significance of that work was erroneously played down through presenting it as a successive – not the first and obviously not the last – version of 'structuralism'.) Three guiding ideas of Lévi-Strauss in particular appear seminal in the present-day search for the new conceptual frame of cultural study.

1. There is no overall 'structure' of culture 'as a whole' (nor of 'society as a whole'). Cultures, like societies, are not 'totalities'. Instead, there are ongoing, perpetual structuration processes in various areas and dimensions of human practice, seldom co-ordinated and subjected to one comprehensive plan. The cultural contribution to nature, or cultural 'superstructure' over nature does not consist in the provision of an artificially produced and reproduced total and normatively regulated way of life, but in the continuous impulse to differentiate, separate, divide, classify: to the conjuring up of new meanings through diacritical practice.

2. The structure which emerges from the above practices (that is, the privilege awarded to certain probabilities over the others; as Pierre Boulez put it, culture consists in transforming the incredible into the inevitable) is not a stationary entity, but a process (Anthony Giddens would later give this process the name of 'structuration'); something akin to the wind, which is nothing but blowing, or to a river, which is nothing but the flow. Culture is nothing but a perpetual activity, and 'structure' is nothing but the constant manipulation of possibilities. The diacritical activity is 'structured' in as far as there is a finite set of the *possible* (realistic) permutations – but which of the possible permutations will occur is in no way 'structurally determined'.

3. One can (and should) narrate cultural practice without referring to 'needs' which culture must supposedly satisfy or pre-established 'meanings' to which it must give an expression. One can (and should) do without assuming the priority of needs over usages and meanings over signs. Needs live and die together with usages, meanings together with signs . . . They come to be together, and together leave the stage. Culture does not serve any purpose; it is not a function of anything; there is nothing it can measure 'objectively' with its success or 'correctness'; there is nothing (except its own inner impulse and dynamics) which can explain its presence.

Between themselves, these three ideas generate a vision of culture starkly different from the one ossified in the orthodox paradigm: a vision of a perpetually restless, unruly and rebellious action, ordering yet itself not ordered, blasphemously disregarding the sacrosanct distinction between the substantive and the marginal, the necessary and the accidental (a mind-boggling attitude, if seen from the order-installing perspective). Admittedly, this is a vision much less attractive and encouraging than the orthodox one: it dashes the hope of ever arriving at a finished and authoritative likeness of any given 'culture', and thus of ever finishing the job undertaken by the student of cultural phenomena. As a matter of fact, this is not a vision of culture at all, but a set of heuristic guidelines for narrating its works. But are such guidelines sufficient to spin a new paradigm of cultural discourse?

I was looking for a metaphor which could ease the way leading to a new paradigm: one that would capture precisely the restlessness, open-endedness, endemic underdetermination and unpredictability of cultural labours. Having considered and rejected several possibilities, I have chosen the model of *consumer co-operative.*

To stave off inevitable voices of protest, I wish to make clear from the start that speaking of consumer co-operative I do not refer to the present-day Co-op, the thoroughly bureaucratized and strictly hierarchical organization much like other business institutions, only (to its own detriment) more so. I go back to the ideal model akin to the one which inspired the spiritual fathers of the Society of Equitable Pioneers when they opened in 1844 their first shop at Toad Lane in Rochdale. It is worth recalling that the shop, meant to be managed by the same people who used it, was invented as a protest (and a remedy against) the logic of overpowering and soulless regimentation, known only too well from the experience of factory life, which was the Pioneers' way of earning their daily bread. That freedom, of which they had been dispossessed in their role of producers, the Pioneers wished to repossess in their role of consumers. To ward off further objections, I admit that the dream of the Pioneers did not quite come true in the distant descendant of the Toad Lane shop, the huge national institution of the Co-op. How to explain this? Perhaps the Pioneers dreamed too early, in a world in which virtually every part of reality pushed and pulled in a direction opposite to the one they dreamed of taking; or perhaps a deadly tendency to ossify is ineradicably present in every free action, and each free stream burrows in time a steady bed . . . If the second explanation fits, the cognitive capacity of our metaphor, if anything, grows in volume . . .

But which traits of the consumer co-operative ideal render it suitable as a metaphor of culture in this form, which in our eyes rises from beneath the debris of the orthodox paradigm?

Let us begin with an observation, that in its premises the consumer co-operative cancels or deprives of sense (just as culture does in practice) the very distinctions which constitute the backbone of the 'order-making' notion of culture. Things which happen inside the ideal consumer co-operative are neither managed, nor random; uncoordinated moves meet each other and become tied up in various parts of the overall setting, only to cut themselves free again from all previously bound knots. Spontaneity here does not exclude, but, on the contrary, demands an organized and purposeful action, yet such action is not meant to tame, but to invigorate spontaneity of initiative. Much like in the Prigoginean plasm, diffuse activities come together and condense from time to time, setting local concentrations or structures, but only for their ways soon to part again and disperse. Actions are not determined unambiguously – either causally, by preceding causes, or teleologically, by assumed goals; what does happen, in fact, is an interplay of both factors, the state of affairs which by itself puts a question mark on the very idea of 'determination'. Under such circumstances it is difficult to decide whether the action was inevitable, or accidental. It is better to speak of the *contingency* of events.

The same observation can be conveyed differently: the 'co-operative' social territory, much like the realm of culture, is neither monocentrically managed, nor the site of anarchy. It is something different from both: a territory of *self-government*. Let me warn the reader right away that this concept has also lost much of its original sense as a result of wear and tear during the long history of its overuse and abuse. We feel entitled today to speak of 'self-government' whenever the legislators and the givers of command are elected by their inferiors rather than appointed by their superiors – regardless of the scope of power concentrated in their hands or the degree of monocentricity of disposition. Let me declare therefore that the term 'self-government' is used here in another, stronger sense. It includes the demand of polycentric power, but also something yet more crucial: the requirement that the sources of disposition must be not only plural and non-hierarchical, but in addition mobile. Their quantity and location must be changeable. In a true self-government power must behave according to Prigogine's pattern: it does not pour, to solidify into established offices or offices-to-be-established, but travels along routes impossible to predict in advance, on the crest of authority – that is of a kind of influence which to implement itself as influence must ever be negotiated anew and ever upheld and accepted anew. It is precisely this emancipation of authority from the network of institutionalized offices and the dispersal of the chances to exert influence which lies at the heart of true self-government. In a self-governed entity there is no way to decide in advance, in which location authority will be born and with which power and in what way it will shape the course of events.

It follows from what has been said thus far that in a consumer co-operative, just as in culture, it is not easy to set apart in its emerging patterns of interaction the 'author' from the 'actor'. Each member is expected to author as much as to act. Authorship and actorship are two aspects of action (aspects present, though with differing intensity, in *every* human action) – not qualities of separate human categories. Actions seldom, if ever, reach that radical and pure repetitiveness which modern technology has achieved in some of its mass-produced artefacts. No human act is a clean and exact imitation, carbon copy, precise reproduction of a pattern or a role scripted in advance. (In Derrida's terms, each act is an *iteration*, not a *reiteration*.) In every act patterns are reproduced anew, in forms never fully identical; every act is to some extent an original *permutation*, a unique version of the pattern. Patterns do not exist in any other way but in the process of continuous and inescapable transformation. With the passage of time transformations attain various degrees of visibility, but changes are scattered – and the moment they acquire salience, as well as the novelty which becomes salient, they are unpredictable, since they emerge from a multitude of tiny, imperceptible and scatttered departures. In the practice of culture, unlike in social theory, there is no separation between 'statics' and 'dynamics', 'continuity' and 'change'.

All traits listed above mark any genuine co-operative. It is not clear so far why the *consumer* co-operative, rather than other forms of co-operation, should fit best the role of the metaphor of culture. One feature of the co-operative invented by the Rochdale Pioneers in particular speaks, however, in favour of this choice: the decision that the share of each member in the common endeavour is measured by the size of his/her consumption, not his/her productive contribution. The more the member consumes, the greater is his or her share in the common wealth of the co-operative. Distribution and appropriation, not production, are therefore the axis of co-operative activity; the efforts to increase consumption and gain more (and keener) consumers is the main source of its dynamics (let us recall that according to Danto and Becker the 'art worlds' that rule the life of arts consist primarily of the consumers of art and those who prompt and serve their consumption). The real productive line of consumer co-operatives is, in principle, the *production of consumers* (ever more numerous, ever more demanding, sophisticated and discerning).

This is not a minor matter. The orthodox models of culture were all creator-centred. Even when not constructed directly around the category of culture creators, they were organized around the spiritual correlate of that category – 'central values', 'philosophical formulae' or 'ethos', whose framing and defence was deemed to be the task and the achievement of a particular class of 'cultural producers'. Even in Clifford Geertz's otherwise original strategy of 'thick description' one can discern a tribute paid to this tradition; demanding the passage from the observed conduct to ever 'deeper layers of culture', Geertz implies that the truth or essence of

culture lies in its 'fundamental assumptions', which give sense to everything else and of which everything else is an expression and/or application. The metaphor of the consumer co-operative suggests, on the other
hand, a decisive shift in emphasis: it is precisely in the acts of consumption, in everyday authorship/actorship of 'ordinary consumers' (they are,
after all, 'ordinary consumers' only in as far as looked upon from the
offices of thinkers, artists' studios or the controlling towers of cultural
managers) that everything cultural acquires its sense. It is here that the
empty shells of signs fill with meaning; here the signs (already made
meaningful) gain or lose value, which reverberates in the vacillations of
the demand. The assumption that the creator and the creator alone is the
author and the judge of meaning and value prompted students of culture
to represent the transformation undergone by meanings and values in
the course of cross-cultural travels of the signs as cases of 'sense
distortion'; but each use of a cultural token contains a measure of
authorship, each is therefore a 'distortion' in exactly the same sense.

The metaphor of the consumer co-operative is quite neutrally comple-
mented by the metaphor of the market. (Only in the market environment
can the model of a consumer co-operative be conceived.) The market in
its turn can be best visualized not as a system, but as a playing field – the
site of the demand-and-offer game. Ostensibly, the selling of commodities is the stake of the game – but in fact something more takes place
here: it is only in the course of the game that tokens are transformed into
commodities. The offer supplies entities meant to become commodities
– but it is the demand which makes them such. Moreover, the process
of 'commodification' is simultaneously the birth act of the consumer:
potential commodities and potential customers realize themselves together. Of culture, as of the market, it is useful to think as a playing field,
a site of the offer-and-demand game. The site is travelled by signs-in-
search-of-meanings and sign-searching-meanings. If for its 'normal functioning' the market requires a certain excess of offer over the existing
demand and if only in the moment of purchase the commodity potential
of market goods is fulfilled – so in culture one can observe a continuous
excess of signs, which only in the activity of their use/consumption stand
a chance of fulfilling their signifying potential, i.e. turn into *cultural
symbols*. Meanings are selected for signs, rather than the other way
round. In this circumstance the essential *non-instrumentality*, the
unmotivated character of cultural phenomena shows itself. Such cultural
phenomena do not serve anything, certainly not at the moment of their
birth; if they come eventually to serve something in social life, this
contrived relationship cannot explain their origins.

As it happened so often before, artists intuited this complex dialectic of signs and meanings well before it was spotted and acknowledged by culture theorists. Before it was described in the scientific prose, it had been dramatized in the theatre of the artistic avant-garde. It was, though, manifested not as a drama, but as tragedy – in the classic, Eurypidean, Racinian or Ibsenian meaning of the word: as the clash of incompatible desires, as salvation and perdition tightly embracing each other, of purity drawing its flavour from pollutions, of life finding its fulfilment only in death, of an epos devoid of the hope of catharsis, of returning to the safe haven of normative order and orderly norms . . . Nothing frightened the avant-garde more than the prospect of the fulfilment of its legislative dream, the sensed proximity of its legislative success – and nothing caused a greater panic than the sound of public applause and the spectre of unanimity. The avant-garde brutally laid bare the inborn emptiness of signs, defining its own freedom as the right to fill them with meaning – but it also (perhaps inadvertently) revealed that freedom consists in the *rights*, not in their fulfilment. Freedom is about fulfilment, but freedom may last only as long as it remains unfulfilled. Packed to the brim with meanings, heavy and inert signs will not roam and hover freely any more. Freedom, the apparent infinity of creative possibilities, accompanies solely the excess of signs, their redundancy, lack of function and purpose – that is a notoriously unpleasant situation, endurable only thanks to the hope that it will be overcome, of finding the presently denied ends and uses. But creative freedom will not survive the fulfilment of that hope . . .

And yet what has been presented as high-brow tragedy at the brightly lit stage of avant-garde art may be after all but the story of the everyday life of culture, of the common and the routine . . . The avant-garde managed to conjure up a loud lament and heroic gesture out of the calm and silent practice of human quotidianity. The chasm between avant-garde adventure and the experience of common culture may be much narrower than the avant-garde spokesmen and script-writers wished their viewers and listeners to believe. The avant-garde construed the common, the ordinary, 'the vulgar' as an opposite of itself. It presented the kind of culture it militated against (one it called 'popular' when in benevolent mood, 'mass' when desperate and in a fury) as an immobile and unmovable, rock-like entity, dug up against everything new and unusual, petrified in its ways and hostile to everything that moved and changed. This image was, though, a fiction at all times. When looked at closely and without blinkers, the day-by-day working of culture proves to be amazingly similar to that of the avant-garde, the lack of histrionics being the sole significant difference. Joanna Tokarska-Bakir, a leading Polish anthropologist, found in the countryside near Przemyśl, a small Polish town, practices not at all unlike the most advanced experiments of an Andy Warhol: cribs built of empty beer cans, for instance. All culture, including the kind least sophisticated by avant-garde standards, is daily engaged in what Lévi-Strauss gave the memorable name of *bricolage*; it construes ever new signs out of anything that happens to be handy, and it pours ever new meanings into everything that happens to be within reach, waiting to become a sign . . .

Jean-François Lyotard wrote that human beings reach their fullest and truest humanity in their childhood (children live in a world full of possibilities, not yet closed, trivialized or discredited, alluring thanks to their mystery and apparent infinity) – but human beings have taken the shedding of childish characteristics for the sign of maturation and as a result use all their efforts to get rid of their most human essences . . . I suggest this idea of Lyotard's should not be played down as another version of the Manichean image of the *homo duplex*: of an entity torn apart by two incompatible essences, two 'natures' or separate origins, engaged in the endless war of attrition. (The most famous, Durkheimian, version of *homo duplex* represented human beings as the battlefield between the legacy of biological evolution and civilizing influences, between nature and culture, between the overpowering might of instincts and emancipating impact of the socially enforced norms of cohabitation.) Lyotard's human being is not a cluster of heterogeneous and contradictory natures, infuriated by their unwanted togetherness. The opposite is at stake here: that contradiction which saturates human life comes whole from the coherent logic of specifically human existence and does not need any other explanations. Both freedom and dependency, both the joy of creation and the bitterness of submission, are born of the same human, all-too-human condition of self-constitution, self-construction and self-assertion, which the idea of culture tries in various ways to capture. Both come from the same stem; moreover, they are not this stem's separate branches, but grow one into the other – one being a continuation, an outgrowth of the other: freedom fulfils itself in incurring dependencies, serfdom in the act of emancipation . . .

The tragedy of signs that live by the search of meaning and begin to expire the moment they found it, despite having been performed in the exclusive theatre of avant-garde art, may be read out in broader terms. One can interpret that tragedy as a story about the fate of culture in general, about its endless self-fulfilment in the act of self-annihilation, about the success which looks uncannily like a defeat, about freedom which may implement itself solely in self-denial. From this fate there is no escape. Culture is neither a cage nor the key which opens it. Or, rather, it is both the cage and the key at the same time.

The image of the consumer co-operative may also help to grasp this *aporia* of culture. The *choice* is the attribute of the consumer, and the co-operative nature of consumer community means *freedom* of choice. The choice is, however, an epitome of everything we said above about the fate of culture; choice is a test-tube of individual life in which one can observe the processes taking place in the grand universe of culture. Freedom of choice rests on the multiplicity of possibilities; yet it would be an empty freedom which denied the right to put one possibility above the others – to reduce the multiplicity of chances, to close and reject the unwanted possibilities – in other words, to trim or to cancel choice altogether. As in the case of signs full of chances as long as they remain free of meanings, the essence of free choice is the effort to abolish the choice.

In this, I suggest, the secret of the perpetual non-satisfaction of the desire for wider consumer choice (and, more generally, of the eternal non-satisfaction of the desire for freedom) can be found. The impetus of consumption, just like the impulse of freedom, renders its own gratification impossible. We always need more freedom than we have – even if the freedom we feel we need is freedom to limit and confine the present freedom. Freedom is always a postulate and expresses itself in a constant reproduction and resharpening of its postulative edge. It is in this openness towards the future, in the running beyond every state of affairs found ready-made or freshly established, in this intertwining of the dream and the horror of fulfilment, that the deepest roots of the obstreperous and refractory, self-propelling dynamism of culture lie.

11

On the Postmodern Redeployment of Sex: Foucault's *History of Sexuality* Revisited

The 'educational revolution' which accompanied the birth of modern society took place in Western Europe between the sixteenth and the eighteenth centuries, although it needed one more century for its fruits fully to mature. The revolution consisted in three seminal departures: first, in setting apart a certain portion of the individual life-process as the stage of 'immaturity', that is a time fraught with particular dangers but also characterized by special needs and thus requiring an environment, regime, and procedure all of its own; second, in the spatial separation of those needing such peculiar treatment and their submission to the care of purposely trained experts; and third, in bestowing upon the family particular supervisory responsibilities in the process of 'maturation'.

As observed by Philippe Ariès,[1] not just Breughel's popular canvases but virtually all iconographic testimonies point out that until roughly the sixteenth century children were treated in Europe as not much else than 'adults of a lesser size'. They differed from the rest of people merely by having weaker muscles and wits. Children were present without restrictions at all adult activities. There was no notion of children's quarters or separate parental bedrooms; neither were there specifically children's or specifically adult games; adult life held no secrets for children. The peculiar blindness towards generational differences expressed itself symbolically as well: there were no culturally acknowledged sartorial signs demarcating a special 'childhood status' – as a rule, children wore clothes outgrown or abandoned by older siblings or relatives, and even if new dresses were ordered for them, they followed the adult fashions of the time.

All this began to change with the dawn of the seventeenth century; first at the top, and then gradually – through osmosis, a trickle-down effect, emulation or status competition – also in ever lower social strata. Sections of family domiciles were set apart and reserved for adult activities and declared 'no-go areas' for children below a certain age; a separate regime and special activities were devised for children; and, to mark it symbolically, children's dresses were designed to stress their inferior, or 'incomplete', status – imitating at first the clothes worn by the lower classes or, in the case of boys, women's dresses.

According to Ariès and other students of popular habits[2] the change in children's treatment went together with the 'discovery' of the child as a creature in its own right and of a somewhat different kind, endowed with peculiar attributes. This discovery was closely connected with the new – modern – perception of social reality, which presented the life career of human individuals as the process of 'maturation', something that would not happen on its own, unassisted and unsupervised, and could not be left to the wisdom of nature. To assist the process and assure its smooth flow one needed a special, child-oriented environment, insulated against accidental leaks from the world of the grown-ups. The longer the child's enclosure in that special environment lasted, the better: together with the positive idea of maturation a negative idea of the 'precocious child' appeared, carrying a decisively pathological flavour. The child was seen as a brittle being, requiring close and constant surveillance and inter-ference: an innocent being, but one that, for the very reason of its innocence, lived under a constant threat of being 'spoiled', incapable of staving off and fighting the dangers on its own. What for adults was a challenge to fight or cope with, for the fragile child was an allurement it could not resist or a trap it could not but fall into. The child needed adult guidance and adult control: a thoughtful, carefully planned supervision, calculated to develop the child's reason as a sort of garrison left by the adult world inside the child's personality. The needs of guidance and control converged onto the idea of a specially designed environment in which the growing-up process ought to take place. Ideally, each stage in the child's development ought to have its own, made-to-measure environment.

Joseph F. Kett[3] found out that except for aristocracy and the upper reaches of the up-and-coming middle classes, the immediate surround-ings of children of all social strata at the beginning of the nineteenth century were still accidental and devoid of structure, instead of being planned and regulated. This state of affairs came to be perceived, however, as one of impermissible laxity, potentially dangerous and calling for urgent reforms. Putting previously 'unsupervised' children (that is, children of the lower classes) under the watchful eye of factory foremen was widely seen under the circumstances as a salutary educa-tional departure; the sole remaining task was to devise the means to control the children's behaviour during the hours in which they were out of the foreman's sight. Hence the quickly gathering force of the move-ment for parish Sunday schools, introduced throughout the country ostensibly in order to provide otherwise lacking instruction, but inspired in the first place by the wish to keep children away from mischief during their 'free', that is unsupervised, time.

There was one category of adults which occupied a position potentially facilitating the continuous, ubiquitous, and pernickety control of every aspect of children's life – the parents. Parental responsibility for child development is today on everybody's lips, and their key role in the child's 'maturation' seems to be a fact of nature. But at the beginning of the nineteenth century it was far from obvious; not a reality, but a dreamed-of solution to the reality's problems, a task for legislators and for the guardians and preachers of morality. After all, in not as yet very distant times, when the corporation – the parish, manor, estate or guild – took care of social integration and order while the ubiquitous neighbourly surveillance was the main (and sufficient) means of social control, the family was not particularly trusted; the children of the nobility were initiated in the arcane skills of noble life by serving in other noblemen's courts, while the sons of artisans spent their apprenticeship years in the households of other masters, often far away from their parents' domicile. From the eighteenth century, hired teachers, academies for young noblemen and boarding schools for the children of the well-off began to replace other people's courts, workshops and offices, but that otherwise dramatic change did not yet cast the family into the centre of the educational effort. And there were other, parallel, departures which pressed in an exactly opposite direction: the separation of the household from business kept fathers away from home for a greater part of the day and further impoverished the face-to-face contacts of children with their fathers. As for the lower classes, poor or destitute, one could hardly speak of family life at all. Both father and mother spent most of their time away from the family home (if there was a family home), earning their living; the same was expected of the children themselves, starting from an age later to be considered tender and in no way fit for the raw conditions of hired labour.

The closure of the family in the family home, fencing the domicile off against neighbourly surveillance, weaving a dense net of intense and emotionally saturated parental and sibling mutual attachments and the elevation of the family to the controlling position in the process of child education was not the outcome of a natural and spontaneous process. The deployment of families in the role of the 'capillary channels' of the societal system of control-through-surveillance, described in detail by Michel Foucault, needed a thorough legislative effort, co-ordinated social action, and intense propaganda of new patterns of intimate cohabitation. The reorganization of social space and repatterning of social relations mobilized many previously uncoordinated factors, too numerous to be

listed here. I shall concentrate therefore on just one of the many factors
of the overall reorganization (though undoubtedly one of the most
effective): on the redefinition of sex and sexual practices. In his *Introduction to the History of Sexuality* Michel Foucault argued convincingly
that in all its manifestations, whether those known since time immemorial or such as have been discovered or named for the first time, sex
served the articulation of new – modern – mechanisms of power and
social control.

The medical and educational discourses of the nineteenth century also
construed, among other notions, the phenomenon of infantile sexuality,
later to be turned by Freud, *ex post facto*, into the cornerstone of
psychoanalysis. The central role in this articulation was played by the
panic contrived around the child's proclivity to masturbate – perceived
simultaneously as a natural inclination and a disease, a vice impossible
to uproot and a danger of an incalculable damaging potential. It was the
task of parents and teachers to defend children against this danger – but
in order to make the protection effective it was necessary to open
children's eyes to the problem, spy its presence in every change of
demeanour, every gesture and facial expression, submit the whole order
of children's lives to the need of making the morbid practice impossible,
to interpret all children's rights and duties in reference to their fatal
inclination. Around the never ending struggle against the threat of
masturbation a whole system was constructed of parental, medical and
pedagogical invigilation and surveillance. In Foucault's words, 'control of
infantile sexuality hoped to reach it through a simultaneous propagation
of its own power and of the object on which it was brought to bear.' The
indomitable and merciless parental control needed to be justified in
terms of the universality and resilience of the infantile vice.

> Wherever there was the chance [that the temptation] may appear, devices of
> surveillance were installed; traps were laid for compelling admissions;
> inexhaustible and corrective discourses were imposed; parents and teachers
> were alerted, and left with the suspicion that all children are guilty, and with
> fear of being themselves at fault if their suspicions were not sufficiently
> strong; they were kept in readiness in the face of this recurrent danger; their
> conduct was prescribed and their pedagogy recodified; an entire medico-
> sexual regime took hold of the family milieu. The child 'vice' was not so
> much an enemy as a support . . .

Let us note that the kind of supervisory power brought into being and
continually reinvigorated by the panic surrounding the phenomenon of
infantile masturbation was resonant with the general tendency of the
typically modern, panoptical power. It epitomized all the crucial traits of
the latter to a degree that permits its treatment as a clinically pure

specimen through which the characteristics of a wider institutional pattern can be best examined.

> More than the old taboos, this form of power demanded constant, attentive, and curious presences for its exercise; it presupposed proximities; it proceeded through examination and insistent observation; it required an exchange of discourses, through questions that extorted admissions, and confidences that went beyond the questions that were asked. It implied a physical proximity and an interplay of intense sensations . . . The power which thus took charge of sexuality set about contacting bodies, caressing them with its eyes, intensifying areas, electrifying surfaces, dramatizing troubled moments. It wrapped the sexual body in its embrace.

Sex was more suitable for such a purpose than any other aspect of human body and soul; natural yet bristling with unnatural temptations, inescapable yet full of dangers, and above all omnipresent and shared by all human beings, sex was as if made to measure for the total and all-penetrating power, bent on the administration of the human body and spirit – a healthy spirit in a healthy body . . . It offered all that such a power might have needed to establish itself and to reproduce simultaneously its mechanism and its object. Foucault spoke of the 'utilization' of sex as a support of the power hierarchy; sometimes he resorted to a military metaphor, speaking of the 'deployment' of various notions construed in the course of the medical-pedagogical discourse in the successive stages of the articulation of modern, panoptical powers.[4]

Sex was deployed in the construction of numerous segments of modern social structure. Its role, though, was particularly great in the building of modern families, those furthest-reaching, all-penetrating capillary extensions of the overall panoptical system of power. Family cells were admittedly tiny and not particularly resourceful, yet decisive for the global success of the whole enterprise, being the only institutions which conducted the combined pressure of the panoptical system down to every single member of the society. (Notably such individuals as escaped the direct disciplining drill of the two most powerful among the panoptical institutions – the factory and the army.)

First and foremost, indeed, the family was the sole training/drilling ground for women and children; that its role towards the male 'head of the family', the bread-provider, the master of the house, was but secondary, confirmed the way in which male sexuality had been articulated. If the natural predisposition of women to hysteria and children to masturbation called for their enclosure in the closely watched space of the family house, where they would always be available for inspection, and justified the continuous demand for confession, vigilance and medical care, the notion of the man's natural proclivity for polygamy and sexual intercourse with more than one woman postulated, on the contrary, a space wider than the family home as well as the right to secrecy and a private space not controlled by other members of the family. The way male sexuality was articulated underlined the fact that the real place of man was in the world extending beyond the walls of the family home. Inside these walls the role of the male master was akin to that of the foreman in the factory or the sergeant in the army.

According to the suggestion contained in Edward Shorter's *Making of the Modern Family*, at some time in the middle of the current century the Western world entered the 'second sexual revolution'. This second revolution consists, roughly speaking, in the dismantling of everything which the first revolution, sketched out above, put together. We witness today a gradual, yet seemingly relentless disintegration (or at least considerable weakening) of the once sacrosant and imperturbable 'family nest'; the cultural correlate of this process is the peeling off of the romantic wrapping from erotic love and laying bare its sexual substance. Let us observe, though, that contrary to the popular beliefs instilled by the way in which this change is presented and discussed, this undoubtedly profound transformation is in no way tantamount to 'sexual emancipation' – to the liberation of sexual activity from the attached social functions which constrained, with often harmful results, the libidinal impulse. It augurs rather a successive 'redeployment' of sex in the service of a new pattern of social integration and reproduction. As before, sex 'has a function'; as before, it is 'instrumental'; only the function has changed, as well as the nature of the process in which the redeployed sex plays its instrumental role.

As in the era of the first sexual revolution, the present transformations are not a historical adventure that happen to sex alone, but part and parcel of a much wider and thorough social change. If two hundred years ago profound changes in sexual patterns went along with the construction of the panoptic system of social integration and control, today equally profound changes accompany the dissembling of that system: a process of *deregulation* and *privatization* of control, of the organization of space and identity problems. The second sexual revolution can be also seen as intimately related to the passage from the social production of the 'producer/soldier' to the cultivation of the 'sensation-gatherer' type (described in the chapter 'A Catalogue of Postmodern Fears' in my *Life in Fragments*).

If in the course of the first sexual revolution sex turned into a major building material of lasting social structures and the capillary extensions of the global system of order-building, today sex serves first and foremost the process of the ongoing atomization; if the first revolution related sexuality to the assumption and preservation of obligations, the second transferred it into the realm of experience collection; if the first revolution cast sexual activity as the measure of conformity with socially promoted norms, the second redeployed it as the criterion of individual adequacy and bodily fitness – the two major self-monitoring devices in the life of the gatherer and collector of sensations.

One side of the present-day sea change is the extrication of sex from the dense tissue of acquired rights and assumed duties. Nothing grasps this aspect better than the concepts of 'plastic sexuality', 'pure relationship' and 'confluent love', all coined by Anthony Giddens.[5] Nothing follows from the sexual encounter, apart from sex itself and the sensations which accompany the encounter; sex, one may say, left the family home for the street, where only accidental passers-by meet who – while meeting – know that sooner or later (sooner rather than later) their ways are bound to part again. As Henk Kleijer and Ger Tillekens sum up the new situation, 'sexual practices not bound by duty, but by pleasure are exported to the domain between the house and labour place.'[6] One is tempted to hypothesize that we witness today a divorce between sex and the family, similar to the divorce between the family and business, pinpointed by Max Weber as one of the main constitutive processes of early modernization. As the Beatles sang prophetically in 1965, 'I don't wanna say that I've been unhappy with you/But as from today, well I've seen somebody that's new/ I ain't no fool and I don't take I don't want/ for I've got another girl.'

Of this 'one side' of the present change one hears most; this is the aspect of the current sexual revolution most widely discussed in the popular press and scholarly studies alike and often represented as the essence of the present transformation of sexual mores. More often than not it is also hailed as the indispensable stage in the process of individual emancipation. And yet this does not seem to be the only aspect of the ongoing redeployment of sex; neither does it seem to be its most seminal aspect. Emphasizing this aspect and this alone, at the expense of other aspects, seems to be rather a manifestation of a 'false consciousness' of sorts; the emphasis helps to turn the eyes away from the 'unanticipated', or rather latent (since absent from the actors' calculations) consequences and side-effects of the new sexuality.

As it happens, the other side of the matter is that the cutting off of sex from other forms and aspects of social relationship, and above all from marital and parental relations, is a powerful *instrument*, not just the *consequence*, of the processes of privatization and marketization. Today individuals are 'socially engaged' primarily through their role as consumers, not producers; the arousing of new desires replaces normative regulation, publicity takes the place of coercion, and seduction makes redundant or invisible the pressures of necessity. In this kind of context the stiff and resilient structures of the 'till death us do part' type, indispensable in the panoptic system of power, lose their usefulness; they even become 'dysfunctional' if measured by the prerequisites of the market-type integration. And so the present-day sexual emancipation reminds one of kicking an adversary who has already fallen. On the other hand, though, it looks like a most powerful blow knocking him down . . .

Sex is being thoroughly cleansed of all 'pollutions' and 'alien bodies' such as assumed obligations, protected bonds, acquired rights. On the other hand, though, all other kinds of human relations are – keenly, vigilantly, obsessively, sometimes in a panic-stricken fashion – purified of even the palest of sexual undertones which stand the slightest chance of condensing those relations into permanence. Sexual undertones are suspected and sniffed out in every emotion reaching beyond the meagre inventory of feelings permitted in the framework of mismeeting (or quasi-encounter, fleeting encounter, inconsequential encounter – see the chapter 'Forms of Togetherness' in *Life in Fragments*), in every offer of friendship and every manifestation of a deeper-than-average interest in another person. (Long before *Oleanna* was written and performed, a friend of mine, an outstanding sociologist, told me that he had decided to keep the door of his office wide open whenever female students came for consultation – to avoid accusations of sexual advances; as he found out very soon, the door had also to be kept open during the visits of male students.) Complimenting the beauty or charm of a workmate is likely to be censured as sexual provocation, and the offer of a cup of coffee as sexual harassment. The spectre of sex now haunts company offices and college seminar rooms; there is a threat involved in every smile, gaze, or form of address. The overall outcome is the rapid emaciation of human relations, stripping them of intimacy and emotionality, and the wilting of desire to enter them and keep them alive.

The switching of sex from cementing partnership to its enfeebling, to ensuring the permanent temporariness of a relationship and its readiness for cancellation at short notice or without notice, is arguably at its most conspicuous, and its most consequential, in the realm of family life. After all, it was precisely in that realm that sex used to provide the essential brick and mortar for structure building: either in its positive version, in articulating marital bonds, or negatively (as the elemental force which needs to be tamed and controlled), in articulating parent–children intimacy. Today sex is turning into a powerful instrument of loosening up the family structure in all its dimensions.

In one country after another the courts legalize the concept of 'marital rape'; sexual services are no more marital rights and duties, and insisting on them can be classified as punishable crime. Since it is notoriously difficult to interpret one's partner's conduct 'objectively', unambiguously, as either consent or refusal (particularly if the partners share a bed nightly), and since to define an event as a rape calls for the decision of one partner only, virtually every sexual act can, with a modicum of good (or rather ill) will, be presented as the act of rape (which certain radical feminist writers were quick to proclaim the 'truth of the matter'). Sexual partners need to remember on every occasion, therefore, that discretion is the better part of valour. The ostensible obviousness and unproblematic character of marital rights, which was once meant to encourage partners to prefer marital sex over sex outside marriage, allegedly a more risky affair, is now more and more often perceived as a trap; as a result, the reasons to associate the satisfaction of sexual needs with marriage become less and less evident or convincing – particularly when 'pure relations' in the Giddensian sense are elsewhere so easy to obtain.

The manifest or latent, awakened or dormant sexuality of the child used also to be a powerful instrument in the articulation of modern family relationships. It provided the reason and the impetus for the comprehensive and obtrusive parental interference with chidren's life; it called on parents to be constantly 'in touch', to keep children constantly within parental sight, to engage in intimate conversations, to encourage confessions and require confidence and secret-sharing. Today the sexuality of children is becoming, on the contrary, an equally powerful factor in parent–children separation and 'keeping one's distance'. Today's fears emanate from the sexual desire of the parents, not of the children; it is not in what children do on their own impulse, but in what they do or may do at the behest of their parents, that we are inclined to suspect sexual undertones; it is what parents like to do with (and to) their children that frightens and calls for vigilance – only this is a kind of vigilance which advises caution, parental withdrawal and reticence. Children are now perceived mainly as sexual *objects* and potential victims of their parents as sexual *subjects*; and since the parents are by nature stronger than their children and placed in the position of power, parental sexuality may easily lead to the abuse of that power in the service of the parents' sexual instincts. The spectre of sex, therefore, also haunts family homes. To exorcise it, one needs to keep children at a distance – and above all abstain from intimacy and overt, tangible manifestation of parental love . . .

Some time ago Great Britain witnessed a virtual epidemic of the 'sexual exploitation of children'. In a widely publicized campaign, social workers, in co-operation with doctors and teachers, charged dozens of parents (mainly fathers, but also a growing number of mothers) with incestuous assaults against their children; child victims were forcibly removed from parental homes, while readers of the popular press were treated to blood-curdling stories about the dens of debauchery into which family bedrooms and bathrooms had been turned. Newspapers brought news about sexual abuse of the infant wards in one care home or borstal after another.

Only a few of the publicly discussed cases were brought to trial. In some cases the accused parents managed to prove their innocence and get their children back. But what happened, happened. Parental tenderness lost its innocence. It has been brought to public awareness that children are always and everywhere sexual objects, that there is a potentially explosive sexual underside in any act of parental love, that every caress has its erotic aspect and in every loving gesture may hide a sexual advance. As Suzanne Moore noted,[7] an NSPCC survey reported that 'one in six of us was a victim of "sexual interference" as a child', while according to Barnardo's report 'six out of 10 women and a quarter of men "experience some kind of sexual assault or interference before they are 18"'. Suzanne Moore agrees that 'sexual abuse is far more widespread than we are prepared to accept', but she points out nevertheless that 'the word abuse is now so over-used that almost any situation can be constructed as abusive'. In the once unproblematic parental love and care an abyss of ambivalence has been revealed. Nothing is clear and obvious any more; everything is shot through with ambiguity – and of things ambiguous one is advised to steer clear.

In a widely publicized case three-year-old Amy was found in school making plasticine sausage- or snake-like objects (which the teacher identified as penises) and talked of things that 'squirt white stuff'. The parents' explanation that the mysterious object squirting white stuff was a nasal spray against congestion, while the sausage-like things were images of Amy's favourite jelly sweets, did not help. Amy's name was placed on the list of 'children at risk', and the parents went into battle to clear their names. As Rosie Waterhouse[8] comments on this and other cases,

> Hugging, kissing, bathing, even sleeping with your children, are these natural patterns of parental behaviour or are they inappropriate, oversexualised acts of abuse?
>
> And what are normal childish pastimes? When children draw pictures of witches and snakes, does this mean they are symbols of frightening, abusive events? These are fundamental questions with which teachers, social work-

ers and other professionals involved in caring for children frequently have to grapple.

Let us note that even the cases of masturbation and children's interest in their own genitals are now ever more widely redefined as the product of parental sexuality, rather than children's own sexual inclinations, and interpreted as indicators of sexual abuse.

To sum up: in the present-day discourse the child appears as the object, rather than subject, of sexual desire. If the casting of the child in the mould of sexual subject justified intimate and comprehensive parental wardenship – the child as a sexual object calls for parental reticence, distance, and emotional restraint. The first served the strengthening (some would say: tightening up) of family bonds. And the second?

The second serves the weakening of bonds, an important condition of the 'monadization' of the future collector of sensations and consumer of impressions. As in its other dimensions (for instance, the 'purification' of sex from contamination by other aspects of inter-human relationship – the process meant to secure a better chance to exploit the hedonistic potential of sex) the current sexual discourse propagates in this case the 'cooling down' of human interaction and freeing it of all erotic (and, more generally, affectual) flavour – in short, its new, more radical 'impersonalization'. If once upon a time the separation of the business from the household allowed the first to be submitted to the stern and unemotional demands of competition while remaining deaf to all other norms and values, notably moral, the present-day separation of sex from other interhuman relations allows it to be submitted without qualification to the aesthetic criteria of strong experience and sensual gratification. First, through 'purifying' the partnership, erotic love has been reduced to sex; then, in the name of purification from unclean sexual intentions, partnership is 'purified' of love . . .

12

Immortality, Postmodern Version

*A free man thinks of nothing less than of death,
and his wisdom is a meditation not of death, but of life.*
Baruch Spinoza, *Ethics*

There is a remarkable story, *The Immortal*,[1] left by the remarkable
Argentinian writer, Jorge Luis Borges. In that story Joseph Cartaphilus of
Smyrna, after a long and arduous voyage, had reached the City of the
Immortals. Wandering through the labyrinthine palace which was the
city, Joseph was overwhelmed first by the impression of breathtaking
antiquity, then by the impression of the interminable, of the atrocious,
and finally by that of the 'completely senseless'. The palace 'abounded
in dead-end corridors, high unattainable windows, portentous doors
which led to a cell or pit, incredible inverted stairways whose steps and
balustrades hung downwards. Other stairways, clinging airily to the side
of the monumental wall, would die without leading anywhere, after
making two or three turns in the lofty darkness of the cupolas.' And so
on. In this palace, built by immortals for immortals, nothing seemed to
make any *sense*, nothing served any *purpose* – but, let us note, in each
detail there was a shadow, a memory of forms conceived in the cities
inhabited by mortal beings, and thus it could express and brandish its
absurdity by blatantly defying the ends for which it was originally
invented. This must have been a city not of any immortals, but of such
immortals who went first through the experience of being mortal,
learned the skills resonant with such an experience, and then, some time
later, acquired immortality. At that moment, they still felt the need to
express their shocking discovery that everything learned before became
suddenly useless and devoid of meaning. By now, however, they had
abandoned even the palace they built at the moment of discovery;
Joseph found them lying in the shallow pits in the sand: 'from
these miserable holes...naked, grey-skinned, scraggly bearded men
emerged...I was not amazed that they could not speak and that they
devoured serpents.' This is not what Joseph, embarking on his expedi-

tion to escape his own dreaded death, hoped to find to be the case in a world ruled by the perpetual bliss of eternal life. But now he understood:

> To be immortal is commonplace; except for man, all creatures are immortal, for they are ignorant of death; what is divine, incomprehensible, is to know that one is immortal ... Everything among the mortals has the value of irretrievable and the perilous. Among the Immortals, on the other hand, every act (and every thought) is the echo of others that preceded it in the past, with no visible beginning, or the faithful presage of others that in the future will repeat it to a vertiginous degree ... Nothing can happen only once, nothing is preciously precarious.

Conclusions are as lucid as they are shattering: everything in human life counts because humans are mortal, and know it. Everything human mortals do makes sense because of that knowledge. Were death ever defeated, there would be no more sense in all those things they laboriously put together in order to inject some purpose into their absurdly brief life. That human culture we know – the arts, politics, the intricate web of human relations, science or technology – was conceived at the site of the tragic yet fateful encounter between the finite span of human physical existence and the infinity of human spiritual life.

The crux of the matter is that knowing of one's mortality means at the same time knowing of the *possibility of immortality*. Hence one cannot be aware of one's mortality without conceiving of the inevitability of death as an affront and an indignity; and without thinking of the ways to repair the wrong. To be aware of mortality means to imagine immortality; to dream of immortality; to work towards immortality – even if, as Borges warns, it is only that dream which fills life with meaning, while immortal life, if ever achieved, would only bring the death of meaning. Perhaps, if asked, Freud would reply that our perpetual drive towards immortality is itself the work of the death instinct ... Or one could speak, following Hegel, of the cunning of reason: it consoles mortals by dangling before them the prospect of immortality – but only by hiding the fact that solely as long as they remain mortal the prospect of immortality may seem like a consolation ...

It is the stern reality of death that makes immortality an attractive proposition, but it is the same reality which makes the dream of eternity an active force, a motive for action. Immortality is, after all, a task – an *unnatural* condition, which will not come by itself unless cajoled or forced into being. It would take a lot of effort and clever strategy to make the dream come true. And human history was filled to the brim with such efforts, dictated by two basic strategies.

The first strategy was collective. Individual humans are mortal; but not those human totalities of which they are part – to which they 'belong'. The Church, the Nation, the Party, the Cause – those, to quote Emile Durkheim's memorable phrase, 'beings greater than myself' – they will all live much longer that any of their members, yet they will live longer, perhaps even forever, solely thanks to each and every member's effort to secure their eternal life at the cost of his own. Thus individual death has been given its meaning: 'It was not in vain.' But the meaning is derivative, and it does not augur preservation of the individual in any shape or form. The concern with individual immortality is dissolved in the task of serving the immortality of the group; with this, individuality itself is dissolved, which helps the group enormously in its ongoing efforts to subordinate individual life-concerns to whatever is declared to be the interest of the group's survival. The tombs of *unknown* soldiers, adorning every capital of the world, encapsulate the gist of this strategy, aiming at the same time at its continuous allure.

The second strategy was individual. Physically, all individuals must die – but some (men described as 'great' for this very reason) may be preserved, as individuals, in the memory of their successors. That other, posthumous life, may in principle last as long as there are humans with memory. But one needs to impress oneself on that memory: through one's deeds, unmistakably *individual* deeds, deeds no one else accomplished. By and large, though not exclusively, two types of deeds were in competition for this kind of immortality – that is, for claiming the right to stay forever in human memory. The first were accomplishments of rulers and leaders of men – kings, law-givers, generals; the second were the achievements of scribes – philosophers, poets, artists. In the words put by Plato into Socrates' mouth, 'the soul is most like the divine and immortal', and hence 'into the family of gods, unless one is a philosopher . . . it is not permitted for any to enter, except the lover of learning'.[2]

Unlike the first strategy, the second was singularly unfit for mass consumption. It was linked to the status of individuality as privilege, as the achievement of the uniquely endowed, extraordinarily meritorious or otherwise exceptional. It was such an individuality which offered the pass-key to immortality, but some people could rise to that individuality only because the others, the multitude, 'the mass', never did and never stood a chance of so doing. Gaining immortality according to the rules of this strategy meant standing out from the crowd and above the ordinary. (Already in Plato the praise of philosophers was underwritten by the contempt for and disparagement of those allegedly living by their flesh alone.)

Their sharp differences notwithstanding, neither of the two strategies could emerge unscathed from the modern revolution, which Michel Foucault described as, first and foremost, the entrenchment of the *individualizing* power, the power that in principle constituted *all* its objects as individuals, deploying techniques of power which required that individual responsibility for the building and exercising of identities was simultaneously the right and duty of all, and saw to it that the requirement was met.[3] Modernity was a democratic (populist?) force – in making all humans into individuals *de facto* or *in spe*. But the formula of collective immortality called for the suppression of individuality; while the formula of individual immortality made sense only as long as individuality remained the privilege of the few.

Democracy was not the sole challenge that the ascent of modernity posited to the customary human ways of coping with the dream of immortality. Modern humanism was another. As John Carroll summed it up in his recent reassessment of the humanist legacy, 'it attempted to replace God by man, to put man at the centre of the universe, to deify him. Its ambition was to found a human order on earth . . . – an entirely human order.' The new Archimedean point on which the earth, and the universe with it, would turn, was to be human will, aided and abetted by human reason. As it turned out, though, 'the humanist will has atrophied to nothing', so that the lofty and arrogant 'I am' 'has degenerated into that of a chronic invalid watching life from the window of the hospital'.[4] How did it come to pass?

Death, modern and postmodern

In the divine order, the harrowing discrepancy between timelessness of thought and the temporality of flesh was an indignity, but not a provocation; a cause of sorrow, but not of umbrage. It could even, though not without the imagination stretched to its limit, be imbued with a deeper sense, or eulogized as the source of all meaning. Not so in the new, human order. Here, everything was to serve human plans and desires, and all that resisted or defied human reason and will was an abomination. The incommensurality of the intellectual and bodily time-spans, and the biological death responsible for it, became now a challenge to human wit and resolve. In a world founded on the promise of freedom to human creative powers, the inevitability of biological death was the most stubborn and sinister of threats poised against the credibility of that promise and so against that world's foundation.

In keeping with the ways and means of modern practice, which always tends to split big and difficult-to-handle issues into a series of smaller and manageable tasks, the awesome and unassailable issue of biological death looming at the far end of life pursuits was in modern times sliced – *deconstructed* – into a multitude of little tasks and concerns filling the total span of life. Modernity did not abolish death – we are as mortal today as we were at the dawn of the 'human order' era; but it did bring enormous advances in the art of fighting off each and any known cause of death (that is, except the cause of all causes, which is innate human mortality itself) – and in preventing such causes from occurring. Busy as we are trying to observe all the prescriptions and proscriptions that modern medicine offers, we think less, if at all, of the ultimate vanity of this observance. The outcome of the deconstruction is that the invisible enemy, death, vanished from view and from speech; yet the price of deconstruction is life policed from the beginning to the end by the banished enemy's ubiquitous garrisons. Having refused to face up to the incompatibility of modern promise with the brute fact of human mortality, we have indeed become, at least for the time being, 'invalids watching life from hospital windows'.

For the time being, or forever? This is, admittedly, a moot problem, and one which I, an outsider to both medical practice and daring biological projects, one who knows of the present and the hoped-for potential of recent bio-technological departures no more than a lay person could or should, have no credentials to consider. I have little if anything to say on the crucial questions on which the answer to the above problem hangs: is the progress of biological understanding and medical know-how likely to step beyond the arresting of the ageing process, and go as far as averting the so far unavoidable onset of the disintegration of life processes? Is it, in other words, able to perform a qualitative leap from merely prolonging life – that is, from postponing the moment when the otherwise inevitable death is faced – to the demotion of the event of death, from its present status of unavoidable fate, to one of contingency (that is, to achieve *practical* immortality)? I leave these questions to the specialists. It is a different question I shall ask: in what form are the discoveries in the field of 'practical immortality' likely to be accommodated within the kind of society we are in? And so, what are their likely cultural meaning and consequences?

Our 'late modern' (Giddens), 'reflexive modern' (Beck), 'surmodern' (Balandier), or – as I prefer to call it – *postmodern* society, is marked by the discreditation, ridicule or just abandonment of many ambitions (now denigrated as utopian, or condemned as totalitarian) characteristic of the modern era. Among such forsaken and forlorn modern dreams is the prospect of doing away with socially generated inequalities, of guaranteeing to every human individual an equal chance of access to everything good and desirable that society may offer. Once more, as at the early stages of the modern revolution, we live in an increasingly polarized society.

Throughout the modern period social deprivation tended to be defined as a temporary hiccup in the otherwise smooth and relentless progress towards equality; it was explained away by the not-yet-rectified, but in principle rectifiable, malfunctioning of the not sufficiently rationalized social system. Those out of work and without earnings were seen as the 'reserve army of labour' – meaning that tomorrow, or the day after, they would certainly be called to active service and join the ranks of producers which in principle would include the whole of society. This is no longer the case. We speak today of 'structural' unemployment (a term which still, counterfactually, alludes to employment being the norm, and suggests that the present massive lack of employment is an anomaly). Those without work are no more a 'reserve army of labour': economic progress does not mean more demand for labour; new investment means less, not more employment; 'rationalization' means cutting work places and jobs. One may say that, at the far end of the spectacular scientific and technological advance, the 'growth' of GNP comes to measure the massive production of redundancy and redundant people. These people are kept alive through what the structure of our economy defines, with more than a hint of the condemnation all abnormality deserves, as 'secondary transfers' – the dependency that stigmatizes them as a burden to the earners, to those actively engaged in economic life, to the 'taxpayers'. Not needed as producers, useless as consumers – they are people which the 'economy', with its logic of needs-arousing and needs-gratifying, could very well do without. Their being around and claiming the right to survival is a nuisance for the rest of us; their presence could no more be justified in terms of competitiveness, efficiency or any other criteria legitimized by the ruling economic reason. There is not enough meaningful employment for all those people alive; and not much prospect of ever matching the volume of work against the mass of those who want it and need it to escape the net of 'secondary transfers' and the attached stigma.

It would be unwise – perhaps ingenuous, but certainly risky – to exclude the possibility of an intimate connection between the premonition of organic redundancy and the present signs of cultural re-evaluation of new life and long life. We live in the time of demographic scare. If during the *Sturm und Drang* era of modernity a high birth-rate used to be seen as a sign of the 'health of the nation', and 'more people' meant more wealth and power, both are dreaded today as a menace to consumer bliss and a vexing tax on 'limited resources'. Increasingly, people are recorded on the debit, not the credit, side of economic calculation. It would indeed be strange were there no link between the economic devaluation of human numbers and the in-built redundancy of population, and the ever more pronounced cultural trend towards refusal at will of the right to live to those who are too weak or insignificant to demand and secure that right. For any serious student of culture it would be naive to take at face value the culturally deployed justifications of behavioural patterns – which, as any serious student of culture knows well, serve to hide rather than reveal the true motives and reasons, in order to gloss over the contradictions between praised values and practised behaviour, and to make palatable what cultural precepts explicitly condemn but life demands. And so we tend to defend abortion of the not-yet-born in terms of the very humane principle of the right to choose of those born already; or euthanasia of the old in terms of the right to choose death over a kind of life to which society has refused to accord meaning. But, as Klaus Dörner reminds us,

> Die meisten der heute lebenden alten Menschen, die sich quantitativ inflationieren und dadurch entwerten, entwerten sich inzwischen auch qualitativ, indem sie im Falle der Pflegebedürftigkeit nicht mehr leben wollen, weil sie es nicht mehr wert seien, sich von Jüngeren abhängig zu machen und deren Genuß ihrer Jugend zu beeinträchtigen. Daher auch die Anziehungskraft der 'Deutschen Gesellschaft für humanes Sterben' für alte und chronisch kranke Menschen, die meinen freiwillig sich suizidieren zu müssen.[5]

It is a paradox (or perhaps not much of a paradox after all), and irony of history (or perhaps not such an irony after all), that a realistic (at any rate, more realistic than ever before) offer of biological immortality is promised by *science* at a time when the *cultural* message is the excess and redundancy of life, and when, accordingly, avoidance, prevention and limitation of life turns into culturally approved and promoted value. Under these circumstances one can expect the offer, if it finally becomes not just realistic but real, to be taken up selectively – and so to become another, possibly the most powerful ever, stratifying and polarizing factor. In doing so, it will only follow the already visible trend to 'privatization' of everything, including the chance of survival or living longer.

With the technology of organ transplant and replacement, contemporary medical science has acquired powerful means to prolong life. But the very nature of that technology – most of all, though not only, its exorbitant cost – precludes its universal application. Access to longer life is already technologically stratified. One could reasonably expect these stratifying effects to become still more pronounced – once the extension of life crosses the threshold of 'practical immortality'. In a drastic reversal of the modern strategy of 'collectivized' survival, biological immortality has every chance of turning into a factor and an attribute of individualization – the preservation of the 'most deserving'. As once was the right to live forever in human memory, the right to perpetuity of biological existence would need to be earned (or inherited, for that matter). It is more than likely to turn into the most valued and coveted stake in the competitive game of individual self-assertion.

A closer look at the postmodern cultural stage strongly suggests such a turn of events. For mass consumption, our culture has a message which, if anything, devalues or dilutes the dream of eternal life; and this through exorcizing the horror of death. This effect is achieved through two seemingly opposite, yet in fact supplementary and converging strategies. One is the strategy of hiding the death of those close to oneself from sight and chasing it away from the memory: putting the terminally ill into the care of the professionals; confining the old to geriatric ghettos long before they are entrusted to the graveyard, that prototype of all ghettos; shuffling funerals away from public places; toning down the public display of mourning and grief; psychologizing away the torments of bereavement as therapy cases and personality problems. On the other hand, though – as Georges Balandier has reminded us recently, death

> se banalise par la prolifération des images; elle s'y insinue, surgit, puis s'efface. Autrefois, la mort donnée à voir avait la qualité d'un spectacle édifiant . . . aujourd'hui, elle devient un moment médiatique, un événement qui libère une émotion fugace, vite affaiblie par son 'peu de réalité' pour ceux qui l'observent. Cette òmni-présence imagière, par quoi la mort se galvaude, fait fonction d'exorcisme; elle la montre et la dissipe dans un même mouvement, car il s'agit toujours d'une mort étrangère et lointaine, celle des autres.[6]

Death close to home is concealed, while death as a universal human predicament, the death of anonymous and 'generalized' others, is put blatantly on display, made into a never ending street spectacle that, no more a sacred or carnival event, is but one among many of daily life's paraphernalia. So banalized death is made too familiar to be noted and much too familiar to arouse high emotions. It is the 'usual' thing, much too common to be dramatic and certainly too common to be dramatic about. Its horror is exorcized through its omnipresence, made absent through the excess of visibility, made negligible through being ubiquitous, silenced through deafening noise. And as death fades away and eventually dies out through banalization, so does the emotional and volitional investment in the craving for its defeat . . .

It is as if the multitude has been surreptitiously yet consistently drilled not to desire what it is unlikely to get at any rate; not to covet eternal life when – if – it becomes feasible. Both those eligible for personal immortality and those left behind would agree that only a certain kind of life deserves to be extended forever – though both sides would accept it, one would surmise, for different reasons and inspired by a different life experience. The kind of society likely to be built on such consensus is not very difficult, but perhaps too awesome, to imagine – for the time being, that is, the time too close to the naive though exciting ambitions of modern, and practices of postmodern, civilization.

Immortality, modern and postmodern

As we noted before, it was the unique and original work/act that through most of human history led towards the individuality of authorship/ actorship and thereby assured, or was hoped to assure, the immortality of the individual *qua* individual – albeit a spiritual one only, woven of memories and commemorative rites. Modernity reinforced and democratized that strategy of individual immortality, once available primarily to princes and philosophers, making it accessible to the growing number of practitioners of ever new trades and professions. Yet the beginning of the distinctly postmodern era coincided with the proclamation of the 'death of the author'; from Roland Barthes through Michel Foucault to Jacques Derrida and Jean Baudrillard, all the most perceptive observers of the convolutions of contemporary culture and the suppliers of its most influential self-interpretations point to the anonymity of the self-evolving texts, to which the authors lost their once cherished privileged access, forfeiting on the way their past monopoly of meaning-making and interpretation.

The most pensive and philosophically acute postmodern artists, when they struggle to represent the spirit and the tendency of their era in their work and in the techniques with which the works are executed, more than anything else portray and express the absence of the 'original'. Composers of pop records record what had already been recorded; Andy Warhol paints what has already been painted; Sherrie Levine photographs what has already been photographed; they and many others quote, collate, reposition, recompose, and above all copy and multiply the already authored icons, floating the question of authorship and originality, and seeing to it that the question cannot be raised again in any meaningful way. Andy Warhol went out of his way to eliminate the 'original' from his own artistic practice. He developed techniques which allowed the creation of any number of copies, but made it impossible to select any one of them as the original or the first.

All of us who commit our thoughts to computers instead of hand-written or typed manuscripts, and converse with the screen, endlessly rewriting and rearranging what we have written, know all too well that each next version makes the past versions non-existent, effacing all traces of the road which led us where we are now. Computer writing puts paid to the once holy idea of the 'original version'; the PhD students of the next century will miss badly the favourite topics of this century's dissertations: tracing the successive stages of the author's struggle with their own thoughts back to the 'beginning', to the original act of inspiration, and thus retelling the drama of individual creation. Thus computers cast a gigantic shadow on our inherited image of the writer as author: does not the very name of the software we use to write suggest a processor of words rather than a composer of ideas, thinker and creator?

In his brilliant insight into the cultural consequences of the 'Second Media Age', which began with the introduction of the interfaced compu-ter networks, the Internet and virtual reality, Mark Poster points out that words and images 'procreate with indecent rapidity, not arborially, . . . as in a centralized factory, but rhyzomically, at any decentred location. The shift to a decentralized network of communications makes senders receivers, producers consumers, rulers ruled [and – let me add – makes the authors into the processors of the increasingly anonymous, parent-less material – Z.B.], upsetting the logic of understanding of the first media age.' Indeed, who '"owns" the rights to, and is therefore respon-sible for, the text of Internet bulletin boards: the author, the system operator, the community of participants?'[7] Or, let me add, the 'system' itself, which certainly involves all those people, but can be reduced to the will and intentions of none of them? Property rights and authorial pretensions lose much of their sense once the information has been set free to move and to multiply, as if of its own accord and by its own momentum, in the no-man's-land of 'cyberspace'. Human operators are not part of that momentum; they trigger processes which they do not direct and are hardly ever able to monitor, let alone to supervise. No one controls the logic of that cultural drive which takes place inside cyberspace – which *is* cyberspace. As Jean Baudrillard once said, this medium converses solely with itself . . . 'The signs evolve, they con-catenate and *produce themselves*, always one upon the other – so that there is absolutely no basic reference which can sustain them.'[8]

The container in which the immortality of individual human deeds was stocked for safe keeping was human memory. The urge to make the container even more foolproof, and capacious enough to accommodate the democratization of individual immortality, must have provided a powerful impetus for the invention and development of computers as, above all, an 'artificial memory'. But the not fully anticipated outcome of that urge was that the human being, alone among the species (and no wonder that he is alone – since all other species are 'immortal' by omission, not by commission, thanks to not being aware of their mortality, rather than through performing the task of self-immortalization), 'is seeking to construct his immortal double, an unprecedented artificial species'. One result was the substitution of the immortality of dead objects for the immortality of living: 'In aiming for virtual (technical) immortality and ensuring its exclusive perpetuation by a projection into artifacts, the human species is precisely losing its own immunity and specificity and becoming immortalized *as an inhuman species*; it is abolishing in itself the mortality of the living in favour of the immortality of the dead.'[9]

But another was the elevation of those 'dead objects' into a virtual species, with its own laws of evolution, its own promiscuous patterns of procreation, its own mutations, mutants, viruses and immunities, and its own tropisms and mechanisms of assimilation, metabolism and adaptation. No one controls that new species, not even the new species itself: the device invented to put paid to the most harrowing of contingencies has itself become, like all species, contingency incarnate. Programmed to make human immortality secure, it emancipated the fate of immortality from human efforts; it expropriated immortality from human individuals craving to make their individual accomplishments eternally alive. Instead of guaranteeing immortality to the authors, it abolished the authorship of eternal life. Individual immortality of great acts and thoughts went the way of the collectivized immortality of the *hoi polloi*. Also the immortality of the individuals *qua* individuals has now been collectivized; entrusted to the vagaries of the species, it feeds itself on the death of the individual. The immortal species of computers proved to be a great equalizer: not because it raised everyone to the ranks once reserved for the 'great men' alone, but because it put paid to the notion of the 'great men' as a race standing a chance of a different kind of immortality from ordinary mortals, such as were always offered immortality-by-proxy through sacrificing their lives at the altar of the species, or of a selected part of the species.

With the infinite capacity and insatiable appetite of artificial memory, being recorded is no longer the reward of the chosen few, nor necessarily the outcome of one's own enterprise. Now everybody has the chance and the likelihood of having his or her name and life record preserved forever in the artificial memory of computers; by the same token, no one has the chance of earning a privileged access to perpetual commemoration. Fame, that premonition of immortality, has been replaced by notoriety, that icon of contingency, infidelity and the capriciousness of fate. When everyone can have a share of the limelight, no one stays in the limelight forever; but no one is sunk forever in the darkness either. Death, the irrevocable and irreversible event, has been replaced by the disappearance act: the limelight moves elsewhere, but it may always turn, and does turn, the other way. The disappeared are *temporarily absent*, not totally absent, though – they are *technically present*, safely stored in the warehouse of artificial memory, always ready to be resuscitated without much ado and at any moment.

If modernity struggled to deconstruct death, in our postmodern times it is the turn of immortality to be deconstructed. But the overall effect is the effacement of the opposition between death and immortality, between the transitory and the durable. Immortality is no longer the transcendence of mortality. It is as fickle and erasable as life itself; as irreal as the death transformed into the disappearing act has become: both are amenable to endless resurrection, but none to finality.

It was the consciousness of death that breathed life into human history. Behind the boundless inventiveness sedimented in human culture stood the awareness of death, which made the brevity of life into an offence to human dignity – a challenge to human wits which called for transcendence, stretched the imagination, spurred into action. Not knowing of death, animals live in immortality without really trying; humans must earn, gain, construct their immortality. They have finally done it, but only through ceding immortality to an artificial species, living its own immortality as a *virtual reality*. With the oppositions between reality and representation, sign and signification, virtual and the 'real' progressively effaced, would not the virtual, technical immortality steal the thunder which immortality as a task, as unfulfilled dream, once held? Is not the new technical, virtual immortality, the immortality-by-proxy, a roundabout, twisted way back to the *a priori* immortality, immortality-by-ignorance of the non-human (and inhuman!) species?

The knowledge of death is the specifically human tragedy. It used also to be the undying source of the specifically human greatness, the motive of the finest of human achievements. We do not know whether the greatness will survive the tragedy: we have not tried it yet, we have not been here before. The world we have inhabited so far is bespattered by marks and traces left by our efforts to escape into immortality. Once we have obtained an electronic equivalent of the portrait of Dorian Gray, we may have earned ourselves a world without wrinkles, but also without landscape, history, and purpose. We may well have found our way to Jorge Luis Borges's City of the Immortals.

13
Postmodern Religion?

'Religion' belongs to a family of curious and often embarrassing concepts which one perfectly understands until one wants to define them. The postmodern mind, for once, agrees to issue that family, maltreated or sentenced to deportation by modern scientific reason, with a permanent residence permit. The postmodern mind, more tolerant (since it is better aware of its own weaknesses) than its modern predecessor and critic, is soberly aware of the tendency of definitions to conceal as much as they reveal and to maim and obfuscate while pretending to clarify and straighten up. It also accepts the fact that, all too often, experience spills out of the verbal cages in which one would wish to hold it, that there are things of which one should keep silent since one cannot speak of them, and that the ineffable is as much an integral part of the human mode of being-in-the-world as is the linguistic net in which one tries (in vain, as it happens, though no less vigorously for that reason) to catch it.

The arrival of postmodern serenity does not mean, of course, that the desperate attempts to 'define religion' are likely to grind to a halt. The postmodern mind did not quite live up to André Breton's pugnacious call 'to deal drastically with *that hatred of the marvellous* which is rampant in some people'.[1] The postmodern mind is too humble to forbid and too weak to banish the excesses of the modern mind's ambition. It only, so to speak, puts them in perspective – lays bare their inner springs as well as their vanity. And so the frantic efforts to 'define religion' will go on unabated, trials long ago discredited yet by now conveniently forgotten (thanks to the 'collective amnesia' and the 'Columbus complex', which, as Pitirim Sorokin observed a long time ago in his *Fads and Foibles of American Sociology*, keep the kind of speech called the social sciences forever vigorous and self-confident) will be rehashed no end and with no greater chance than before of passing the test of time.

More often than not, 'defining religion' amounts to replacing one ineffable by another – to the substitution of the incomprehensible for the unknown ... This is the case with most popular definitions, which served mainly to placate the scientific conscience of sociologists eager to declare the embracement of the unembraceable: the definitions which 'defined religion' pointing to its relation to the 'sacred', 'transcendental', 'enchanted' or even, in the tamed and thereby vulgarized renditions of Rudolf Otto,[2] the 'tremendous'.

Define, *and* perish

What worries the obsessive definition-makers is the belief that if we fail to coin a 'rational definition' of religious phenomena (that is, a definition which would pass the test of that rationality through which social science constitutes and legitimizes itself), we would enter the postmodern world ill prepared to tackle the questions proclaimed central by the sociological descriptions of historical trends. Is the world we inhabit more religious than it used to be? Or less? Do we witness a decline, redeployment or renaissance of religiosity? The way to resolve (or, perhaps, by-pass) the problem leads through the tested stratagem of the cleverly chosen definition. By this reckoning, two types of definitions may get us out of trouble. One removes the problem of historical trends from the agenda – by dissolving the issue of religion in some unquestionably universal and eternal traits of the human existential predicament; the other, on the contrary, tapers the definition in such a way that religiosity becomes as precisely measurable as one's waist size, and therefore the elusive issue of socio-cultural trends is replaced with a thoroughly manageable problem of statistical tendency.

As it happens, we find examples of both types of stratagem in the records of the European Conference held in 1993 in Amalfi. On the one hand, Jeffrey C. Alexander believes that by an expedient of circumcision (cutting off the final 'n' from 'religion') we move 'away from the mundane and commonsensical to a more fundamental understanding of religion', and then we can see better that religion (now returned to its 'latinate form' as 'religio', exotic and mysterious, and thus containing presumably untapped supplies of illumination) 'is the name we give to the activity that allows us to feel we are in contact with this noumenal world "beyond our own", which to be sure is a world of the imagination, of projected fantasy and the sensibility of the unconscious mind. In this precise [sic!] sense, and no other more ontological one, religion allows transcendence.' The statement that religion is 'the most omnipresent of the qualities that distinguishes humankind' follows therefore as no surprise, being a foregone conclusion. Religion in Jeffrey Alexander's rendering is the most universal of human qualities simply because everything human, from painting through orgasm to writing sociology – has been defined as a religious phenomenon. On the other extreme, we find in the same volume Bernard Barber's and Alan Segal's declaration of an intent to make the definition 'rigorously analytic, useful for picking out the religious aspect or component in a complex of concrete activities and beliefs'. *If* such a definition is coined (not very convincingly, for reasons spelled out earlier, Barber and Segal want to reach it through the far from obvious concept of the 'transcendental'), then one can be satisfied that 'much that goes on in churches, synagogues and mosques is not religious by our analytical definition', and – we may say – one can compose an inventory of things religious with something approaching the chartered accountant's standard of precision.[3]

Whether one 'defines' religion through things *transcendental,* or through things *ultimate* – the practical application of the definition remains as tall an order, and in the end as contentious, as the definition itself. As Thomas Luckmann pointed out, 'matters that come to be of "ultimate" significance for the members of later generations are likely to be congruent only to a limited extent with matters that were of "ultimate" significance to earlier generations.'[4] One can avoid this difficulty by trying to obtain the description of the 'transcendental' or 'ultimate' from the institutionalized religious spokesmen, but then, for practical and theoretical purposes, one ends up with a tautology: churches are about religion, and religion is what churches do. Or one wishes to walk without institutional crutches, pinpointing the relevant phenomena according to one's own interpretation or the popular intuitions of the 'transcendental' or 'ultimate' – and then one ends up with a conceptual net either too tight or too porous, catching too many or leaving out too many human thoughts and actions in the unexplored remainder of the pool of life.

But let me repeat: the postmodern mind is altogether less excited than its modern adversary by the prospect (let alone moved by the urge to do so) of enclosing the world in a grid of neat categories and clear-cut divisions. We are somewhat less horrified today by the nasty habit of things of spilling over their definitional boundaries, or even by the premonition that the drawing of such boundaries with any degree of lasting reliability defies human resources. We are also learning to live with the revelation that one cannot articulate all one knows, and that to understand – to know how to go on – does not always require the availability of a verbalized precept. We are not all that appalled by the necessity to settle for 'family resemblances' where the modern pursuit of transparency goaded us to seek the shared 'distinctive features'. I propose therefore, that in opposition to the traditional concerns of the 'sociology of religion', what comes at the head of our interests when we wish to understand the phenomena of religion and religiosity is not so much the need to 'define them clearly', as the need to find out 'how up till now social mechanisms were able to operate', 'pointing out on what kinds of assumptions, what kinds of familiar, unchallenged, unconsidered modes of thought the practices that we accept rest' (Foucault).[5] Perhaps in the case of religion more than in all other cases, because religiosity is, after all, nothing else but the intuition of the limits to what we, the humans, being humans, may do and comprehend.

God, or insufficiency of self-sufficiency

In his classic and in my view unsurpassed analysis of the way in which religiosity is gestated by the human existential condition, Leszek Kołakowski proposes that religion is not 'a collection of statements about God, Providence, heaven and hell';

> Religion is indeed the awareness of human insufficiency, it is lived in the admission of weakness . . .
> The invariable message of religious worship is: 'from the finite to the infinite the distance is always infinite . . .'
> [W]e face two irreconcilable ways of accepting the world and our position in it, neither of which may boast of being more 'rational' than the other . . . Once taken, any choice imposes criteria of judgement which infallibly support it in a circular logic: if there is no God, empirical criteria alone have to guide our thinking, and empirical criteria do not lead to God; if God exists, he gives us clues about how to perceive His hand in the course of events, and with the help of those clues we recognize the divine sense of whatever happens.[6]

The suspicion that there are things that humans cannot do and things that humans cannot understand when left to their own wits and muscles, however stretched by the contraptions which they may invent using the same wits and muscles they have been endowed with, is hardly ever removed far from the level of consciousness; yet not very often does it reach that level. Most of the time we (and that 'we' includes philosophers working full time with the 'ultimate' and insoluble questions of being) live in the state of what Anthony Giddens called *ontological security* – 'a sense of reliability of persons and things', aided and abetted by the 'predictability of the (apparently) minor routines of day-to-day life'.[7] The opposite of ontological security is *existential anxiety*, which dawns upon the trustful or merely happy-go-lucky at the rare moments when it becomes evident that the ability of daily routine to self-perpetuate has its unencroachable time-limits. I suggest that by far the most seminal of the accomplishments of daily routine is precisely cutting the life-tasks to the size of human self-sufficiency. In as far as the routine may go on undisturbed, it offers little occasion to ruminate on the causes and purposes of the universe; the limits of human self-sufficiency can be kept out of sight.

We have come to believe the churches far and wide which, whenever pressed, insist that they provide the service necessitated by the overwhelming human urge to get answers to 'fundamental questions' of the purpose of life and to placate the fears that arise from the absence of a good answer. One wonders, though; there is little in daily routine which prompts such eschatological inquiry. Cattle must be fed, crops harvested, taxes paid, dinners cooked, roofs repaired; or the brief must be written or studied, letters mailed, applications filed, appointments kept, videos repaired, tickets bought . . . Before one has the time to think of eternity, bedtime is coming, and then another day filled to the brim with things to be done or undone. One wonders: it may well be that churches, like other producers of goods and services, had to occupy themselves first with the production of their own consumers: they had, if not to create, then at least to amplify and sharpen up the needs meant to be satisfied by their services, and so to make their work indispensable.

Of the pastoral power, whose techniques Christianity elaborated and brought to perfection, Michel Foucault wrote that

> [a]ll those Christian techniques of examination, confession guidance, obedience, have an aim: to get individuals to work at their own 'mortification' in this world. Mortification is not death, of course, but it is a renunciation of this world and of oneself: a kind of everyday death. A death which is supposed to provide life in another world.[8]

It stands to reason that only once such a mortification has been implanted as the duty of the individual, once an 'everyday death' came to be accepted as the good, 'value for money' price for the promised 'life in another world', the shepherd's role 'to ensure the salvation of his flock'[9] may be acknowledged, respected, and endowed with power-generating capacity. People have to become first concerned with personal salvation, to desire the posthumous reward and fear the posthumous punishment, to need the shepherd – and need him in *this* life, now endowed with an added value of the continuous rehearsal for the life to come. If this is the case, then 'religion' had to be *inserted* into the *Lebenswelt* of the individual, rather than being *born out of it* or sited inside it from the beginning. The worry about eternity does not 'come naturally' (much as the philosophical worry about the ultimate foundations of knowledge is not born, as Husserl was at pains to show, from the 'natural attitude' in which we are, daily and with no interruption, 'immersed naively', taking things as 'a matter of course'[10]). Great effort is needed for that worry to outweigh the gravity of daily concerns aimed at the tasks to be performed and results to be consummated in this one and only life which men and women know directly, since they make it out of their own daily work.

The hope of eternal life, the dream of heaven and the horror of hell are not the issue of parthenogenesis, though this is what the philosophers of religion have well-nigh succeeded in convincing us of. That excruciating terror of insufficiency which, as Kołakowski suggests, makes us susceptible to a religious message, could only follow the setting of tasks which went *beyond* the reach of tools developed to tackle the tasks of daily life and therefore *created* human insufficiency. Far from laying to rest the worry about the 'ultimate', now translated as the question of salvation, churches saw to it that the worry saturated every nook and cranny of the human mind and conscience, as well as presided over the totality of life activities.

Modernity, or doing without God

I propose that the case of the 'innateness', of the 'natural' presence of the religious drive in the universal human predicament, in the species-bound way of 'being in the world', has not been proven. It was only relentlessly insinuated; explicitly, through the acceptance of the ecclesiastical self-legitimation formula as the explanation of religiosity, or obliquely, through describing the new (or rather newly discovered) paucity of interest in eschatology as the outcome of 'secularization' (that is, of a process defined by its starting point, a process of 'departure' from the 'norm'). Above all, it has been 'made plausible' by the 'there must be religiosity somehow, somewhere' attitude of philosophers and sociologists who seek eagerly the way of redefining modern and postmodern concerns as religious 'in their essence' or 'in the last instance'.[11]

I propose that not all strategies of human being-in-the-world must be ultimately religious (that is, grounded in an intuition of the unassailable insufficiency and weakness of human powers), and that not all of them were. Most notably, the modern formula of human life on earth has been articulated in terms of a sharply alternative strategy: by design or by default, humans are alone to take care of things human, and therefore *the sole things that matter to humans are the things humans may take care of.* Such a premise may be perceived as sad and a reason to despair, or on the contrary – as a çause for exhilaration and optimism; both perceptions, though, are decisive only to the lives devoted to philosophical reflection, while appearing only at rare 'philosophical moments' in ordinary lives.

The organization of daily life is by and large independent of philosophical sadness and joy, and evolves around concerns which seldom, if ever, include the worry about the ultimate limits of things which humans, as humans, could reasonably (and effectively!) be concerned about. The modern revolution consisted precisely in the rejection of that latter type of worries, or taking them off the agenda altogether, or constructing the life agenda in such a way that little or no time was left to attend to such worries; one may also say that it consisted in plugging the ears to the homilies of redemption and salvation and closing the eyes to pictures of posthumous bliss or doom. The concerns which have filled human life since the beginning of modernity relate to *problems* – and 'problems' are, by definition, such tasks as are cut to the measure of the genuine or assumed human skills, tasks 'one can do something about' or 'one may and should find out what to do about'. It was that modern strategy which Marx extrapolated into a 'law of history', when he proposed that 'no historical era sets itself tasks it cannot fulfil'. Whether this proposition is true as a timeless principle is debatable. But it certainly applies to the modern era.

In his recent study of the cultural consequences of the modern revolution, which he calls 'humanism', John Carroll composed a poignant description of that alternative strategy of life:

> Its ambition was to found a human order on earth, in which freedom and happiness prevailed, without any transcendental or supernatural supports – an entirely human order . . . To place man at the centre meant that he had to become the Archimedean point around which everything revolved . . .
> The axiom on which the humanist rock was to be forged was put as well by Pico della Mirandola in 1486 as by anyone: 'We can become what we will' . . . So the humanist fathers put their founding axiom: man is all-powerful, if his will is strong enough. He can create himself. He can choose to be courageous, honourable, just, rich, influential, or not.[12]

I believe that Carroll's apt description of the humanist ambition would gain from a further clarification. In that world made to the human measure and guided entirely by human needs which the humanists proposed to create, not everything was to be subjected to human will; but that will was to be directed solely towards things which could be mastered, controlled, improved by human means. Contrary to Carroll's suggestion that the humanist creed drew inspiration from Archimedes, who believed that he stole the secrets of the gods, rather it turned Protagoras' contemplative idea that 'man is the measure of all things' into a declaration of practical intent. No wonder that in Carroll's list of all the things men can become, one 'thing', crucial to the religious promise – that of eternal life – is missing. Humanism was not so much about being able to become whatever one may will, as about willing to become what one truly can (given the ample, though not necessarily infinite, richness of human potential): willing only those things that one can do something concrete and practical about making true. The afterlife clearly did not belong in this category of things. The idea of human self-sufficiency undermined the grip of institutionalized religion not by promising an alternative way to eternal life, but by drawing human attention away from it; by focusing instead on tasks which humans may perform and whose consequences they are able to experience as long as they are still 'experiencing beings' – and this means here, in this life.

The celebratory mood of humanist writers was not the cause of modernity. It was but a philosophical gloss over the collapse of the old order and the emergence of a new one – differing from the one it was about to replace by being understood from the start as something which needs to be *constructed* and *designed* – not found and protected. In the absence of any *given* order of things, it was clear that there would be as much (and no more) sense and order in the world as its human inhabitants managed to insert into it; and that the ordering work at the top must be replicated by the work at the bottom – each individual having to shape and direct his or her own life, which otherwise would remain shapeless and bereft of purpose. Modern life strategy was not a matter of choice, wise or foolish, but of a rational adjustment to totally new life conditions never visited before.

In this process of rational adjustment there was little use for religion. As Alain Touraine pointed out, the 'uses' of religion are of three kinds.[13] First, religion may serve the dependence on and routine subordination to a rhythm of life interpreted as natural or supernatural, but in both cases experienced as invariable and invulnerable. Such a rhythm, let us observe however, has been most conspicuously broken, and the name 'modernity' stands for its collapse; there was not much left which religion, with its message of the preordained, one-off created world, could serve. Second, membership of a church or a sect may play an important role in keeping the walls of social divisions solid and impenetrable, and thus served well a social structure marked by low mobility and permanence of stratifying factors. But, let us observe again, such a stiff *structure* has been gradually eroded in the ever more vigorous and flexible, diffuse and decentred processes of *structuration*, and again religion with its message of the 'divine chain of being' was ill fitted to make sense of the new situation and new challenges. For reasons spelled out above, one can agree with Touraine's opinion that the 'importance of the first two aspects of religious life' has been greatly reduced; but in opposition to Touraine one would point out that the reduction in question was not the outcome of 'de-christianization' but of those deep transformations in life conditions and viable life strategies of which the alleged 'de-christianization' was itself one of the effects.

The third use of religion Touraine describes as 'the apprehension of human destiny, existence, and death'. In case of that latter function, Touraine notes its ongoing 'isolation': 'like the dance and painting, religion becomes a leisure activity, that is, deliberate, unregulated behaviour, personal and secret.' This statement can be accepted with a proviso that it is the interest in 'existence and death' itself which has been relegated to leisure pastimes, such as bear only a marginal impact on the way the day-by-day and serious life activities are organized. Whether the extant 'churches and sects', and particularly those among them which boast the greatest and the fastest-growing numbers of followers, can be similarly marginalized as leisure commodities, is debatable. The important point is that, in order to resist such a marginalization, churches and sects which have managed to do just that need to appropriate other functions than catering for the preoccupation with the mysteries of existence and death.

Anti-eschatological revolution

Not unlike late-modern modernist art, which – having pushed the modern obsession with pure and perfect form to its logical end – reached the brink of the destruction of art as such, and thereby paved the way for the postmodern aesthetic equanimity and formal tolerance, the late-premodern 'art of pious life' had pushed the church-inspired obsession with death and posthumous salvation to a radical extreme beyond which continuation of life became virtually impossible, thereby making some sort of psychological 'neutralization' of death imperative. In his exhaustive study of the late-medieval and early-modern culture of sin and fear, Jean Delumeau found the fascination and infatuation with posthumous life, and the demands of salvation-oriented piety, raised to heights no longer attainable by people still engaged in normal life-pursuits. The monks, preachers and other 'artists of religious life' set standards of piety which collided not just with popular 'sinful' inclinations, but with the maintenance of life as such, and thereby placed the prospects of 'eternal life' out of reach of all but a few saints; the care for salvation rapidly became a luxury for the chosen few, able and willing to opt out of normal life, and practise otherworldly asceticism, and by the same token ceased to be a viable proposition for ordinary people who wished or were obliged to carry on their business of life as usual.

The macabre derives from the ascetic contemplation of monks entirely turned towards the otherworld and who sought to convince themselves – and to persuade others – of the wicked character of our illusions here below. This ecclesiastical discourse then spread out of the monasteries through preaching and iconography, that is, through the evangelism of fear . . . The insistence on the macabre, in the wake of the *contemptus mundi*, thus stood within the logic of a vast enterprise of guilt-infliction aimed toward salvation in the afterlife.

The life of self-immolation, mortification of the body, rejection of worldly joys was what salvation, according to its prophets and devoted practitioners, demanded: they urged 'penitence and detachment from worldly things such as honours, wealth, beauty, and carnal desire'. As could only be expected, the sheer exorbitance of such a demand had effects that were not at all resonant with the preachers' intentions. One effect was a morbid taste 'for spectacles of suffering and death', 'culminating in willfully pernicious scenes of tortures, executions, and slaughters. Departing from the moral and religious lesson, there was a gradual sliding into sadistic pleasure.' The *macabre* turned, one may say, into an art for art's sake. On the other hand, and more seminally, *memento mori* showed the pronounced tendency of turning into *memento vivere* . . . 'Since life is so short, let us hasten to enjoy it. Since the dead body will be so repulsive, let us hurry to gain all possible pleasure from it while it is still in good health.'[14] All the more so, as the earning of spiritual salvation by rules excruciatingly difficult to obey was becoming an increasingly nebulous prospect for most.

At their radical extreme, the exacerbation of the fear of death and the fomenting of the dream of eternal life proved, so to speak, counterproductive. They gave rise to altogether different yearnings, which could hardly be tied down to religious purposes and were thus blatantly unfit for employment in the service of ecclesiastical power. More importantly, they jarred with the prerequisites of daily life and of the reproduction of its conditions. If life this side of death was to continue, concerns with 'honours, wealth, beauty and carnal desire' had to gain an upper hand over such concerns with life-after-death as required their renunciation – and they did. Modernity undid what the long rule of Christianity had done – rebuffed the obsession with the after-life, focused attention on the life 'here and now', redeployed life activities around different narratives with earthly targets and values, and all-in-all attempted to defuse the horror of death. There followed the toning down of the impact of the awareness of mortality, but – more seminally yet – detaching it from religious significance.

This effect has been achieved in modern times through the application of three not necessarily coherent, yet closely intertwined and in the end complementary strategies.

1 Like everything else in modern life, death has been subjected to a division of labour; it has become a 'specialized' concern. For the rest, the non-professionals, death has become a somewhat shameful and embarrassing affair, somewhat akin to pornography (as Geoffrey Gorer observed), an event not to be discussed in public and certainly 'not in front of the children'. The dead and particularly the dying have been removed beyond the confines of daily life, assigned separate spaces not accessible to the public, and entrusted to the care of 'professionals'. The elaborate and spectacular public ceremony of funerals has been replaced by the brief and on the whole private event of the burial or incineration of the body under the efficient supervision of experts.

2 Similarly to all other 'wholes', the total and unassailable prospect of death has been sliced and fragmented into innumerable smaller and smaller threats to survival. One cannot do much with that prospect as such, and it would be utterly foolish to concern oneself with things one can do nothing about. But the little threats may be fought back, pushed aside, even defeated. And fighting them back is an activity so time- and energy-consuming, that no time or energy is left for musing on the ultimate vanity of it all. Death no longer appears to modern men and women as a scythe-wielding skeleton in a black gown, who knocks at the door only once and cannot be barred an entry. Significantly, modernity has not produced another symbol to replace the sinister figure of Death; it has no need for an alternative 'unified' symbol, since death itself has lost its past unity – it is now dissolved in minute, yet innumerable traps and ambushes of daily life. One tends to hear it knocking now and again, daily, in fatty fast foods, in listeria-infected eggs, in cholesterol-rich temptations, in sex without condoms, in cigarette smoke, in asthma-inducing carpet mites, in the 'dirt you see and the germs you don't', in lead-loaded petrol and the lead-free, and thus uncleaned, fumes, in fluoride-treated tapwater and fluoride-untreated water, in too much and too little exercise, in over-eating and over-dieting, in too much ozone and the hole in the ozone layer; but one knows now how to barricade the door when it knocks, and one can always replace the old and rusty locks and bolts and alarms with 'new and improved ones'.

3 While the death of the near and dear has become a thoroughly private and semi-secret event, human death as such has turned into a daily occurrence, too familiar and ordinary to arouse horror or any other strong emotions; just a spectacle among other spectacles which combine into the *Lebenswelt* of the modern cinema-goer and video-borrower. Like all other spectacles, death 'as seen on TV' is a drama played in *virtual*

reality, no less but no more tangible and 'given to hand' than the exploits of the Star Trek heroes, gun-slinging cowboys or trigger-happy Rambos and Terminators. The death game is like other games – dangerous perhaps, but amusing, and amusing because dangerous. It holds a considerable measure of fascination; like the late-medieval *danse macabre*, it tends to develop into an art for art's sake. And, just as the sight of a crowd of naked bodies does not arouse sexual passions which are easily triggered by a solitary nakedness, people dying 'like flies', in droves, take the sting of dread from the sight of death. In a form yet more impressive than Aldous Huxley imagined, his vision of 'death conditioning' (showing children people in their death-throes, while feeding them their favourite sweets) came to be practised with effects not far different from those he envisaged.

The overall effect of the modern way of responding to the factuality of death by its domestication-cum-estrangement, or by dissolving the *issue* of the inevitability of death in the plethora of practical *problems* related to the effectivity of health-protecting techniques, has been a considerable weakening of the conception of life as life-towards-death (as Heidegger famously articulated it, with retrospective – or was it rather posthumous? – wisdom). Death, deployed once by religion as a kind of extraordinary event which nevertheless imparts meaning to all ordinary events, has itself become an ordinary event – even if it is, admittedly, the last in a chain of ordinary events, the last episode in a string of episodes. No more a momentous happening, ushering in the existence of another, of longer duration and graver significance, but merely the 'end of a story' – and stories hold interest only as long as they envelop and hold open the possibilities of surprise and adventure. Nothing happens after the story is over – and so those who put themselves in charge of that *nothing*, the religious experts, do not have much to offer to those who are engrossed in living the story . . .

And the stories lived by modern men and women are, indeed, engrossing.

Uncertainty, non-ontological

With a good deal of simplification, we can say that the lives of pre-modern men and women held little uncertainty. In a world virtually unchangeable within the horizon of individual life, its residents assigned from their birth to clearly charted life-tracks expected little surprise as long as they lived. The time of death, impossible to predict and coming from nowhere and unannounced, was the only window through which they could get a glimpse of uncertainty; and the uncertainty they might have glimpsed had they been brought to that window and made to look through it, was the uncertainty of existence as such, the ontological uncertainty, one uniquely suitable to be grasped and told in eschatological narrative.

With the progress of modern medicine, which supplied virtually every instance of death with its specific, 'rational' and 'logical' cause, death is no longer a caprice of blind fate, no longer as utterly haphazard and unpredictable as it used to be. Having become a natural, not at all mysterious and even partly manageable occurrence, it offers little ground to eschatological ruminations. On the other hand, it is the *life before death* that offers daily insights into uncertainty. Only what is glimpsed through the many windows offered by the vagaries of modern life, by the brittleness of achievements and the fragility of human bonds, is not the *ontological* variant of uncertainty, and so the eschatological narrative is ill fitted to unlock its mysteries and vent the anxieties such mysteries foment. The puzzle most frighteningly and ubiquitously present in all daily pursuits is the course of one's life, not the moment of death. It is the ebbs and flows of luck, the rise and fall of values one has become used to cherishing, the eccentricity of ever changing expectations, the capriciousness of the rules which keep altering before the game is finished, the cacophony of voices in which it is hard to pinpoint the leading motif – which most painfully, with the most immediate and tangible effects, defy understanding. All these challenges to understanding, to 'knowing how to go on', are human products; they bear witness not to human insufficiency, but to human omnipotence (even the sinister vagaries of climate, the premonitions of a new ice age or of the planet's overheating, are traceable to what humans do or neglect to do); and my poor response to human-made challenges is the fault of the human, all-too-human faculties of one human being – myself. The uncertainty I suffer from is the outcome of human potency, and it is human potency that I need to guide me on the road to certainty.

Already in 1957, in *Die Seele im technischen Zeitalter*, Arnold Gehlen noted that

> fewer and fewer people act on the basis of personal, internalized value orientations . . . But why are there fewer such people? Clearly because the economic, political, and social atmosphere has become hard to grasp intellectually, and hard to live up to morally, and because it changes at an accelerated pace . . .
>
> In a world where such things go on, any belief in constant principles of orientation is in danger of being denied that minimum of external confirmation without which it cannot survive.

People whose already internalized orientations keep being devalued, even ridiculed, by the day, need authoritative guidance; but the guidance they seek and may reasonably expect, a guidance adequate to the kind of agony they experience, is one likely to call on their own resources, aimed at reforming (correcting, improving, developing) their own know-how, attitudes and psychical predispositions. 'As soon as the *polis* ceased to lay down the law about everything, the way opened up for the emergence of previously unthinkable stirrings of the psyche',[15] observes Gehlen (quoting Ernst Howald's *Die Kultur der Antike*); but the 'stirrings of the psyche' to which Gehlen alludes are the prodromal symptoms of the birth of *identity*, that most seminal of all modern creations/inventions. The birth of identity means that from now on it is the individual's skills, power of judgement and wisdom of choice that will decide (at least need to decide; at any rate are expected to decide) which of the infinite number of possible forms in which life can be lived become flesh, and to what extent the desultory and wavering choice may fulfil the role once played by the *polis*-purveyed and protected 'constant principles of orientation'.

It is the uncertainties focused on *individual identity*, on its never complete construction and on the ever attempted dismantling-in-order-to-reconstruct, which haunt modern men and women, leaving little space and time for the worries arising out of the *ontological* insecurity. It is in this life, on this side of being (if there is another side at all . . .), that existential insecurity is entrenched, hurts most and needs to be dealt with. Unlike the ontological insecurity, the identity-focused uncertainty needs neither the carrot of heaven nor the stick of hell to cause insomnia. It is all around, salient and tangible, all-too-protruding in the rapidly ageing and abruptly devalued skills, in human bonds entered until further notice, in jobs which can be taken away without *any* notice, and the ever new allures of the consumer feast, each promising untried kinds of happiness while wiping the shine off the tried ones.

Postmodern men and women do need the alchemist who is able, or claims to be able, to transmogrify base uncertainty into precious self-assurance, and the authority of approval (in the name of superior knowledge, or access to wisdom closed to the others) is the philosophical stone these alchemists boast of possessing. Postmodernity is the era of experts in 'identity problems', of personality healers, of marriage guides, of writers of 'how to reassert yourself' books; it is the era of the 'counselling boom'. Postmodern men and women, whether by their own preference or by necessity, are *choosers*. And the art of choosing is mostly about avoiding one danger: that of *missing an opportunity* – because of not seeing it clearly enough, or not chasing it keenly enough, or being too inexperienced a runner to catch it. To avoid this danger, postmodern men and women need counselling. Uncertainty postmodern-style begets not the demand for religion; it gestates instead the ever rising demand for identity-experts. Men and women haunted by uncertainty postmodern-style need not preachers telling them about the weakness of man and the insufficiency of human resources. They need reassurance that they *can* do it – and a brief about *how* to do it.

I have argued elsewhere[16] that in postmodern, consumer-oriented society individuals are socially formed under the auspices of the pleas-ure-seeker or sensation-gatherer role, instead of the producer/soldier role formative for the great majority of society members (at least, the male society members) in the modern era. I also argued that the criteria by which performance in a sensation-gatherer role is assessed are notoriously resistant to all quantification – and by the same token defy 'objective', that is cross-individual, comparisons. Unlike the performance of a producer or a soldier, the sensation of the experience-seeker cannot be with any degree of self-assurance assessed as 'adequate' or 'normal', let alone as the most intense or most satisfying, accessible in principle to one's own self or particularly to other people. There is always a fly of self-doubt and suspicion of inadequacy, 'falling short of the possible', in any barrel full of the sweet sensual honey. This circumstance opens up a wide new area of uncertainty – and generates ever growing demands for the 'teachers of experience', or their technical products which may help to enhance, deepen or intensify sensations.

This-worldly transcendence

Abraham Maslow pointed out that, with the benefit of hindsight, the cases of personal illumination, revelations or ecstasy recorded in the lives of the saints, and then replicated more broadly, though perhaps in a somewhat more attenuated form, in the lives of the rank-and-file faithful, can be reinterpreted as, 'in fact, perfectly natural, human peak-experiences'. Ecclesiastical institutions, one may say looking back, 'can be seen as a kind of punch card or IBM version of an original revelation or mystical experience or peak-experience to make it suitable for group use and for administrative convenience . . . [O]rganized religion can be thought of as an effort to communicate peak-experiences to non-peakers'.[17] With great insight and analytical skill, Maslow uses concepts which could be gestated and fully formed solely in the greenhouse of late-modern or postmodern culture, to reinterpret *a posteriori* an experi-ence which was lived without the benefit of the much later discovered proper names . . . It 'makes sense' to us to recognize in the religious ecstasy of the past the intense and 'total' experience which the precepts of 'libidinal economy' (or 'conatus toward satisfaction' – Edith Wyschogrod),[18] so prominent in postmodern culture, prompt us, individuals constructed as sensation-gatherers, to seek and find. The question is, though, whether the reverse procedure equally 'makes sense'? Whether one can legitimately recognize the orgasmic experience of the postmodern sensation-gatherers as essentially religious?

I propose that the postmodern cultural pressures, while intensifying the search for 'peak-experiences', have at the same time uncoupled it from religion-prone interests and concerns, privatized it, and cast mainly non-religious institutions in the role of purveyors of relevant services. The 'whole experience' of revelation, ecstasy, breaking the boundaries of the self and total transcendence, once the privilege of the selected 'aristocracy of culture' – saints, hermits, mystics, ascetic monks, *tsadiks* or dervishes – and coming either as an unsolicited miracle, in no obvious fashion related to what the receiver of grace has done to earn it, or as an act of grace rewarding the life of self-immolation and denial, has been put by postmodern culture in every individual's reach, recast as a realistic target and plausible prospect of each individual's self-training, and relocated at the product of life devoted to the art of consumer self-indulgence. What distinguishes the postmodern strategy of peak-experience from one promoted by religions, is that, far from celebrating the assumed human insufficiency and weakness, it appeals to the full development of human inner psychological and bodily resources and presumes infinite human potency. Paraphrasing Weber, one may call the postmodern, lay version of peak-experience 'the this-worldly ecstasy'.

Obviously, it is no more the 'religious organizations', with their message of the perpetual insufficiency of man, who are best suited to 'communicate the peak-experience to non-peakers'. Whoever comes to replace it, must first and foremost abolish the concept of 'non-peakers' altogether and declare peak-experience a duty and a realistic prospect for everybody. 'You can do it.' 'Everybody can do it.' 'Whether you do it is entirely up to you.' 'If you fail to do it, you have only yourself to blame.' Second, having uncoupled the dream of peak-experience from religion-inspired practices of self-denial and withdrawal from worldly attractions, it must harness it to the desire of worldly goods and deploy it as the driving force of intense consumer activity. If the religious version of peak-experience used to reconcile the faithful to a life of misery and hardship, the postmodern version reconciles its followers to a life organized around the duty of an avid, perpetual, though never definitely gratifying consumption. The paragons and prophets of the postmodern version of peak-experience are recruited from the aristocracy of consumerism – those who managed to transform life into a work of the art of sensation-gathering and sensation-enhancement, thanks to consuming more than ordinary seekers of peak-experience, consuming more refined products and consuming them in a more sophisticated manner.

The promise of new, overwhelming, mind-boggling or spine-chilling, but always exhilarating experience, is the selling point of food, drinks, cars, cosmetics, spectacles or holiday packages. Each dangles the prospect of 'living through' sensations never experienced before and more intense than any tested before. Each new sensation must be 'greater', more overpowering and exciting than the one before, with the vertigo of 'total', peak, experience looming always on the horizon. It is hoped, and overtly or tacitly suggested, that moving along the road of quantitative accretion of sensual intensity one would arrive eventually at a qualitative breakthrough – at an experience not just more profound and enjoyable, but 'totally different'. And in that journey one would be helped by 'meta-experiential' goods and services – those aimed at the enhancement of psychic and bodily 'sensation-receiving' powers and skills. It is not just that more sublime pleasures ought to be offered – one needs also to learn how to squeeze the potential they contain, the potential that opens up in full solely to the past masters of the art of experiencing, the artists who know how to 'let themselves go' and who made their mind and body, through diligent training, fit to receive the full impact of the overwhelming sensation. The purpose of such training is provided by the metaphor of multiple orgasm: a fit body, served by an equally well-trained mind, is a body capable of repeated, even continuous, intensity of sensations, a body forever 'on the high', constantly open to all chances of experience which the world around may provide – a sort of *well-tempered clavier* always ready to emit tunes of sublime beauty.

It is such a 'meta-experiential' function which is performed today by numerous 'self-improvement' movements, deriving their seductive powers from the promise of developing the sensuous potential of the body through exercise, contemplation, self-concentration, breaking psychic blocks and convention-induced constraints, letting free the suppressed instincts or cleansing out hidden injuries, developing the skills of self-abandonment and passive submission of the 'flow' of sensations, or embracing the esoteric, best of all exotic, mysteries able to teach and guide all those efforts. The axiom which underpins all such movements is that experiencing, like all other human faculties, is above all a *technical* problem, and that acquiring the capacity for it is a matter of mastering the appropriate *techniques*. It goes without saying that any similarity between such movements and religious churches or sects is purely superficial, reduced at best to their organizational patterns. Rather than sharing their character with religious institutions, they are products and integral parts of the 'counselling boom' – though they are not, like other branches of counselling, meant to serve directly the consumer choices of assumedly fully fledged consumers, but are aimed rather at the training of 'perfect consumers'; at the developing to the full of the capacities which the experience-seeking and sensation-gathering life of the consumer/chooser demands.

Back to the future

There is, though, a specifically postmodern form of religion, born of the internal contradictions of postmodern life, of the specifically postmodern form in which the insufficiency of man and the vanity of dreams to take human fate under human control are revealed. This form has come to be known under the English name of *fundamentalism*, or the French name of *intégrisme*, and shows its ever more weighty presence all over the part of the world once dominated by the Christian, Islamic and Judaist religions.

I propose that the rise of a religiously dressed form of fundamentalism is not a hiccup of ostensibly long chased away yet not fully suppressed mystical cravings, not a manifestation of eternal human irrationality, immune to all healing and domesticating efforts, and not a form of escape back into the pre-modern past. Fundamentalism is a thoroughly contemporary, postmodern phenomenon, embracing fully the 'rationalizing' reforms and technological developments of modernity, and attempting not so much to 'roll back' modern departures, as to 'have one's cake and eat it' – make possible a full enjoyment of modern attractions without paying the price they demand. The price in question is the agony of the individual condemned to self-sufficiency, self-reliance and the life of never fully satisfying and trustworthy choice.

It is difficult not to agree with Gilles Kepel's diagnosis, that the present-day fundamentalist movements are

> true children of our time: unwanted children, perhaps, bastards of compu-
> terization and unemployment or of the population explosion and increasing
> literacy, and their cries and complaints in these closing years of the century
> spur us to seek out their parentage and to retrace their unacknowledged
> genealogy.
>   Like the workers' movements of yesteryear, today's religious movements
> have a singular capacity to reveal the ills of society, for which they have
> their own diagnosis.[19]

One needs to make it clear, however, that the 'ills diagnosed' are different from those once laid bare by the workers' movements, and thus the movements which diagnose them (which *are*, knowingly or unknowingly, their diagnosis) attract a different kind of converted and faithful. True, one should not play down the role of the traditional constituency – the deprived and the impoverished, whose ranks grow rather than shrink in the world of global free trade, where all stops have been pulled and all bars delegalized. Unlike in the case of the workers of yesteryear, though, the misery of the present-day deprived (the present-day form of the 'hidden injuries of class', to recall the apt phrase coined by Richard Sennett and Jonathan Cobb) appear to them (in most cases adequately) not as the outcome of exploitation, but as a result of having been left behind in the scramble for the entry tickets to the consumers' party. The poor of today are first and foremost *flawed consumers*, unable to take advantage of the treasures displayed tantalizingly within their reach, frustrated before the act, disqualified before even trying; while they are unfulfilled producers, or people cheated at the division of surplus value but a distant second.[20] It is this quality which makes them, potentially, a constituency from which fundamentalist movements, which are triggered and kept on course by above all the agonies of the postmodern, self-reliant by appointment, free agents, may draw its reserves. A message of human insufficiency, or resentment of self-sufficiency, incubating in the bitter experience of fully fledged postmodern consumers, may be telling also to their differently tuned ears.

The bitter experience in question is the experience of *freedom*: of the misery of life composed of risky choices, which always mean taking some chances while forfeiting others, or incurable uncertainty built into every choice, of the unbearable, because unshared, responsibility for the unknown consequences of every choice, of the constant fear of foreclosing the future and yet unforeseen possibilities, of the dread of personal inadequacy, of experiencing less and not as strongly as others perhaps do, of the nightmare of being not up to the new and improved formulae of life which the notoriously capricious future may bring. And the message arising from that experience is: no, the human *individual* is not self-sufficient and cannot be self-reliant. One cannot go by one's own judgement; one needs to be guided, and directed, and told what to do. This is a message of insufficiency; but, unlike the message carried by pre-modern religion, it is not the message of the weakness of the human *species* – but of the irreparable weakness of the human *individual*, compared to the human species' omnipotence.

In this respect, fundamentalism brings into the open the underground anxiety and premonition normal and well-nigh universal under the postmodern condition. It gives public expression to what many people suspect all along although they are authoritatively told not to believe or led not to think of it. On the other hand, the framework of life offered by fundamentalism merely brings to its radical conclusion the cult of specialist counselling and guidance and the preoccupation with expert-assisted self-drill, both of which the postmodern consumer culture daily promotes. In this respect, fundamentalism is the supreme (though radically simplified) embodiment of a tendency aided and abetted by the whole thrust of postmodern culture. One may conclude that religious fundamentalism is a legitimate child of postmodernity, born of its joys and torments, and heir to its achievements and worries alike.

The allure of fundamentalism stems from its promise to emancipate the converted from the agonies of choice. Here one finds, finally, the indubitably *supreme* authority, an authority to end all other authorities. One knows where to look when life-decisions are to be made, in matters big and small, and one knows that looking there one does the right thing and so is spared the dread of risk-taking. Fundamentalism is a radical remedy against that bane of postmodern/market-led/consumer society – risk-contaminated freedom (a remedy that heals the infection by amputating the infected organ – abolishing freedom as such, in as far as there is no freedom free of risks). Fundamentalism promises to develop all the infinite powers of the group which – when deployed in full – would compensate for the incurable insufficiency of its individual members, and therefore justify the unquestionable subordination of individual choices to the rules proclaimed in the group's name.

Islamic *intégrisme* of ayatollahs or Muslim Brothers' style, the Lubavich sect of the present-day Chassidic movement, evangelist churches of the Bible Belt, belong to a wider family of postmodern responses to those postmodern fears which have been visited upon the individuals *qua* individuals by the progressive deregulation and privatization of all 'secular' insurance/protection nets, once state-provided through the entitlements of state citizenship. In a world in which all ways of life are allowed, yet none is safe, they muster enough courage to tell those who are eager to listen what to decide so that the decision will remain safe and stand up in all courts that matter. In this respect, religious fundamentalism belongs to a wider family of totalitarian or proto-totalitarian solutions offered to all those who find the burden of individual freedom excessive and unbearable. Apart from religious fundamentalism, that family includes many forms of ethnic, race-oriented, or tribal fundamentalisms, all constituted in opposition to the secular state and to the indiscriminate and non-discriminating (denigrated as 'abstract') citizenship, which come now to replace the by-and-large discredited political totalitarian movements (like communism or fascism) – thoroughly modern (or pre-postmodern) in their appeal to state-managed solutions and the state legislative and ordering powers.

Far from being an outburst of pre-modern irrationality, religious fundamentalism, much like the self-proclaimed ethnic revivals, is an offer of an *alternative rationality*, made to the measure of genuine problems besetting the members of postmodern society. Like all rationalities, it selects and divides; and what it selects differs from the selection accomplished by the deregulated market forces – which does not make it less rational (or more irrational) than the market-orientated logic of action. If the market-type rationality is subordinated to the promotion of freedom of choice and thrives on the uncertainty of choice-making situations, the fundamentalist rationality puts security and certainty first and condemns everything that undermines that certainty – the vagaries of individual freedom first and foremost. In its fundamentalist rendition, religion is not a 'personal matter', privatized as all other individual choices and practised in private, but the nearest thing to a *compleat mappa vitae*: it legislates in no uncertain terms about every aspect of life, thereby unloading the burden of responsibility lying heavily on the individual's shoulders – those shoulders that postmodern culture proclaims, and market publicity promotes, as omnipotent, but many people find much too weak for the burden.

Religious fundamentalism, Kepel has suggested, has 'a singular capacity to reveal the ills of society'. How true. With the market-induced agony of solitude and abandonment as its only alternative, fundamentalism, religious or otherwise, can count on an ever growing constituency. Whatever the quality of the answers it supplies, the questions which it answers are genuine. The problem is not how to dismiss the gravity of the questions, but how to find answers free from totalitarian genes.

14

On Communitarianism and Human Freedom, or How to Square the Circle

In the Spring 1994 (vol. 8, no. 2) issue of *Critical Review* a number of prominent political philosophers published their thoughts on the chances of embracing the liberal and communitarian principles in one coherent, non-contradictory system of thought. Since on the occasion virtually all the arguments most favoured by each of the two sides have been rehearsed, restated and summarized, this collection of statements offers an excellent starting point for the consideration of moot issues, stakes and prospects of the ongoing liberal/communitarian *querelle*.

The exchange was prompted by the publication of Will Kymlicka's *Liberalism, Community and Culture* (Oxford: Clarendon Press, 1991) – 'a penetrating, highly illuminating, and exceptionally lucid book' as Ronald Beiner (himself the author of another influential study, *What's the Matter with Liberalism?* (University of California Press, 1992)) writes, and other writers agree. What, in their opinion, made Kymlicka's book so interesting and worthy of extended comment is that it confronted point-blank the arguments raised against the liberal theory by the most influential spokesmen of communitarianism (thinkers like Alasdair MacIntyre, Michael Sandel, Charles Taylor or Michael Walzer) with the intention to defuse such arguments by either showing that their opposition to liberal tenets is wholly illusory, or by accommodating them into a 'new and improved' version of liberalism; as well as the book's overall peace-making tone, its underlying conviction – refreshing and welcome after years of acrimony – that short of merger and unity, at least a lasting truce and friendly cohabitation between adversaries are feasible.

Among Kymlicka's propositions, the one his commentators like most (though some, on the communitarian side of the argument, think it is not going far enough to cure liberalism of its ills – to whit, making it more communitarian-minded) is that, in fact, the plurality of cultures and cultural allegiances is something which liberalism, far from frowning upon, considers an asset: as cultures multiply, so do the choices open to the individual, and liberalism is all about freedom of choice. The liberal, therefore – so Kymlicka suggests – should be interested in actively promoting variety and resisting all homogenizing pressures.

Why this opinion is seen as 'highly illuminating' by the reviewers seems at first glance to be something of a mystery, since on the same ground cultural (even moral) pluralism has been defended and praised by foremost liberal thinkers for a long time now.[1] Perhaps, however, the excitement is less mysterious than it seems; the arguments, stated in liberal thought in a generalized and thus relatively uncontroversial and inoffensive form, Kymlicka extended as an olive branch to the communitarian critics of liberalism. By the same token, he suggested that the repeatedly declared liberal devotion to difference may be stretched far enough to embrace the kind of difference which the communitarians promote and so renders their charges against liberal thought null and void. In order to do so, Kymlicka gives the liberal call for variety a wording meant to placate the communitarian grievances without offending the liberal conscience: 'Liberals should be concerned with the fate of cultural structures, not because they have some moral status of their own, but because it's only through having a rich and secure cultural structure that people can become aware, in a vivid way, of the options available to them.' So the liberals may stay happy, since the 'cultural structure' now, as before, has not been recognized as a finite value in its own right; but the communitarians may feel appeased, since whatever their motives, liberals promise to respect and even promote the kind of difference so dear to the communitarian heart. (They manage to do so by imputing to the 'cultural structure' an instrumental value in promoting liberal goals.) The communitarian joy may well be rendered even more complete by the hand-on-hip acceptance, by a liberal writer, of what they used to aver all along as an argument *against* liberalism – namely, that 'having a rich and secure cultural structure' is a good and humane thing. (They may be worried, though, as well as baffled, by a surprising suggestion that a 'secure structure' is a good thing because it prompts the awareness of options – but then what it does or does not promote is an empirical statement, not an issue of policy, and thus may be quietly left to future quarrels between social-scientific archivists. And if this is how the liberals prefer, for the sake of convenience, to couch their surrender, why should the people whose point has been thereby granted object?)

It seems that Kymlicka's stratagem is to get both sides to agree on a joint policy statement through making each believe that not only has the pursuit of their goals not been compromised, but that the signing of the agreement testifies to the intention of going on pursuing them to yet better effect.

This is, however, glossing over the genuine bone of contention, not resolving the controversy. The difference loved (or declared to be loved) by the liberals is not the difference loved (or declared to be loved) by the communitarians. All similarities, one is tempted to say, are purely coincidental . . . The difference the liberals esteem and hold dear is external to the human individual; 'difference' stands here for the profusion of choices between various ways of being human and living one's life. The difference for which the communitarians clamour is of the internalized kind; 'difference' stands here for the refusal, or inability, to consider other forms of life as options – for being *determined* or *fated* to remain what one is, to stay this way whatever happens, and resist all temptation to the contrary. To put it in a nutshell, the liberal 'difference' stands for individual freedom, while the communitarian 'difference' stands for the group's power to *limit* individual freedom. What the communitarians' postulate amounts to is a licence for groups to exercise such power without interference.

The communitarian theorists, notably MacIntyre, complain about the skin-deep, volatile and insecure nature of the identities obtainable under the liberal regime of free choice and 'disentrenchment' of formative structures. They hanker after identities which are neither phony nor shallow (that is – to deploy Weber's metaphor – identities more like iron cages than cloaks lying lightly on the individual's shoulders), which they, for reasons not at all obvious, yet never argued explicitly, consider equivalent to the *meaningful* identity. Again for reasons not at all clear and even less convincing, the communitarians want the outcome of the choice to be settled before the act of choosing takes off: to a communitarian mind, a good choice is a choice of what is already given (exactly what Barrès or Fichte used to say about nationality) – the discovery and giving conscious expression to 'historical identity' transmitted through birth. (This time one may recall Mao's understanding of the once famous policy of 'let a hundred flowers bloom'; the blooming was innocuous to Mao in as far as there was certainty that one flower, the sole one deserving to bloom forever, would overwhelm and stifle all the others.) The tribute paid to individual choice is here no more than lip service. Ideally, freedom ought to be employed solely to choose unfreedom; voluntariness here means using individual volition to abstain from exercising free will. The true choice has been made and signed before the individual's birth. The life that follows the birth is (should be) all about finding out what that choice was, and behaving accordingly.

Communitarian theory (just like liberalism, for that matter) is a *modern* ideology, constructed and preached under modern conditions – that is, under the circumstances when choice is not only a possibility, but a reality difficult to escape from; modern individuals are 'sentenced' to a lifetime of choosing. And so the communitarian hints about the irretriev- ably 'encumbered' nature of individual identity stop short of developing a fully fledged theory of ascriptive determinism. Communitarian-style determinism is not automatic; paradoxically, its work cannot be com- pleted without an active role played by human will and choice. Fate runs its full course only when willingly (joyfully!) embraced by the fated individual. But admitting this, the communitarian philosophy places willy-nilly the communities of tradition and history it promotes at one footing with all other 'groups of belonging' (including those in direct or oblique competition with 'rooted' reference groups); all such groups 'hold' their members only as far as the members 'stick' to them; the perpetuation of all such groups depends on the intensity and resilience of their members' active allegiance. It is therefore risky to leave the destiny of the favoured, 'rooted' reference groups ('communities of tradition') to the vagaries of open competition. One would much prefer to have the favourable outcome of the competition guaranteed in advance – but this means *privileging* one choice over all the others; making the odds against other choices overwhelming, and increasing the stakes entailed in making the 'right' choice. At this point, though, communitarianism leaves the ostensibly philosophical discussion of human existential predicament to enter the realm of practical politics.

The paradox is not new, of course, and not of the communitarians' making. It has haunted from the start modern nationalism, of which the present-day communitarianism is, so to speak, a discontinuous continu- ation (racism was then, as it is now, a constantly tempting path of escape from the paradox which nationalism and communitarianism share). Maurice Barrès, one of the most insightful and influential philosophers of nationalism, struggled with the same problem: nationalist beliefs are pointless without an assumption, that there is a point 'from which all things can be seen in true proportions' – but also without the premise that this point cannot be designed, but only found, recovered or lost; this must be a point fixed *beforehand* – but (and here comes the crux) it must be yet dug up and fortified by each individual, using his skills, reason and will. In other words, the human lot is *inevitable*, but this inevitability of fate works through *voluntary* efforts . . .

I must place myself at the point demanded by my eyes, as they have been formed in the course of centuries, at the point from which all things make themselves to the Frenchman's measure. The assembly of just and true relations between the objects and the concrete man, the Frenchman, are French truth and justice: to discover these relations is French reason. Pure nationalism is nothing else than being aware of such a point's existence, searching it, and – having reached it – clinging to it in our arts, our politics, and all our activities.[2]

We know where this lyrical encomium of the roots has pointed to, with an irresistible momentum of its own: to an overwhelming urge to *make sure* that the 'I must' means what it says, that the 'discovery' is made by everybody, and that everyone 'clings' to what has been discovered in 'all activities'. And there was but one way of making sure: using the state prerogative of legislated coercion to render 'missing the point' as unlikely as possible, and 'finding the point' virtually inescapable. The nation without a state would be, after all, just one 'reference group' among many – like them forever uncertain of its survival, like them buffeted by cross-waves of changing fashions, like them having to appeal daily to flickery loyalties, and like them having to lean over backwards to deliver proofs of the advantage of its benefits over the offers of the competitors. The nation-state (the idea of a nation made into the state's flesh) could, on the other hand, *legislate* for loyalty and determine in advance the results of free choice. The postulated roots could be legislated into existence and taken care of by the state agencies of law and order, the state-defined canon of cultural heritage and the state-authorized curriculum of history teaching.

Let us recall that the purpose of all that was to put paid to the grip in which 'communities' (*local* traditions, customs, dialects, loyalties) held the would-be patriots of the one and indivisible nation. The idea guiding all these efforts of the nation-state was to superimpose one kind of allegiance over the mosaic of communitarian 'particularisms' in the name of the nation's interest which overrides and puts in abeyance all other interests, including what this or that individual might believe was his or her 'own', individual, interest. In terms of practical politics, this meant the dismantling or legal disempowering of all *pouvoirs intermédiaires*, of the self-government of any such unit less than the nation-state as claimed to be more than the executor of the nation-state's will, and claimed more than delegated power.

From Charles Taylor's contribution to the *Critical Review* debate we learn that, after all these (as it transpired later, inconclusive) efforts of national unification, 'minority communities' are 'struggling to maintain themselves'. They struggle to maintain themselves, that is, as *communities*. And this means in turn that 'these people are striving for more than their rights as individuals'. Taylor is undaunted by the fact that it is only thanks to the old stratagem of *petitio principii* that his statement makes sense: what was to be proved has been entered as an axiomatic premise. If there is something more than the 'rights as individuals' (that is, if there is something so important that it justifies the suspension of the rights of individuals *qua* individuals), then, of course, struggle is inevitable and any benevolent person owes the fighters sympathy and assistance. But what is that 'something more'?

'Something more' (let us repeat: that 'something' which makes certain restrictions of the individual right to choose palatable and even welcome) is the 'goal of *survivance*'; and this means in turn 'the continuance of the community through future generations'. Put in simpler, and above all *practical*, terms, the pursuit of the 'goal of survivance' calls for the right of the community to limit or pre-empt the choices of younger and not-yet-born generations, to decide for them what their choices should be like. In other words, what is demanded here is the power of enforcement, the power to make sure that people would act in a certain way rather than in other ways, to taper the range of their options, to manipulate the probabilities; to make them do what they otherwise would probably not do (if they would, why all this fuss?), to make them less free than they would otherwise be.

Why is it important to do so? Taylor points out that this is to be done in people's own well-understood interest, since 'human beings can only make meaningful choices of their way of life against a background of alternatives which can only come to them through the language and cultural tradition of their society'. A similar idea was expressed over and over again by the generations of prophets and court poets of states acting in the name of majority nations, and it is not immediately obvious why under Taylor's pen it should be an argument in favour of the 'struggling minorities' cause. For the change of address to become justified, one needs first to reveal a hidden corollary: namely, the realization that the nation-state has not delivered on its promise, that for one reason or another it is now bankrupt as a fount of 'meaningful choice of the way of life', that nationalism devoid of its state foundation has lost the authority without which the overriding of individual rights of choice is neither feasible nor felt acceptable, and that in the resulting void it is the 'struggling minorities' which are now believed to be the second line of trenches where 'meaningful choice' can be protected from slaughter; it is now hoped that they will succeed in the task which the nation-state has definitely failed to perform.

The striking similarity between the nationalist and the communitarian hopes and paradoxes is not at all accidental. Both 'future perfect' visions are, after all, the philosophers' reactions to the widespread experience of acute and abrupt 'disembeddedment', caused by the accelerated collapse of the frames in which identities were habitually inscribed. Nationalism was the response to the wholesale destruction of the 'cottage industry of identities', and the ensuing devaluation of the locally (and matter-of-factly) produced and endorsed patterns of life. The nationalist vision arose from the desperate hope that clarity and security of existence can be rebuilt at a higher, supra-local level of social organization, around the national membership and state citizenship melted into one. For reasons too vast and numerous to be listed here, that hope failed to come true. The nation-state proved to be the incubator of a modern society ruled not so much by the unity of feelings as by the diversity of unemotional market interests. Its thorough job of uprooting local loyalties looks in retrospect not so much like a production of higher-level identities, but like a site-clearing operation for the market-led confidence game of quickly assembled and even faster dismantled modes of self-description.

And so, once more, 'meaningful' identities ('meaningful' in the sense once postulated by nationalists, now by the communitarians) are hard to come by, while keeping them in place and intact, for however brief a moment, taxes the taught and learned juggling skills of the individuals far beyond their capacity. Since the idea that 'society' institutionalized in the state will lend a helping hand does not hold much water now, it is no wonder that eyes shift in a different direction. By an irony of history, however, they drift towards entities whose radical destruction were seen since the beginning of modernity as the condition *sine qua non* of 'meaningful choice'. It is now the much-maligned 'natural communities of origin', *necessarily lesser than the nation-state*, once described by modernizing propaganda (not without reason) as parochial, backwater, prejudice-ridden, oppressive and stultifying, which are looked to hopefully as the trusty executors of that streamlining, derandomizing, meaning-saturating of human choices which the nation-state abominably failed to bring forth.

There is no denying that the life of a free agent is not all roses. The torments, which the critics of life no more securely founded in ascription try to capture in the image of 'shallow and meaningless identity', are genuine. The torments are many, but they all boil down to the noxious, painful and sickening feeling of perpetual uncertainty in everything regarding *the future*. The fast and continuously accelerating pace of change makes one thing certain: that the future will not be like the present. But the quick succession of futures dissolving into a succession of presents also teaches as well – beyond reasonable doubt – that today's present (at least its subjectively mastered, 'domesticated' and 'tamed' part) does not bind the future, that tomorrow's present – and so there is little the individual can do today to make sure that the results he or she wishes to hold tomorrow will be achieved. Living in a *Risikogesellschaft* (the extremely apt term coined by Ulrich Beck), we may say, rebounds in personal experience as *Risikoleben*. As Ulrich Beck and Elisabeth Beck Gernsheim put it, 'certainties have fragmented into questions which are now spinning around in people's heads. But it is more than that. Social action needs routines in which to be enacted.' But it is

> precisely this level of pre-conscious 'collective habitualizations' of matters taken for granted, that is breaking down into a cloud of possibilities to be thought about and negotiated. The deep layer of foreclosed decisions is being forced up into the level of decision-making. Hence the irritation, the endless chafing of the open wound – and the defensive-aggressive reaction . . . Life loses its self-evident quality.[3]

Trying to grasp the infuriatingly evasive identity, demanded with the same superhuman power as it is denied, individuals fight a losing battle. Hence the irritation that punctuates and poisons the delights of their successive avatars. What makes the prospect of a radical cure dimmer still is the fact that individuals, torn between intoxicating freedom and horrifying uncertainty, desire the impossible; they want no less than eating their cake and having it – relishing and practising their freedom of choice while having the 'happy end' guaranteed and the results insured. Whatever name they select to call their worry, what individuals truly resent is the risk innate in freedom; however they describe their dreams, what they desire is a *risk-free freedom*. The trouble is, however, that freedom and risk grow and diminish only together. Thus the ultimate solution to the plight of the modern individual is not on the cards.

Pseudo-solutions, on the other hand, abound, thanks to an inexhaustible demand for straightening out the twisted loop of contradictory pains and desires. At times when the continuous uncertainty is, dramatically, pushed a notch or two further, the dream of homely security prevails over the allure of adventure. This happened at the onset of the modern restructuring of structures and re-evaluation of values, paving the way to the early success of the nationalist promise of homely tranquillity. This is happening again today, with the onset of the postmodern stage of the modern revolution – with the radical change in the rules by which the game of livelihood is played, with the thorough redefinition of all particular, acquired skills and of the meaning of skill as such, with the disavowal of the habitualized patterns of partnership and the devaluation of the social know-how which that pattern required – and is paving the way for the sudden popularity of communitarianism, that 'nationalism mark two'.

Admittedly, the old-fashioned nationalism is far from having run its course, particularly in the post-colonial world, in Africa or in Eastern

Europe, among the debris left by the collapsing capitalist or communist empires alike. There, the idea of a nation providing a home for the lost and the confused is still fresh and, above all, untried. It is all in the future (even if nationalism, just like communitarianism, deploys with gusto the language of heritage, roots and shared past), and the future is the natural place in which to invest one's hopes and cravings. For Europe (with the exception of its currently post-colonial part), on the other hand, nationalism together with its crowning achievement, the nation-state, lies fairly and squarely in the past. It failed to resolve in the past what once more is to be resolved now, and it would be foolish to expect that the second time around it will perform any better. Europe knows too what the post-colonial world does not know or does not care much about: that the closer the nation-state's works approach the ideal of solid foundations and a secure home, the less freedom there is to move around or out of the house, and the air inside the house gets rank and foul. For these, and for other reasons which I have tried to explain elsewhere,[4] nothing which the present-day nation-states are used, able or willing to do seems adequate to the anguish of uncertainty which devours the psychic resources of the postmodern individual.

Under the circumstances, what makes the visions of 'natural community' conjured up in communitarian writings so attractive is, above all, the fact that it has been imagined independently from, and even in opposition to, the state. It looks as if the state, in resonance with popular feelings, has been abandoned by communitarian philosophers to the 'risk-producing' side of human existence: it takes care of freedom, but in so doing it leaves individuals to their patently inadequate resources in their struggle to navigate among the risks of freedom in order to sail into the haven of 'meaningful choice'. As once the nation did, so now the 'natural community' stands for that dream of a safe heaven. This haven is located away from the explored itineraries, having been moved to places which lonely sailors were discouraged from visiting. However eager the communitarians are to 'root' such places in a genuine or invented premodern past, it is the modern spirit of adventure, of exploring the unexplored, of trying the untried, which makes them attractive to the philosophers and their readers alike. Perhaps this time . . .

The 'community' of the communitarian philosophers is expected to enchant and attract for the same reason that the nations of the nationalist philosophers once did: for their homely cosiness, the promise of mutual support and understanding, the harmony of interests, the unity of desires. Once more, the dilemma as old as modernity itself is left out of account or glossed over:

- either 'community' is a *result* of individual choices, an entity made and freely chosen (in Roberto Unger's words – 'accidental, made up, pasted together' as the result of unpredictable coalitions, unforeseen conse- quences, and missed opportunities),[5] and thus their very existence, and the choices of loyalty which sustain that existence, are incurably burdened with the same anxieties of risk-taking as all other aspects of life of the thoroughly individualized persons acting under the condi- tion of permanent uncertainty;
- or this 'community' *precedes* all choice, in the sense of *a priori* predisposing the individuals to stay loyal to its values and behavioural precepts (through indoctrination, drill, control) – and thus the commu- nity membership comes into direct conflict with the individual freedom of self-constitution, self-assertion and self-definition.

This dilemma signals a trade-off situation; the value acquired and cherished needs to be sacrificed in order to gain the value missed. But the homely cosiness of no-choice owes its allure solely to the hardships of daily freedom. Without that freedom, the plight of no-choice has all the attraction of prison life.

Today this dilemma remains as genuine and unsolved as it ever was, and no amount of argument is likely to square this particular circle. It preoccupies the philosophers, but it also saturates the experience of the postmodern individual reiterated daily in a world which is fragmented, episodic and hostile to consistent, consequential action; the individual burdened with the task of daily choices and the daily task of getting the choices 'confirmed' and validated among the cacophony of contradictory and ephemeral ideals and precepts. Such an experience gestates an acute need of reassurance, which in contemporary society is sought in two kinds of authority – the authority of the experts, or the authority of numbers.

There is today a proliferation of analysts, advisers and counsellors basking in the glory of the 'latest word' of science, as well as of the teach- yourself textbooks they produce; their overall message is: 'Choose, but choose wisely.' And there is the reassurance derived from the awareness that many 'others like me' share my predicament and choose similar 'solutions' to similar 'problems'. Here, the message is: 'Choose what others have chosen, and you cannot go wrong.' Between themselves, the two authorities draw a line separating the torments of individuality from the agony of madness.

It is the search for the second kind of authority, that of numbers, which sediments the 'neo-tribes' (or, more precisely, *postulated* tribes) – wholes which in the last account (and contrary to their promise) seldom prove to be more than the sum of their parts, and whose imputed authority is measured by the determination of each part to make sums. Such 'neo-tribes' are products of multiple choices and are no more durable than the choices which made them – as long, that is, as the choosers retain their freedom of choosing, so that they are free to revoke their decision when the need arises. Neo-tribes, conjured up with the intention of giving those choices that solidity the choosers sorely miss, share in the *inconsequentiality* of choices, and change little in the episodicity of the chooser's life.

These are the problems which haunt those who are in a position to choose. Freedom of choice is, however, a graduated quality; indeed, it has become a major (arguably *the* major) stratifying variable in our multi-dimensionally stratified society. In the postmodern/consumer society choosing is everybody's *fate*, but the ranges of *realistic choices* differ, and so do the supplies of *resources* needed to make them. It is the individual *responsibility* for choice that is equally distributed, not the individually owned *means* to act on that responsibility. Notoriously, casting everyone equally into the situation of the 'chooser by necessity' does not promote equality of the practical ability to choose. For all we know, the effect is exactly the opposite. As Jerzy Jedlicki pointed out, what the liberal vision of the universal and equally awarded right to choose failed to take account of, is that 'adding freedom of action to the fundamental inequality of social condition will result in inequality yet deeper than before'.[6] What liberal society offers with one hand, it tends to take back with the other; the duty of freedom without the resources that permit a truly free choice is for many a recipe for life without dignity, filled instead with humiliation and self-deprecation.

This is all too real a problem in a society organized around liberal principles, and one which the communitarians purport to assault and tackle. Yet the problem consists in matching the practical ability to choose against the requirements imposed on individuals by the necessity of choosing; while the communitarians propose, instead, to heal the painful consequences of the mismatch not by raising the rights to the level of the possibilities which the condition of freedom entails *in potentia*, but by making a virtue out of the restrictions imposed on the exercising of the right to choose, and thus to make the actualization of that potential of freedom still more difficult. As so often in the practice of social engineering, the medicine proposed has every chance of rendering the ailment more acute.

'Values are more important than the rights of individuals', or the task of 'survivance' which ought to take precedence over individual entitlements, are slogans which appeal to the humane conscience, and have every right to trouble the liberal complacency, as long as they come from the deprived quarters which agonize over their lack of the possibility of choosing in a society in which being an individual is tantamout to being a free chooser, yet practical freedom of choice is a privilege, and as long as these slogans are deployed as reminders that the job of freedom-promotion is far from complete and that its completion will require doing something to rectify the present distribution of resources which deprives large sectors of would-be individuals from exercising their individuality. It is, however, all too easy to overlook the fact that, apart from being effective 'bargaining points' in the legitimate struggle for the redistribution of resources serving individual freedom, these slogans carry a proposition which, if accepted uncritically, will have exactly the opposite effect: namely, the curtailing of that freedom. Ronald Beiner justly points out that, in his zeal to accommodate the communitarian postulates in the liberal promotion of freedom, Kymlicka 'does not fully face up to the fact that what he is advocating as an entailment of liberalism is assistance for a community to fend off liberalization of its way of life'. One recalls willy-nilly the Soviet rulers' proposition that the ultimate communist goal of the abolition of the state was to be achieved through radically increasing the coercive power of the state. And one recalls also the consequences of that particular instance of double-think.

Philosophical well-wishers on both sides of the liberal/communitarian divide are all too often blackmailed or cowed to courteously close their eyes to the realities of those 'minorities' whose cause they are prompted to advocate by their laudable sympathy for the left-behind and deprived. But all too often the reality, when contemplated at close quarters, and particularly from inside, looks rather unprepossessing. More often than not the 'survivance' postulate turns into an awesome weapon of sub-jugation and tyranny, exercised by the sometimes acclaimed, more often self-proclaimed, guardians of the 'community' (ethnic, racial, religious) traditional values in order to exact obeisance from their hapless wards and to stamp out every inkling of an autonomous choice. The values of rights and freedom, dear to the liberal heart, are appealed to promote the demotion of individual rights and the denial of freedom. 'Minorities' are products of the illiberal practices of the state; but they are all-too-fit to be deployed in the service of the illiberal practices of the 'community leaders'.

Communitarianism is not a remedy for the inherent defects of liberal-ism. The contradiction between them is genuine, and no amount of philosophical gymnastics may heal it. Both communitarianism and liber-alism are projections of dreams born of the real contradiction inherent in the plight of autonomous individuals. Each one is but a one-sided projection, which for the sake of its own coherence tends to gloss over the fact that none of the virtues of the individual's plight may survive the elimination of its banes. For better or worse, the life of the autonomous individual cannot but be navigated between the two equally unattractive extremes, and this navigation demands that freedom is accepted together with the risks it carries. Steering clear of the temptation of sacrificing freedom in the name of the risk-free condition is all the chance of meaningful and dignified life human individuals may reasonably hope for, however much the philosophers do to bar them from facing that truth.

Afterword: The Last Word – and it Belongs to Freedom

There are winners and losers in every game. In the game called freedom, though, the difference tends to be blurred or obliterated altogether. The losers are consoled by the hope of a win next time, while the joy of the winners is clouded by the premonition of loss. To both, freedom means that nothing has been settled for ever and that the wheel of fortune may yet turn around. The vagaries of fate make both the winners and the losers feel uncertain; but uncertainty conveys different messages to different people: it tells the losers that not everything has been lost yet, while whispering to the winners that all triumphs tend to be precarious. In the game called freedom the losers stop short of despair and the winners stop short of self-assurance. Both sides have a stake in freedom – and both have reasons to complain. Neither side would take the curtailment of freedom lightly – yet neither is totally deaf to the allurements of certainty, which promises to cure the pains of freedom by killing the patient.

The experience of those engaged in the game called freedom is as uncertain, contingent and inconclusive as their fate. It brings joy and sorrow; it feeds solidarity and selfishness; it promotes love of change and its hate. It is this ambivalence of fate and the contradictory attitudes it nourishes that prompts many an observer (see for instance 'Un monde sans cap' by Ignacio Ramone, in *Le Monde diplomatique* of October 1995) to speak of the 'crisis of intelligibility'; the roots of the experiential ambivalence are traced to the collapse of order at all its theorized levels – global, national, institutional, environmental – and to the absence of a vision of a good society able to command a universal or near-universal consent. We lack the conceptual means – so it is being said – to straighten out the convoluted and straggly picture, to conjure up a cohesive model from the confused and incoherent experience, to string together the scattered beads of events. Indeed, if what we are after is the logic of things (read: determination of things, their *a priori* destination, certainty of the end obtained before the beginning) then 'the laws of the market' are a poor substitute for 'the laws of nature' or 'the laws

of history', let alone 'the law of progress'. No wonder that the ambivalence of experience and the resulting incoherence of desires and attitudes
are projected as the débâcle of the world order and the failure of
intellectual nerve and understanding.

One wonders, though. One wonders what conceptual means are
needed (and what conceptual means would suffice) to return the exiled
and homesick thinkers back to the Lost Paradise of certainty. Were not
'the laws of history' so cosily obvious, so easy to spot and to spell out,
thanks to the presence of powers bent on *making* history law-abiding
and determined to state the laws by which it would have to abide? Was
not 'the law of progress' so much in evidence thanks to powers sufficiently skilful, resourceful and unscrupulous or callous to make the
'progressive' live and spread and the 'backward' shrink and die? Was it
not the case that laws of history and progress came to rule thought when
such powers came to rule the world? And is it not the case that, short of
the return of such powers, the modern certainty of progress and, more
generally, of historical direction, are unlikely to rise from the postmodern
ashes?

For numerous reasons, the restoration of modern certainty is not on
the cards. For better, or for worse? The argument is likely to be endless
and in all probability inconclusive, all the indubitable attractions of
certainty notwithstanding; and not because it is not clear whether the
benefits of certainty's vanishing act do or do not balance the losses, but
because too many people have learnt the costs of the war against
ambivalence and the price to be paid for the comforts of certainty, and
because too many people have had their fingers (and not only fingers!)
singed in the process and are wary of bearing those costs once more. If
history proves anything, it has proved – and abundantly – one thing,
which any future balancing of accounts must bear in mind. As Odo
Marquard, the author of *Apologie des Zufälligen* (1987) and *Abschied vom
Prinzipiellen* (1991) put it in his own inimitable way: 'If – regarding a
holy text – two interpreters, contradicting each other, assert: I am right,
my understanding of the text is the truth, and a truth imperative for
salvation – it may come to a fight.' But if they agree instead that 'the text
can be understood in a different way and, if this is not enough, in
another way, and yet another' – they may rather start to negotiate – 'and
who negotiates, does not kill'. The 'pluralizing hermeneutics', unlike the
'singularizing hermeneutics', augurs a 'being towards the text' in lieu of
the 'being towards murder'.

History is fraught with mass murders committed in the name of the
one and only truth. (The latter expression is a pleonasm, to be sure: truth
can either be 'one and only' or untrue; the idea of truth needs to be

resorted to and is resorted to when the falsehood of all other beliefs is implied; 'truth' in the plural is a contradiction in terms.) It is hard to point out, though, a single case of a cruel deed perpetrated in the name of plurality and tolerance. The intrepid conquerors of the infidels, the cardinals of the Holy Inquisition, the commanders of religious wars were no more notorious for their relativism and love of plurality than Hitler or Stalin. And yet one hears again and again that 'If there is no God, everything is allowed', though one learns from history that the opposite is the case: if there is God, then there is no cruelty, however atrocious, which is not allowed to be committed in His name. And, most crucially, it is not then the human perpetrators of cruelty who bear responsibility, and thus fear to be censured by their conscience for the atrocity committed.

We are not engaged here in a theological dispute about the existence or non-existence of God. In what has been said above (and, more importantly, in the political as much as philosophical use/abuse of his name) 'God' stands for the idea of the 'one and only', for the 'thou shalt have no other gods before me' idea in all its countless renditions and costumes: of *Ein Volk, ein Reich, ein Führer*, of one party, one verdict of history, one line of progress, one way of being human, one (scientific) ideology, one true meaning, one proper philosophy. In all such cases 'one and only' conveys the one and only message: the right to the monopoly of power for some, the duty of total obedience for others.

It is solely in the struggle against such one-and-onliness that the human individual, and the human individual as a moral subject, a responsible subject and a subject taking responsibility for his responsibility, may be born. 'Variety,' says Marquard, 'exactly variety, is the chance of human freedom.' Marquard uses the etymological kinship of the German *Zweifel* (doubt) with *zwei* (two): the presence of *two* (or more) beliefs – which through their controversy lose much of their force – allows the human being 'as a laughing or crying Third, to emancipate from the power of each'. It is beneficial for the individual *qua* individual 'to have many convictions', 'to have many traditions and histories, and many souls – oh! – in one's breast', 'to have many gods and many orientation points'.

If monotheism means unfreedom, freedom born of polytheistic reality does not, contrary to its detractors, mean nihilism. To be free does not mean believing in nothing; what it does mean is believing in too many things – too many for the spiritual comfort of blind obedience; it means being aware that there are too many equally important or convincing beliefs for the assumption of a careless or nihilistic attitude to the task of responsible choice between them; and to know that no choice would save the chooser from the responsibility for its consequences – and that therefore having chosen does not mean having settled the matter of choice once and for all, nor the right to put one's conscience to rest.

The voice of conscience – the voice of responsibility – is audible, as it were, only in the discord of uncoordinated tunes. Consensus and unanimity augur the tranquillity of the graveyard (Habermas's 'perfect communication', which measures its own perfection by consensus and the exclusion of dissent, is another dream of death which radically cures the ills of freedom's life); it is in the graveyard of universal consensus that responsibility and freedom and the individual exhale their last sigh.

The voice of responsibility is the birth-cry of the human individual. Its audibility is the sign of the individual's life. Not necessarily, though, is it a sign of a happy life – if happiness means the absence of worries (a highly debatable, though widely popular, definition of happiness, to be sure). The acceptance of responsibility does not come easy – not just because it ushers in the torments of choice (which always entails forfeiting something as well as gaining something else), but also because it heralds the perpetual anxiety of being – who knows? – in the wrong.

And so the freedom of the free, the individuality of the individual are threatened not only by the power-holders. The latter support individual freedom as the noose supports the hanged man – the individual taking responsibility in his/her own hands is every power's nightmare. Power-holders, current and *in spe*, recognize but one form of their subjects' responsibility: to be responsible, in the language of power, is to follow the command, while 'to have power' means, in essence, taking away someone else's right to any other responsibility, that is their freedom. The trouble, however, does not end here. Forces eager to take freedom away do not always need coercion to achieve their purpose. As the experience of our totalitarian age has demonstrated beyond reasonable doubt, all too often the wish to take freedom away meets with the wish to give it away. All too often freedom is used to escape from freedom: to escape from *having* conscience into *being* conscience, and from the need to defend one's point into the faith that all points worth making have been already made.

But the excruciating task of resisting the allurements of escape is not the end of the story either. There is yet another trap, another temptation, and a temptation most difficult to resist, one to which we all surrender time and again: a temptation to have one's cake and eat it, to taste in full the joy of choosing without fear of paying the penalty for a wrong choice, to seek and obtain a foolproof, patented and guaranteed recipe for the right choice – for freedom without anxiety . . . There must be someone, somewhere, who knows how to set apart the right decision from the wrong one – a grandmaster of the art of being free, a supreme practitioner and/or a supreme theorist of the right choice . . . The trick is to find him or her, to get or buy the magic formula, to learn it and to follow it in every detail . . .

The snag is, though, that foolproof recipes are to freedom, to responsibility and to responsible freedom, what water is to fire. There is no such thing as a prescription for freedom, though the constant demand breeds a growing supply of people willing to write it. And there is no such thing as freedom without anxiety, though this being the perennial dream of so many of us there is little wonder that so many of us wish the dream come true while so many others find it profitable to keep the wish alive.

All in all, it is by no means certain what most of us would have chosen were they given the choice – the anxiety of freedom, or the comforts of such certainty as only unfreedom can offer? The point is, though, that the choice has not been and is unlikely to be given us. Freedom is our fate: a lot which cannot be wished away and will not go away however keenly we may avert our eyes. We do live in a diversified and poly-phonic world where every attempt to insert consensus proves to be but a continuation of discord by other means. This world has undergone for a long time (and in all probability will continue to undergo for a long time to come) a process of thorough and relentless 'uncertainization'[1] (the widely described 'disappearance of the job' is but one, highly symbolic, dimension of the process – and one exerting an enormous psychological impact, as it tends to be projected upon the perception of all other aspects of existence. In France, for instance, 70 per cent of all new employment in 1994 was temporary or fixed-term; by that year the proportion of jobs with some degree of in-built stability fell from 76 per cent of the active population in 1970 to 58 per cent.[2] In the USA 90 per cent of vacancies offered in 1993 were part-time, without insurance and pension rights attached[3]). It is with such an increasingly uncertain world that its inhabitants struggle to grapple, and it is for living in such a world that they brace themselves and wish to prepare when looking feverishly for the skills of 'making the best' of their perhaps unchosen, yet all-too-real freedom.

Some writers portray the world of free, 'untied' and increasingly self-reliant individuals as utopia come true; some others prefer to talk about the descent of a dystopia. Neither of the two camps suffers a shortage of convincing arguments to support its verdict. The dispute between the eulogists and the detractors is bound to remain inconclusive, much as the process of 'uncertainization' is bound to continue. Rather than try vainly to resolve the differences of evaluation, it is more reasonable to take an inventory of gains and losses which the new situation brings – and to

accept that whatever cure or partial improvement might be thought of
would have to start from the already thoroughly 'individualized' world;
will have to rely, in other words, on the strategies which individuals
thrown into the condition of freedom and self-reliance are likely to
choose and have the means to pursue. Wherever one wishes to go – all
roads start from here.

One universally admitted side-effect of the progressive untying of the
individual freedom of choice[4] is the ever more profound division between the haves and the have-nots. On the inter- as well as the intra-
societal scale, it now reaches proportions unheard of for almost a century
and until recently 'culturally forgotten' (see chapters 3 and 4). The
relative poverty of those excluded from the consumer feast grows, as the
hope of its alleviation at the next turn of prosperity fades; hence the
deepening despair of the excluded, and the vehement efforts of all the
rest, saved as yet from their lot, to 'culturally cancel' the moral significance of the return of the poor and the desolate – through the surreptitiously induced brutalization of the poor and the subsequent
'criminalization' and 'medicalization' of poverty after the pattern widely
practised in the nineteenth century but later, during the welfare-state
episode, condemned and abandoned. The postmodern dismantling of
modern institutions removes the last barriers to the initiative of those
who can afford it; but it also uncovers once more the unacceptable face
of early-modern ruthlessness and lack of compassion.

As the expenditures on collective and individual welfare and social
wages are cut, the costs of police, prisons, security services, armed
guards and house/office/car protection grow unstoppably. The welfare
cuts, once started, soon become self-propelling, while poverty redefined
as law-and-order or a medical problem develops an inexhaustible appetite for resources. Those already excluded or on the brink of exclusion
are as a result hurled into the invisible, yet all-too-tangible, walls of their
exclusion camps and firmly locked inside. But the individual freedom of
those already free gains nothing much from the shift of resources either.
The universally shared and overwhelming sensation of insecurity seems
to be the only winner.

Cutting down on the freedoms of the excluded adds nothing to the
freedom of the free; it detracts quite a lot from their *feeling* of being free
and their ability to *rejoice in* their freedoms. The road of welfare cuts
may lead everywhere except to a society of free individuals. As far as the
needs of the free are concerned, this is altogether a blind alley. It distorts
the balance between two sides of freedom: somewhere along this road
the joy of free choice fades while fear and anxiety gather force. The
freedom of the free requires, as it were, the freedom of all.

In the classic formulation of Guido de Ruggiero[5] 'freedom is the ability to do what one likes, a liberty of choice implying the individual's right not to be hampered by others in the development of his own activity'; freedom expresses itself therefore in resistance to oppression – in 'critical energy'. Let us note that the decisive role has been allotted here to the *ability* to do and the *ability* to resist; but that ability requires more than the awarding of rights – ability is a *practical* quality, which does not come in equal measure to all individuals sharing in the equal rights of the citizen. I have argued elsewhere[6] that freedom is a social relation; I have argued also in this book (see chapter 2) that the oppressive, paralysing, incapacitating strength of 'others' is not so much the feature of external conditions, of the abominable quality of the 'others' – as the outcome or a projection of the resourcelessness of those amenable to incapacitation. It is in recognition of this link of freedom with resourcefulness that Sir William Beveridge[7] proclaimed his grand projects of state-guaranteed welfare to be 'essentially Liberal things – a carrying forward into the new world of the great living traditions of Liberalism'. He added that it is in the name of the freedom of everyone, *and not just those incapable for one reason or another of exercising their liberty*, that one needs to ensure that every citizen 'has an income sufficient for the honourable subsistence of himself and all who depend on him, an income sufficient though he has nothing else of his own and not cut down by any means test if he has anything of his own'. Such a guarantee – extended to *everyone*, including those who at that moment stood firmly on their own two feet and to whom the need of collective insurance seemed at that moment irrelevant or at least remote – was in Beveridge's view the only preventive medicine against the *fear* of want and idleness, the fear which begins to eat up souls long before the want and idleness themselves start to bite and which devours first and foremost that confidence, daring and determination which supply Ruggiero's 'critical energy' and are necessary to keep want and idleness at a safe distance.

It was obvious to Beveridge, the 'radical liberal', that individual freedom needs collective protection. The present-day self-proclaimed *spokesmen* for liberalism attempt to make equally obvious the opposite: that individual freedom needs the tearing apart of all collectively woven protective nets – partly because the nets hamper self-assertive moves, but mostly because they are costly (i.e. their maintenance costs cut down on the amount of ready cash available to individuals for the purpose of self-assertion). As if to prove the point, the self-proclaimedly liberal *politicians* make the nets ever more ragged, paltry and squalid so that more and more people wonder what sort of joy or benefit one could get from falling into them. Whether 'money in your pocket' grows as the protective nets fall apart is a moot question; what is indubitable is that want and idleness return in force, making the unlucky homeless and haunting the homes of the lucky.

I am as far as one can be from suggesting that the obvious faults of one strategy are sufficient proofs of the unclouded virtues of the other. I believe that hard-won, sad, yet liberating postmodern wisdom tells us that no strategy is foolproof – and least of all such strategies as claim to be such and are accordingly oblivious to the dangers they carry and the damages they may incur. Our legislating zeal has been mitigated by learning the hard way the truth contained in Thomas Mann's 1939 warning that the reconciliation of liberty and equality 'is never completed and finally achieved. It remains a humanitarian task to be solved again and again', or in Michael Walzer's conclusion that morality is and will forever remain 'something we have to argue about' and this we can – must – do, taking care that there is a continuous possibility to argue.[8]

The point which needs to be underlined again and again, since it is all too easily belied or forgotten, is that the present debate is not an updated version of the old, barren and, in the end, phony argument about the alleged conflict of interest between individual and society and about the line along which a reconciliation, compromise or armistice between them could or should be established. Few if any participants of the debate would demand today the sacrifice of individual freedoms 'for the sake of society'; it is the society that needs to legitimize itself in terms of the service done to individual freedom – not the individual freedom in terms of its social utility. In postmodern politics individual freedom is the supreme value and the yardstick by which all merits and vices of society at large are measured. But thanks to many keen trials and even more costly errors we now stand the chance of realizing, and accepting, and agreeing, that individual freedom cannot really be achieved by individual efforts alone; that for some to be able to secure and enjoy it, something must be done to secure the possibility of its enjoyment to all, and that doing this is the task in which free individuals may engage only jointly and through their common achievement: through the *political community*.

> The political community should be conceived as a discursive surface and not as an empirical referent. Politics is about the constitution of the political community, not something that takes place within it. The political community . . . requires a correlative idea of the common good, but a common good conceived as a 'vanishing point', something to which we must constantly refer but that can never be reached . . .
> [A] fully inclusive political community can never be realized . . . [T]he

condition of possibility of the political community is at the same time the
condition of impossibility of its full realization.[9]

This is how Chantal Mouffe spells out what can be tried and how can
one try it if the never ending, forever inconclusive yet indispensable and
salutary effort to create and keep alive the political community of free
individuals is to be undertaken. Now, the idea of 'the common good'
which stands a chance of serving as that 'vanishing point' that constitutes
such a community (perhaps the sole idea which stands such a chance)
is, undoubtedly, not the idea of the sacrifice of individual liberty for the
sake of the genuine or putative 'interests of the whole', but the idea that
the freedom of every individual, and the free enjoyment of that freedom,
requires the freedom of all; and that the liberty of each needs to be
secured and guaranteed by the joint efforts of all. For each free individual
to be free from the *fear* of want and idleness, it is necessary that
everybody is free from *genuine* want and idleness.

We have more than enough reasons to be wary of calls to sacrifice the
individual on the altar of the 'social whole' – invariably a code name for
domination and oppression. And we have accumulated over the years
more than enough arguments with which to resist and fight off the
demands for such a sacrifice. We know that attempts to build a 'political
community' on those grounds boil down as a rule to the imposition of
unwanted powers on some but also the practical disempowerment of all.
Vacating the political scene of our shared memories in order to stage
once more the drama of the legislatively enforced happiness-by-design
seems to be, under the circumstances, an unrealistic and improbable
prospect; if undertaken, it may prove a tall order. But it is no such
community, poetically described by modern thought as 'something
greater than the sum of its parts' and for that reason entitled to demand
meekness and submission from each and every one of its parts, which is
at stake in postmodern politics. A politics informed by postmodern
wisdom can only be oriented towards the *reassertion of the right of free
individuals to secure and perpetuate the conditions of their freedom.*

Postmodern politics aimed at the creation of a viable political community needs to be guided (as I suggested in the conclusions of *Modernity
and Ambivalence*) by the triune principle of Liberty, Difference and
Solidarity; solidarity being the necessary condition, and the essential
collective contribution, to the well-being of liberty and difference. In the
postmodern world the first two elements of the triune formula have
many overt or covert allies, not least in the so-called 'deregulatory' and
'privatizing' pressures of increasingly globalized markets. One thing
which the postmodern condition is unlikely to produce on its own – not

without a political intervention, that is – is solidarity; but without solidarity, as we have argued before, no freedom is secure, while the differences and the kind of 'identity politics' they tend to stimulate end up more often than not, as David Harvey pointed out,[10] in the internalization of oppression.

It is all too easy to abuse the principle of solidarity; it is not easy, perhaps impossible, to assert with confidence where the requirement of solidarity with difference ends and connivance at oppression begins. As with all principled politics, so the postmodern politics is replete with risks of defying its own principles; in this respect its only advantage over other varieties of politics is that it is fully aware of such danger and therefore inclined to monitor carefully its own accomplishments. Above all, it is reconciled to the absence of perfect solutions and guaranteed strategies, to the infinity of its own tasks and to the probable inconclusiveness of its efforts: this is perhaps the best available protection against the trap in which modern political attempts at community construction used to fall so often – that of promoting oppression in the guise of emancipation.

'There is beauty and there are the humiliated' – Albert Camus noted in 1953 in *Retour à Tipasa*. 'However difficult this may be, I would not like to be disloyal either to the first or to the others.' One could only add to this profession of faith that the attempt at selective disloyalty would be doomed, as there can be hardly any beauty without solidarity with the humiliated.

Notes

Chapter 1   The Dream of Purity

1 Cynthia Ozick, *Art and Ardour* (New York: Dutton, 1984), p. 165.
2 Klaus Dörner, *Tödliches Mitleid: zur Frage der Unerträglichkeit des Lebens* (Gütersloh: Verlag Jakob van Hoddis, 1993), p. 13.
3 Michel Foucault, *Histoire de la folie* (Paris: Plon, 1961). Here quoted after the English translation by Richard Howard, *Madness and Civilization: A History of Insanity in the Age of Reason* (London: Tavistock, 1967), pp. 13, 11.
4 Mary Douglas, *Purity and Danger* (Harmondsworth: Penguin, 1970), pp. 12, 53.
5 See in particular Alfred Schütz's 'Common-sense and scientific interpretation of human action', *Collected Papers*, vol. 1 (The Hague: Martinus Nijhoff, 1967).
6 Alfred Schütz, 'The social world and the theory of social action', *Studies in Social Theory*, vol. 2 (The Hague: Martinus Nijhoff, 1967), p. 13.
7 See Alfred Schütz, 'The stranger: an essay in social psychology', *Studies in Social Theory*, vol. 2, pp. 95ff.
8 See Zygmunt Bauman, *Life in Fragments* (Oxford: Blackwell, 1995).
9 Georges Balandier, *Le Dédale: pour en finir avec XXe siècle* (Paris: Fayard, 1994), p. 20.
10 Nils Christie, *Crime Control as Industry: Towards Gulags, Western Style?* (London: Routledge, 1993), pp. 166–7, 171, 172.

Chapter 2   The Making and Unmaking of Strangers

1 See the chapter 'A catalogue of postmodern fears' in my *Life in Fragments* (Oxford: Blackwell, 1995).
2 See *Street Wars: Space, Politics and the City*, ed. G. Crysler and C. Hamilton (Manchester University Press, 1995).
3 David Bennett, 'Hollywood's indeterminacy machine', *Arena*, 3/1994, p. 30.
4 (Harmondsworth: Penguin, 1970), p. 53.
5 See Jean-Paul Sartre, *Being and Nothingness: An Essay on Phenomenological Ontology*, trans. Hazel E. Barnes (London: Methuen, 1969), pp. 608–10.
6 Alain de Benoist, *Dix ans de combat culturel pour une Renaissance* (Paris: GRECE, 1977), p. 19.
7 Julius Evola, *Éléments pour éducation raciale* (Paris: Puiseaux, 1985), p. 29.

8 Richard Stevers, *The Culture of Cynicism: American Morality in Decline* (Oxford: Blackwell, 1994), p. 119.
9 See chapters 10 and 11 of my *Legislators and Interpreters* (Cambridge: Polity, 1987).

Chapter 5   Parvenu and Pariah

1 Albert Camus, *Carnets, janvier 1942 – mars 1951* (Paris: Gallimard, 1964), p. 111.
2 Edmond Jabès, *Un étranger avec, sous le bras, un livre du petit format* (Paris: Gallimard, 1989), p. 34.
3 Robert Musil, *The Man without Qualities*, trans. Eithne Wilkins and Ernst Kaiser (New York: Capricorn Books, 1965), vol. 2, p. 174.
4 Wylie Sypher, *Rococo to Cubism in Art and Literature* (New York: Vintage Books, 1960), p. 104.
5 Hannah Arendt, *Rahel Varnhagen: La Vie d'une Juive allemande à l'époque du Romantisme*, trans. Henri Plard (Paris: Tierce, 1986), p. 247.
6 Arendt, *Rahel Varnhagen*, p. 31.
7 Agnes Heller and Ferenc Feher, *The Grandeur and Twilight of Radical Universalism* (New Brunswick: Transactions, 1991), p. 303.
8 Pierre V. Zima, 'L'Ambivalence dialectique: entre Benjamin et Bakhtine', *Revue d'Esthétique*, 1/1981, p. 137.
9 Theodore W. Adorno, 'Introduction to Benjamin's *Schriften* (1955)', *On Walter Benjamin, Critical Essays and Recollections*, ed. Gary Smith (MIT Press, 1988), p. 14.
10 Gerschon Scholem, *Walter Benjamin: The Story of Friendship* (New York: Faber & Faber, 1982), pp. 229, 234.
11 Richard Rorty, *Objectivity, Relativity and Truth: Philosophical Papers*, vol. 1 (Cambridge University Press, 1991), pp. 14, 13.

Chapter 8   The Meaning of Art and the Art of Meaning

1 John Rahn's English translation, under the title 'Contemporary music and the public', appeared in *Perspectives of New Music*, vol. 24 (1985); reprinted in Michel Foucault, *Politics, Philosophy, Culture: Interviews and Other Writings, 1977–84*, ed. Lawrence D. Kritzman (London: Routledge, 1988), pp. 314–22.
2 François Lyotard, *Le Postmoderne expliqué aux enfants: Correspondance 1982–85* (Paris: Galilée, 1988), pp. 30–1.
3 Jean Baudrillard, 'The work of art in the electronic age', interview with *La Sept*, and 'Fractal theory', interview with Nicholas Zubrugg. Quoted from the texts reprinted in *Baudrillard Live: Selected Interviews*, ed. Mike Gane (London: Routledge, 1993), pp. 147, 165. Of simulation, Baudrillard writes the following: 'Simulation is no longer that of a territory, a referential being or a substance. It is the generation by models of a real without origin in reality: a hyperreal. The territory no longer precedes the map, nor survives it. Henceforth, it is the map that precedes the territory – *precession of simulacra* – it is the map that engenders the territory' (see Jean Baudrillard, *Selected Writings*, ed. Mark Poster (Cambridge: Polity, 1988), p. 166).
4 Anna Jamroziak, *Obraz i Metanarracja: Szkice o postmodernistycznym obrazowaniu* (Warsaw, Instytut Kultury, 1994), pp. 49–50.

5 Piotr Kawiecki and Romuald Piekarski, *Zagadnienia Estetyki Współczesnej: Sztuka – Wartości – Poznanie* (Gdańsk: Gdańsk University Publishers, 1994), p. 33.
6 Suzi Gablik, *Magritte* (New York: Thames & Hudson, 1985), pp. 75, 72.
7 Anna Zeidler-Janiszewska, 'Oblicza eksperymentowania: O awangardowych impulsach w kulturze współczesnej', *Czy Jeszcze Estetyka? Sztuka współczesna a tradycja estetyczna*, ed. Michał Ostrowicki (Kraków: Instytut Kultury, 1994), p. 144.
8 Michel Foucault, 'The art of telling the truth', quoted after Alan Sheridan's translation in *Politics, Philosophy, Culture*, p. 95.
9 Michel Foucault, 'Practicing criticism', quoted after Alan Sheridan's translation in above, pp. 154–5. The new understanding of critical activity throws in a new light the role of the 'critical intellectual' (a pleonasm, to be sure). This role, in Foucault's opinion, is 'to see how far the liberation of thought can make . . . transformations urgent enough for people to want to carry them out and difficult enough to carry out for them to be profoundly rooted in reality'.

Chapter 9 On Truth, Fiction and Uncertainty

1 See William James, *Pragmatism* (Indianapolis: Hachett, 1981), p. 100.
2 Richard Rorty, 'Pragmatism, Davidson and Truth', *Objectivity, Relativism, and Truth* (Cambridge University Press, 1991), pp. 127–8.
3 Richard Rorty, 'Heidegger, Kundera, and Dickens', *Essays on Heidegger and Others* (Cambridge, University Press, 1991), pp. 70–1.
4 Immanuel Kant, *Critique of Pure Reason*, trans. J.M.D. Meiklejohn (London: Dent, 1969), pp. 3–4, 17, 481.
5 Kant, *Critique of Pure Reason*, p. 6.
6 Martin Heidegger, 'On the essence of truth', *Basic Writings*, ed. David Farrell Krell (London: Routledge, 1978), pp. 117–18.
7 Heidegger, 'On the essence of truth', pp. 135–6.
8 Kant, *Critique of Pure Reason*, pp. 19–21.
9 See Hilary Putnam, *Realism and Reason* (Cambridge University Press, 1983).
10 Donald Davidson, 'A coherence theory of truth and knowledge', as quoted in Rorty, *Objectivity, Relativism, and Truth*, p. 136.
11 Rorty, 'Heidegger, Kundera, and Dickens', pp. 68, 77, 81, 75.
12 Milan Kundera, *The Art of the Novel*, trans. Linda Asher (New York: Grove Press, 1986), p. 160; quoted in Rorty, 'Heidegger, Kundera, and Dickens', p. 73.
13 See lecture 5, 'Possible woods', in Umberto Eco, *Six Walks in the Fictional Woods* (Harvard University Press, 1994).
14 Ortega y Gasset, *En torno a Galileo (1550–1650). Ideas sobre las generaciones decisivas en la evolución del pensamiento europeo* (a series of lectures delivered in 1933); here quoted after Polish translation (Warsaw: Spacja, 1993), pp. 150–1.
15 See his *La Fin des certitudes: Temps, chaos et les lois de la nature* (Paris: Odile Jacob, 1995). It is only now, says Prigogine – after centuries of determinism, of the efforts to scrap the difference between the past and the future – that we come to view reality, also the natural reality, as continuous invention ruled not by unchangeable laws, but contingency and probability.

16 See Martin Heidegger, 'The origin of the work of art', *Basic Writings*, pp. 164–81.

17 Jean Baudrillard, 'Simulacra and simulation', trans. Paul Foss, Paul Patton and Philip Beitchman, *Sémiotext(e), 1983*. Here quoted after *Jean Baudrillard, Selected Writings*, ed. Mark Poster (Cambridge: Polity Press, 1988), p. 168.

Chapter 11   On the Postmodern Redeployment of Sex

1 See Philippe Ariès, *Centuries of Childhood* (London: Jonathan Cape, 1962), esp. pp. 10–50.

2 See the works of Edward Shorter, David Hunt, Jack Goody, or Mark Poster's *Critical Theory of the Family* (London: Pluto Press, 1978).

3 Joseph F. Kett, *Rites of Passage* (New York: Basic Books, 1977), p. 111.

4 Michel Foucault, *The History of Sexuality*, vol. 1 (Harmondsworth: Penguin, 1990), pp. 40–4, 103–7.

5 See Anthony Giddens, *The Transformation of Intimacy: Sexuality, Love and Eroticism in Modern Societies* (Cambridge: Polity Press, 1992).

6 See Henk Kleijer and Ger Tillekens, 'Passion, pop and self-control; the body politic and pop music', *ZSE*, 1994/1, pp. 58–75.

7 Suzanne Moore, 'For the good of the kids – and us', *The Guardian*, 15 June 1995.

8 Rosie Waterhouse, 'So what is child abuse?', *Independent on Sunday*, 23 July 1995.

Chapter 12   Immortality, Postmodern Version

1 Jorge Luis Borges, *Labyrinths: Selected Stories and Other Writings*, ed. Donald A. Yates and James E. Irby (Harmondsworth: Penguin, 1974), pp. 140–1, 138, 144, 146.

2 'Phaedo', in *Great Dialogues of Plato*, trans. W.H.D. Rouse (New York: Mentor Books, 1956), pp. 484, 487, I.V. Vishev (*Problema lichnogo bessmertia* (Novosibirsk: Nauka, 1990), p. 126) quotes a papyrus going back to the fifteenth century BC, expressing already ideas later to be canonized by Plato: 'Their [the writers'] servants have gone away, their gravestones are covered with mud, their abodes are forgotten. But their names are spoken about thanks to the books they created; their memory will live forever.' It may be guessed that the link between intellectual work and individual immortality-through-public-memory is as old as the invention of writing.

3 See Michel Foucault, *Politics, Philosophy, Culture: Interviews and Other Writings, 1977–84*, ed. Lawrence D. Kritzman (London: Routledge, 1988), p. 60.

4 John Carroll, *Humanism: The Wreck of Western Culture* (London: Fontana, 1994), pp. 2–6.

5 Klaus Dörner, *Tödliches Mitleid: zur Frage der Unerträglichkeit des Lebens* (Gütersloh: Vertrag Jakob van Hoddis, 1993), p. 129.

6 Georges Balandier, *Le dédale: pour en finir avec le XXᵉ siècle* (Paris: Fayard, 1994), pp. 110–11.

7 Mark Poster, 'A second media age?', *Arena*, 3/1994, pp. 76, 81.

8 Jean Baudrillard, 'The evil demon of images', interview with Ted Colless, David Kelly and Alan Cholodenko, in *Baudrillard Live: Selected Interviews*, ed. Mike Gane (London: Routledge, 1993), p. 141.
9 Jean Baudrillard, *The Illusion of the End*, trans. Chris Turner (London: Polity Press, 1994), p. 84.

Chapter 13 Postmodern Religion?

1 Quoted after Susan Gablik, *Magritte* (London: Thames & Hudson, 1985), p. 66.
2 Rudolf Otto's fundamental *The Idea of the Holy* (first published in 1917, here quoted from John W. Harvey's 1923 translation (Penguin, 1959)) is in actual fact a closely argued statement about the *impossibility* of a 'rational definition' of religious experience. We may only try to approximate it in our descriptions, yet need to remember all the time that its complexity cannot really be grasped: 'like every absolutely primary and elementary datum, while it admits of being discussed, it cannot be strictly defined' (p. 21). The imagery of that experience cannot be 'taught', it can be only 'evoked'. What appears in the religious experience Otto gives the name of *mysterium tremendum*: 'it may burst in sudden eruption up from the depths of the soul with spasms and convulsions, or lead to the strongest excitements, to intoxicated frenzy, to transport, and to ecstasy. It has its wild and demonic forms and can sink to an almost grisly horror and shuddering' (p. 27). The absence of structural logical coherence is paralleled by the absence of the behavioural logic it provokes. *Mysterium tremendum* is at the same time 'daunting' and 'fascinating' – these two qualities combining 'in the strange harmony of contrasts, and the resultant dual character of the numinous consciousness' which brings together what cannot be rationally tied together – 'horror and dread' on the one hand, 'potent charm' on the other (p. 45). According to Mircea Eliade (see his *Traité d'histoire des religions* (Paris, 1956)), the sole thing one can say about the nature of hierophany (and everything can acquire hierophanic value; that is, become the 'expression' of *sacrum*) is that it always signals a *selection*; it divides the world into the 'sacred' and the rest. One is tempted to say that, by this description, all attempt at definition also contains a sizeable measure of hierophanic value . . .
3 See *Religio: Ruolo del sacro, coesione sociale e nuove forme di solidarietà nella società contemporanea*, ed. Carlo Mongardini and Marieli Ruini (Rome: Bulzoni Editore, 1994), pp. 15, 31. In the same volume Johan Goudsblom rightly points out that most of our discussion of religious phenomena remains, even if unknowingly, under the influence of theology – hopelessly mixing 'emic' and 'etic' elements in its descriptions (p. 89). We may add that the same applies to the 'rationalizing ideology', which also weighs heavily, even if as a tacit premise, on all attempts to define religious phenomena. As a result, the discourse finds itself in a virtual 'double bind', forced or cajoled to absorb elements from two mutually exclusive cognitive universes. In the discourse of 'religious science' the emic elements drawn from theology coexist uneasily with emic elements inserted by the 'rationalization' discourse which for the last couple of centuries has striven to estrange and reify religious experience as the *wholly other* of reason. Present-day efforts to

'define religion' bear all the signs of the influence of the Enlightenment's war against superstition – *à rebours*...

4 Thomas Luckmann, *The Invisible Religion* (London: Macmillan, 1967), p. 82.

5 Michel Foucault, *Politics, Philosophy, Culture: Interviews and Other Writings, 1977–84*, ed. Lawrence D. Kritzman (London: Routledge, 1988), pp. 50, 154.

6 Leszek Kołakowski, *Religion: If there is no God ... On God, the Devil, Sin and other Worries of the so-called Philosophy of Religion* (London: Fontana, 1982), pp. 194, 199, 202. These are, of course, statements describing the common and distinctive attributes of *religion*, not necessarily those of the manifold religious *institutions*. The latter would be better described by a reference to their functions, rather than to their constitutive creeds or recruiting slogans – and functions are more varied than the essentially intellectual response of 'explanation' or 'making sense' to genuine or induced confusion, queries or fears of the faithful. Thus, for instance, churches and sects may perform integrative/assertive/enabling/political functions towards politically and economically oppressed minorities; parishes, chapels and congregations are known for their important sociating role played in cementing closely knit communities and securing their continuous self-reproduction.

7 Anthony Giddens, *The Consequences of Modernity* (Cambridge: Polity Press, 1990), p. 82. As Giddens points out, 'philosophers pose questions about the nature of being, but they are not, we may suppose, ontologically insecure in their ordinary actions' (p. 93). Indeed, Arthur Schopenhauer, while overwhelmed with questions like 'Why there is not nothing at all rather than this world', and agonizing over the fact that 'No ground, no final cause can be found' (*The World as Will and Representation* (New York: Dover, 1966), p. 637), led an orderly and secure *bürgerliche* life and was truly appalled when its leisurely rhythm was abruptly broken by the events of the 1848 revolution. Schopenhauer went far beyond the call of duty to restore the 'groundless' world without a final cause to the routine pursuit of its daily causes – including the invitation of government soldiers to his house from which the insurgents were clearly visible and could thus be shot at with ease (see his *Gesammelte Briefe*, ed. A. Hübscher (Bonn, 1978)). He returned to eschatology and ontological insecurity when the revolution had been safely put down.

8 *Politics, Philosophy, Culture*, p. 70.

9 *Politics, Philosophy, Culture*, pp. 70, 62.

10 See Edmund Husserl, *The Paris Lectures* (The Hague: Martinus Nijhoff, 1967), p. 14; Edmund Husserl, *The Idea of Phenomenology* (The Hague: Martinus Nijhoff, 1968), p. 13.

11 Statements to this effect abound to such an extent that one is all too often misled into taking the frequency of repetition for a sign of self-evidence. They are all shaped according to a similar pattern: true, religion changed its form beyond recognition, and people live their lives without giving religious signification to what they do, but this is only because they do not see through their motives as well as we, the social scientists, do ... And so we read in Jeffrey C. Alexander's paper, that 'sacrality and the demand for experience of transcendence remain fundamental features of life ... The referents are no longer in heaven, but the signifiers and the signifying process remain religious: their aim [whose aim? – Z.B.] is to place an actor, group or society in

touch with the pure and impure forces from which the world seems, in the mythic and existential imagination [whose imagination? – Z.B.], to ultimately derive' (*Religio*, p. 19). Thomas Luckmann, for his part, suggests that it is 'religious themes' that have been 'taken up' by virtually all institutions which today serve the running of daily life: 'syndicated advice columns, "inspirational" literature ranging from tracts on positive thinking to *Playboy* magazine, *Reader's Digest* versions of popular psychology, the lyrics of popular hits, and so forth, articulate what are, in effect, elements of models of "ultimate" significance' (*The Invisible Religion*, p. 104).

12 John Carroll, *Humanism: The Wreck of Western Culture* (London: Fontana, 1993), pp. 2–3. Carroll sees the humanist upheaval as ushering in a relatively brief, and certainly time-limited, period which now comes to its end. He also considers its consequences as uniformly disastrous for the quality of Western civilization. I propose to separate Carroll's perceptive diagnosis of the humanist strategy from both, highly contentious, opinions.

13 See Alain Touraine, *The Post-Industrial Society: Tomorrow's Social History: Classes, Conflicts and Culture in the Programmed Society*, trans. Leonard F.X. Mayhew (London: Wildwood House, 1974), pp. 213–4.

14 Jean Delumeau, *Sin and Fear: The Emergence of a Western Guilt Culture, 13th–18th Centuries* (New York: St Martin's Press, 1990), pp. 112–13.

15 Quoted after the English translation by Patricia Lipscomb, *Man in the Age of Technology* (New York: Columbia University Press, 1980), pp. 52–3, 75.

16 See Zygmunt Bauman, 'A catalogue of postmodern fears', *Life in Fragments*, chapter 4 (Oxford: Blackwell, 1995).

17 Abraham H. Maslow, *Religions, Values, and Peak-Experiences* (Columbus: Ohio State University Press, 1964), pp. 19–24. Maslow left ample accounts of the narratives he obtained from people reporting their 'peak-experiences'. Among elements which keep repeating in their reports we find many features which characterize the ideal type of experience as promoted by postmodern culture: for instance, sensations of unusual concentration of attention and gathering of all spiritual powers, the effacing of the difference between figure and ground (the impression of the 'wholiness'), the ego-transcending, self-justifying nature of the moment which felt like 'end-experience' rather than 'means-experience', lack of consciousness of time and space, perception of the world as beautiful, good and desirable – and above all the experience of 'a loss, even though transient, of fear, anxiety, inhibition, of defense and control, of perplexity, confusion, conflict, of delay and restraint' (p. 66) – that is, all the most sinister nightmares haunting postmodern individuals afflicted with identity-anxiety.

18 See Edith Wyschogrod, *Saints and Postmodernism: Revisioning Moral Philosophy* (University of Chicago Press, 1990), pp. 252ff.

19 Gilles Kepel, *The Revenge of God: The Resurgence of Islam, Christianity and Judaism in the Modern World*, trans. Alan Braley (Cambridge: Polity Press, 1994), p. 11. I also fully endorse Kepel's working assumption that 'what these movements say and do is meaningful, and does not spring from a dethronement of reason or from manipulation by hidden forces; rather it is the undeniable evidence of a deep malaise in society that can no longer be interpreted in terms of our traditional categories of thought' (p. 11).

20 For a fuller argument, see the chapter 'Two nations, mark two: the oppressed', in my *Legislators and Interpreters* (Cambridge: Polity Press, 1987).

Chapter 14   On Communitarianism and Human Freedom

1 For instance, both the necessity and desirability of pluralism have been emphatically argued by John Rawls – for whom the multiplicity of religious, philosophic and moral beliefs which are all rational yet mutually incompatible, is the trade-mark of liberal/democratic society. Rawls points out that the variety of views is by itself a good thing – in a well-constructed society members are right, wishing their plans to be diversified (see his 'A Theory of justice', *Liberalism and its Critics*, ed. Michael Sandel (New York University Press, 1984)). What goes without saying is that liberal thinkers never condemned the will to defend freely chosen beliefs, while decrying state attempts to impose choices by force. As Jerzy Szacki sums it up as succinctly as convincingly, pointing out that the two questions – whether the government can be a side in moral conflicts; and whether such conflicts can be ever overcome – 'liberalism answers in the negative' (Jerzy Szacki, *Liberalizm po Komunizmie* (Kraków: Znak, 1994), p. 245).
2 See Maurice Barrès, *Scènes et doctrines du nationalisme* (Paris: Émile Paul, 1902), pp. 8–13. There is only one thing which I may, according to Barrès, will with any effect: to be in all I think and do determined by *la terre et les morts*; to say to myself 'I wish to live with these masters, and, by making them consciously objects of my cult, to partake fully of their strength' (p. 16). The alternative is *déracinement* – a horrifying state of disempowerment, a limp body without a backbone.
3 See Ulrich Beck and Elisabeth Beck-Gernsheim, 'Individualization in modern societies – perspectives and controversies of a subject-orientated sociology', *Detraditionalization* (Oxford: Blackwell, 1995). The process of 'individualization', understood as primarily an unstoppably rising level of uncertainty and 'subjectivization' of risks, has been most extensively and persuasively analysed in other works of the above authors, notably in *Das ganz normale Chaos der Liebe* (Suhrkamp, 1990), which they jointly wrote, and *Riskante Freiheiten: Individualisierung in moderne Gesellschaften* (Suhrkamp, 1994), which they jointly edited. In that latest book they pithily summarize their findings: 'Take whatever you like – God, Nature, truth, science, technology, morality, love, marriage – modernity transformed everything into "risky freedoms" . . .' For instance, 'marriage – like driving with excessive speed on a winding road – a personal, risky undertaking, not eligible for insurance' (pp. 11, 25). Consult as well Christopher Lasch's essential *The Minimal Self: Psychic Survival in Troubled Times* (London: Pan Books, 1984).
4 See my *Life in Fragments* (Oxford: Blackwell, 1995), chapter 'Europe of nations, Europe of tribes'.
5 Roberto Unger, *Politics: A Work in Constructive Social Theory*, vol. 1 (Cambridge University Press, 1987), p. 167. Unger points out that 'If the triumph of certain institutions and ideas was relatively accidental, their replacement can also more easily be imagined as realistic'. Compare Will Kymlicka's discussion of Unger in the reviewed issue of *Critical Review*.

6 Jerzy Jedlicki, 'Antynomie liberalnej koncepcji wolności', *Źle urodzeni, czyli o doświadczeniu historycznym* (London: Aneks, 1993), p. 35.

Afterword: The Last Word – and it Belongs to Freedom

1 The term 'l'insécurisation' was coined by Jean-Luc Mathieu (see his *L'insécurité* (Paris: Presses Universitaires de France, 1995)).
2 See André Gorz, 'Vers une société post-marchande', *Transversales science culture*, September/October 1955; Bernard Cassen, 'Chômage, des illusions au bricolage', *Le Monde diplomatique*, October 1995.
3 See Jeremy Rifkin, *The End of Work: The Decline of the Global Labour Force and the Dawn of the Post-Market era* (New York: Tarcher-Putnam, 1995).
4 This process is usually dubbed 'deregulation'. One wonders, though, to what extent this uncritically accepted name conceals, rather than reveals, the true nature of the process. Certainly, some kinds of activity are 'deregulated', while other kinds – or entire classes of life activities – are subjected simultaneously to ever stricter, sometimes oppressive, regulation; and the coincidence of the two opposite processes does not seem at all contingent. All in all, states do not today pass fewer laws than they used to in the past; they do not 'regulate' less; and the part of national income used to back up the regulatory efforts shows no signs of curtailment. It is only that the objects and the strategies of regulation are redefined, and the state-managed expenditure earmarked for different uses. Most notably, the new poor are the subject of ever more stern and pernickety legislation, aiming at tying-up, rather than untying, their freedom of choice and their right to an initiative. As Martin Woollacott put it aptly (see his 'Dismembering values', *The Guardian*, 9 December 1995), the costs 'migrate from caring to guarding, from the welfare state to lock-up state'.
5 Guido de Ruggiero, *The History of European Liberalism*, trans. R.G. Collingwood (Boston: Beacon Press, 1959), pp. 350–1.
6 See my *Freedom* (Milton Keynes: Open University Press, 1989).
7 See Sir William Beveridge, 'Liberal radicalism and liberty', *Western Liberalism: A History in Documents from Locke to Croce*, ed. E.K. Bramsted and K.J. Melhuish (London: Longman, 1978), pp. 712–17.
8 Michael Walzer, *Interpretation and Social Criticism* (Cambridge, Mass.: Harvard University Press, 1987), p. 32.
9 Chantal Mouffe, 'Liberal socialism and pluralism: which citizenship?', *Principled Positions: Postmodernism and the Rediscovery of Value*, ed. Judith Squires (London: Lawrence & Wishart, 1993), p. 81.
10 David Harvey, 'Class relations, social justice and the politics of difference', *Principled Positions*, p. 118.

Index

Adorno, Theodor 76, 117
Alexander, Jeffrey C. 166, 214–15
ambivalence 69, 78, 81, 123, 200
anxiety 122–3
Arendt, Hannah 73–4
Ariès, Philippe 141–2
Aristotle 83
ascetic priests 85, 113, 117–18
author/actor 135–7, 160
avant-garde 98, 138

Badie, Bertrand 64
Bakhtin, Michail 68
Balandier, Georges 13, 19, 156, 159
Barber, Bernard 167
Barrès, Maurice 189, 216
Barthes, Roland 160
Baudelaire, Charles 101
Baudrillard, Jean 25, 101–2, 106, 125, 160–1
Beck, Ulrich 19, 156, 192–3, 216
Becker, Harold 101, 136
Beck-Gernsheim, Elisabeth 193, 216
Beiner, Ronald 186, 197
Benjamin, Walter 12, 76–8, 99
Bennett, David 24
Benoist, Alain de 31
Bentham, Jeremy 80
Berlin, Isaiah 79
Beveridge, William 205
Bloch, Ernst 84
Bonger, Willem Adriaan 44
Borges, Jorge Luis 152–3, 164
Boulez, Pierre 103, 133
Bourdieu, Pierre 99
Breton, André 165
brutalization of the poor 59–62, 204
Bürger, Peter 99

campaign politics 66–8
Camus, Albert 71, 208
Canetti, Elias 17
Carey, John 98
Carroll, John 155, 171
Cassen, Bernard 217
child, image of 149–50
Christie, Nils 15, 42
Cicero 128
Clarke, David 22
Clinton, Bill 42, 44
Cobb, Jonathan 183
communitarianism 31–2, 79–82, 186–96
consensus 202–3
consumerism 13–15, 23–4, 28–9, 39–42, 59–61, 147, 180–4, 204
counselling boom 178, 182–4
Cragg, Tony 110
culture 77–8, 96, 101, 128–38

Davidson, Donald 117
death 163, 175
Delumeau, Jean 173
democracy 63–4
deregulation 2, 13–16, 22, 38–44, 60, 120, 123, 146, 184, 207, 217
Derrida, Jacques 33, 77, 138, 160
detemporalization of space 86
Dickens, Charles 84
Diderot 128
disembeddedment 32–3, 122–3, 146, 191
Doel, Marcus 22
Dörner, Klaus 5, 44, 158
Douglas, Mary 7, 26
Drucker, Peter 39

Durkheim, Emile 21, 154

Eaton, Marcia 101
Eco, Umberto 100, 119–20, 124
Eliade, Mircea 213
emancipation 32–3
episode 91
Erzensberger, Hans Magnus 22
ethics, macro 46, 50, 52–7, 62, 65, 68–9
exclusion 18, 34, 59, 62, 82, 204
experience-collectors 30, 179–82
experimentation 108–9, 126

family 141–51
Feher, Ferenc 76
flawed consumers 41
Foucault, Michel 5, 38, 77, 103–4, 109, 109–11, 133–4, 145, 160, 168–9
freedom 2–3, 14, 27–9, 33, 59, 90–3, 120, 124, 138–40, 183–8, 191–207
Freeman, Richard 43
Freud, Sigmund 1–3, 12, 77, 124, 153
Frisch, Max 28, 75
fundamentalism 182–4

Gablik, Susan 108, 111
Gadamer, Hans 108
Galbraith, John Kenneth 62, 67
Gasset, José Ortega y 121
Gautier, Theophile 102
Geertz, Clifford 136
Gehlen, Arnold 177–8
Giddens, Anthony 4, 19–23, 88, 133, 147–9, 156, 168
globalization 65
Goethe, Wolfgang 73
Goffman, Ervin 29
Gorer, Geoffrey 175
Gorz, André 217
Goudsblom, Johan 213
Gudmundsson, Kristjan 110

Habermas, Jürgen 84, 107
Harvey, David 208
Hebdidge, Dick 29
Hegel, Georg 83, 153
Heidegger, Martin 47, 83–5, 114, 117,
125, 176
heterophilia 30
heterophobia 82
Horkheimer, Max 117
Hunter, James Davison 83
Husserl, Edmund 47–8, 76, 113, 169
Huxley, Aldous 176

identity 20–1, 24–6, 34, 71, 75, 78, 88–9, 120–3, 178, 188, 191–3
individuality 155, 159–62, 183–5, 197, 201–2, 206–7
inequality 57–60
inner demons 38–9, 42, 93

Jabès, Edmund 72
James, William 112
Jamroziak, Anna 106
Jaukkuri, Maaretta 105, 109
Jedlicki, Jerzy 196
Jonas, Hans 53–6
justice 48–65

Kafka, Franz 74–5
Kant 54, 114–16
Kawiecki, Piotr 107
Kepel, Gilles 182, 215
Kett, Joseph T. 142
Kierkegaard, Søren 75
King, Martin Luther 32
Kleijer, Henk 147
Kołakowski, Leszek 168–70, 214
Kosseleck, Reinhart 128
Kuhn, Thomas 131
Kundera, Milan 91, 117–19, 124
Kymlicka, Will 186–7, 197, 216

Lasch, Christopher 88–9, 216
Le Pen, Jean Marie 75, 79, 81
Levinas, Emmanuel 46–57, 62, 65, 68
Levine, Sherrie 160
Lévi-Strauss, Claude 18, 77, 132, 139
liberalism 19, 50, 186–8, 196–7, 205
Linebaugh, Peter 42–3
lock-up state 217
Lotman, Iuri 96
Luckmann, Thomas 67, 215
Lukács, Georg 76–7
Lyotard, François 104, 139

MacIntyre, Alasdair 20, 186–8
Maggiori, Robert 33
Magritte, René 108, 111
Mann, Thomas 206
Mannheim, Karl 76
market 14, 23–4, 137, 185, 192, 199
Marquard, Odo 200–1
Marx, Karl 76, 79, 171
Maslow, Abraham 179, 215
mass 138
Mathieu, Jean Luc 217
meaning 107–8, 111, 125–6, 160, 171–2
metaphor 132
Meyer, Reinhard B. 95
Minc, Alain 22
Mitchell, Margaret 120
mixophilia/mixophobia 881
modernism 96–8, 101, 105, 109, 173
modernity 10–13, 16–21, 30–3, 71, 77–8, 84–7, 96–100, 118–19, 122, 128, 155–7, 174, 188, 192
Moore, Barrington Jr. 57
Moore, Susanne 150
moral responsibility 49, 51–3, 56, 62–5, 69–70, 185, 196, 201–2
moral self 47–8, 51
Morawski, Stefan 96–7
Mouffe, Chantal 207
movement politics 65–8
Musil, Robert 73

nationalism 12, 19, 29, 189–94
nation-state 12–13, 18–20, 31, 45, 52–6, 64–5, 82, 191
new poor 23, 29, 34–7, 43–4, 57–8, 60, 157, 183, 204, 217
Nietzsche, Friedrich 113

Offe, Claus 22
order, social 1, 3, 6–7, 10–13, 18–19, 38–9, 129–34
Orwell, George 17
Otto, Rudolph 166, 213
Ozick, Cynthia 5

pariah 78–81
Parsons, Talcott 80
parvenu 72–8, 81
Perec, Georges 123

pilgrim 90, 93
Plato 113, 154
player 88–9, 123
pleasure principle 2–3
pluralism, cultural 121–2, 186–7, 201–3
Poirié, François 50
polarization, social 58, 157
political community 206–7
Poster, Mark 161
Prejean, Helen 43
Prigogine, Ilya 122, 135, 211
privatization 13–16, 37, 44, 146–7, 158, 180, 184
progress 200
purity 1–8, 11–13
Putnam, Hilary 117

Quine, Willard van Orman 119

racism 31–2, 82
Ramone, Ignacio 199
Rawls, John 216
reality principle 2
risk 193–5, 198
Riviere, Joan 1
Roberts, David 4
Rorty, Richard 65–9, 79–80, 83–5, 112, 117–18
Ruggiero, Guido de 205
Russell, Bertrand 80

Saint-Just, Louis Antoine, 128
Sallenave, Danièle 55
Sandel, Michael 186
Sartre, Jean-Paul 20, 26, 55, 87
Scheler, Max 9
Scholem, Gershon 76, 78
Schönberg, Arnold 102
Schopenhauer, Arthur 214
Schütz, Alfred 8–9
security 2–3, 124
Segal, Alan 167
self-government 135
Sennett, Richard 183
sex 144–6, 148, 151
Shorter, Edward 146
Simmel, Georg 3
simulacrum 125, 210
slimy 26–9, 34

sociology 81–2
Socrates 154
solidarity 63, 81, 207–8
Sorokin, Pitirim 165
Spinoza, Baruch 152
Steiner, George 100
Stevers, Richard 32
Stone, Norman 22
Strachey, James 1
stranger 10, 13, 17–19, 25, 28–31
structure, social 131, 135
sublime 104
Sypher, Wylie 73
Szacki, Jerzy 216

Taguieff, Pierre André 31
Taylor, Charles 186, 190–1
technoscience 65
Thual, François 64
Tilekens, Ger 147
Tokarska-Bakir, Joanna 138
tolerance 14, 63–4, 81, 103, 121
totalitarian tendencies 12, 31, 50,
    126, 184–5, 202
Touraine, Alain 172–3
tourist 89–94

tradition 97
tribalization 65, 79–81, 195–6
truth 85, 112, 116, 124

uncertainty 13, 17, 21, 35, 42, 69, 94,
    119–20, 124, 176–82, 192–4, 199,
    203–4
Unger, Roberto 195, 216
Urbonas, Gediminas 110

vagabond 92–4
Vishev, I. V. 212

Walzer, Michael 186, 206
Warde, Ibrahim 45
Warhol, Andy 102, 139, 160
Waterhouse, Rosie 150
Weber, Max 75, 93, 147, 188
welfare state 23, 36–7, 42–4, 59–60,
    63, 204, 217
Wittgenstein, Ludwig 7, 104, 121
Woollacott, Martin 217
Wyschogrod, Edith 180

Zeidler-Janiszewska, Anna 108–9
Zima, Pierre V. 76